LOUISIANA WILD TURKEYS:

HISTORY, SCIENCE, MANAGEMENT, & HUNTING

By:

Norman J. "Jimmy" Stafford, III

Quotes from the *Holy Bible* include the following translations the 1611 King James Version (KJV), the 1993 English Standard Version (ESV), and the 1985 New International Version (NIV).

Louisiana Wild Turkeys: History, Science, Management, and Hunting is published by:

Claitor's Law Books and Publishing Company

P. O. Box 261333

Baton Rouge, Louisiana 70826-1333

(800)-274-1403 or (225)-344-0476

Fax (225)-344-0480

www.claitors.com

First Edition

Edited by Jeffrey Duguay Ph.D.

Associate Editor: Tina W. Stafford

Front cover photograph *"East Feliciana Tom"* by David W. Moreland

Back cover photograph of a Washington parish gobbler track by the author

ISBN: 978-0-692-78157-9

Table of Contents

Common Acronyms

LDWF = Louisiana Department of Wildlife and Fisheries
LDAF = Louisiana Department of Agriculture and Forestry
USFS = U. S. Department of Agriculture Forest Service
WMA = Wildlife Management Area
CRP = Conservation Reserve Program
EGCP = East Gulf Coastal Plain
WGCP = West Gulf Coastal Plain
MAV = Mississippi River Alluvial Plain
SMZ = Streamside Management Zone
LSU = Louisiana State University
DR = Direct Recovery
n = Number in Sample

NRCS = Natural Resource Conservation Service
USFWS = United States Fish and Wildlife Service
KNF = Kisatchie National Forest
NWR = National Wildlife Refuge
WRP = Wetland Reserve Program
UEGCP = Upper East Gulf Coastal Plain
UWGCP = Upper West Gulf Coastal Plain
BA = Basal Area
ROW = Rights of Way
UGA = The University of Georgia
RD = Ranger District
D.B.H. = Diameter at Breast Height

Introduction

It is important for readers to know that the author of this book is first a turkey hunter. Long before attention turned to study, wild turkey hunting captivated me more than the pursuit of any other quarry. Later blessed to work with wild turkeys for more than 33 years while employed by the Louisiana Department of Wildlife and Fisheries (LDWF), I served my last years before retiring as Louisiana's Wild Turkey and Resident Small Game Program Leader. It is with knowledge gained during hunting, research, management, and in-depth study that this book is written.

This writing focuses on the eastern wild turkey (*Meleagris gallopavo silvestris*) in Louisiana. It examines wild turkey history, biology, habitats, habits, management, local research, and multiple facets of turkey hunting within the state. Input from numerous wild turkey experts is included, as well as facts and informed opinions. Upon reading, it is hoped that Louisiana turkey enthusiasts will better understand the past, present, and future status of this great bird. This book seeks to dispel myths, prioritize meaningful habitat restoration efforts, divulge new information derived from recent research, and encourage steps needed to ensure that wild turkeys continue to be hunted in Louisiana for years to come.

The United States Fish and Wildlife Service (USFWS) reported a 4.1-billion-dollar nationwide economic impact related to management and pursuit of wild turkeys (USFWS 2010). The USFWS found wild turkey hunting second only to deer hunting in the U. S. with some 2.6 million turkey hunts per year. From 1996 – 2006, while all other hunting declined by 19%, wild turkey hunting increased by 15%. This increase is believed to be due to expanding turkey numbers and the special allure of wild turkey hunting.

In 2015 the wild turkey was selected by the U.S. Treasury to represent Louisiana on U. S. currency. The *"Kisatchie Wild Turkey"* quarter, featuring the wild turkey, also included Louisiana's vanishing longleaf pine habitat as its background. More than 2,000 people attended the official coin dedication ceremony held by the U.S. Forest Service in Alexandria, Louisiana. This was yet another example of the esteem at which the wild turkey is held in Louisiana.

Figure 1: Rear side of the Kisatchie Quarter (U. S. Forest Service)

The allure of the wild turkey comes from its many unique characteristics. Its iridescent feathers, that when displayed while strutting, demonstrate a beautiful metallic shine unlike any other native bird. The unique male gobble demands instant attention and can resound with greater prominence than any other bird of spring. Wild turkeys also possess a wariness and unpredictable response when pursued that challenges even the most skilled hunter. These wonderful traits, and more, add to the addictive nature of its hunting and captivates sportsmen in mass.

One of my earliest childhood memories involves a wild turkey in St. Tammany Parish, Louisiana. Only four years old, my dad brought me along on a wild turkey hunt. As he stalked a roosted turkey (not considered unsporting in those days), he placed me beneath a large pine along a dim logging trail so that he could approach closer without the noise and movement of a four-year-old. I still remember the point at which he walked around a wet area in the trail and rounded a bend leaving my sight. Frightened, I began to call out to him causing the turkey to fly. As dad fired 3 times at the bird it fell and I ran toward dad as fast as I could. He then began to yell *"stop"* and started running back to me. Little did I know that he had earlier stepped around a large cottonmouth in the wet spot while sneaking on the turkey, exactly where I was running. The loud shots, poisonous snake, and beautiful wild turkey all left a permanent impression on my young mind. By the age of eight (during the late 1960s) I was regularly turkey hunting in southeast Louisiana with my dad. Turkeys were very scarce then, but so were turkey hunters. During some years I would fail to hear even a single gobble. It was the late 1970s before local turkey numbers increased to the point where I consistently harvested gobblers. Since those early days I have hunted or worked in every parish within Louisiana that has a turkey season. From 1977 until the writing of this book I have been blessed to harvest a Louisiana wild turkey gobbler every season, most taken on public lands. I mention this not to boast of personal accomplishments but to demonstrate a passion for hunting in Louisiana and consistency in successful hunting tactics. Hired in 1982 by the LDWF as a wildlife specialist then later as a wildlife biologist, I soon became involved in the Louisiana wild turkey research and restocking effort. In those early years I relished every moment working with experienced LDWF personnel like Turkey Study Leader Dan Dennett, Dave Moreland, Robert Helm, Bob Love, Lloyd Cutrer, Mark Bible, Keith Hemsteter, and so many others. Through the 1980s, 1990s, and early 2000s other similar LDWF district/region crews across the state also worked tirelessly to find and trap wild turkeys for restocking the state. This statewide effort was a continuation of efforts started in the 1940s to restore turkeys to Louisiana. Through the years these dedicated LDWF employees, who overcame countless obstacles and at times were maligned by some turkey hunters, are the unsung heroes that deserve primary credit for restoring wild turkeys across the state. This book is dedicated to those hard working individuals that made wild turkey restoration in Louisiana a reality.

The first fulltime LDWF Turkey Study Leader Dan Dennett (left) and LDWF trapper Lloyd Cutrer (right) in St. Helena Parish (D. Moreland)

By the 1990s, in addition to wild turkey restocking, trapping efforts were increasingly directed at research in an effort to answer questions about Louisiana wild turkeys. It is during these decades that this author learned most about Louisiana turkey habits. From 1989 through 2007 district supervisors and wildlife division administrators encouraged efforts in southeast Louisiana to conduct the largest gobbler study done to date in Louisiana. The author, together with hard working LDWF staff of that area, captured, banded, and monitored over 500 gobblers. Similar important gobbler mortality studies were conducted in northcentral Louisiana, southwest Louisiana, Tunica Hills WMA, Big Lake WMA, Sherburne WMA, Three River/Red River (Richard K. Yancey WMA), Peason Ridge WMA, Tensas River National Wildlife Refuge, and on various private lands by Danny Timmer, Larry Savage, Dr. Jim Dickson, Fred Kimmel, John Robinette, Lowery Moak, Harry Cook, Curtis Parker, Len Bennett, James C. Davis, Dr. Michael Chamberlain, and many others. Beginning in 2010 I would again oversee a similar gobbler study on Kisatchie National Forest (KNF), netting and monitoring some 140 gobblers. Additional studies I participated in or supervised include telemetry studies of turkey habitat use in St. Helena parish, a GPS telemetry study of gobbler movement in relation to hunter movements in West Baton Rouge, West Feliciana, and Washington Parishes, a GPS telemetry study of turkey movements during high water in the Morganza spillway (Sherburne WMA), a GPS telemetry nesting study on Bens Creek WMA, a wing marked hen study in Washington Parish, hen nesting ecology study at Sherburne WMA, a GPS telemetry study of hens and broods in relation to large scale prescribed burning at Kisatchie National Forest, a GPS study of newly released turkeys in Caddo Parish, the Peason Ridge WMA GPS telemetry study of movements in relation to small scale habitat modifications, gobbler banding/mortality in East Feliciana Parish, Fall harvest-banding study on Peason Ridge WMA, turkey population monitoring post-hurricane Katrina at Pearl River WMA, annual turkey production studies statewide, food habits studies statewide, disease studies statewide, and numerous smaller studies. It is this experience placing hands on thousands of Louisiana trapped and/or harvested wild turkeys, as well as knowledge gained from working with some of the best turkey experts in the country, that has given me unique insight into Louisiana wild turkeys that I wish to share. It is hoped that the benefits to the reader of this lifetime of experience overshadows the lack of literary aptitude and political correctness demonstrated within this text.

West Feliciana parish gobblers (J.C. Davis)

Acknowledgements

This sometimes overlooked section of any book is to me, the most important. For it is in this section where one realizes how so many others have been such a blessing. I am blessed to have spent a lifetime in the great state of Louisiana, a state with such a diversity of habitats, cultures, and outdoor pursuits that it is without a doubt "The *Sportsman's Paradise*". I have been blessed to work for the Louisiana Department of Wildlife and Fisheries, an agency that historically has been made up of some of the greatest conservation professionals in the world. It has been a privilege to be associated with people that love wildlife and seeing others enjoy hunting, fishing, and other outdoor activities, most of these being people of good character, not afraid to take a stand for what is right even when such a stand is difficult.

The following is an incomplete list of present and former LDWF employees that have had a positive influence on turkeys in Louisiana during the past 60 years and/or contributed to this writing: Joe Herring, Dan Dennett, Jr., David Moreland, Hugh Bateman, Tommy Pricket, Danny Timmer, Larry Savage, Cody Cedotal, Fred Kimmel, Robert Barham, Charlie Melancon, Clark Hoffpauer, Leslie Glasgow, J. D. Hair, L. D. Young, Burton Angelle, Virginia Van Sickle, Jessie Guidry, Dwight Landreneau, Randy Myers, Jimmy Anthony, Kenny Ribbeck, Tommy Tuma, John D. Newsom, Richard K. Yancey, Robert Murray, Dewey Wills, Raymond Moody, John Haygood, Bob Love, Flavil D. Hollis, Dr. George H. Bick, J. B. Kidd, Louis Brunett, Reggie Wycoff, Jerald Owens, John Robinette, Kerny Sonnier, Jonathan Bordelon, Shannon Soileau, Randy Corlew, Brad Launey, Joe Shows, Cliff Ortis, Dave Fisher, Francis Bordelon, Greg Lachney, Vic Blanchard, John Sturgis, Tony Vidrine, John Mullins, Dave Morrison, Robert Gosnell, Mike Olinde, Jeff Duguay, Steve Smith, Duck Locascio, Mark Bible, Robert Helm, Lloyd Cutrer, Alvin Frierson, Henry Roberts, Curtis Parker, Charles "*Chili*" Baur, Pat Jones, Ray Palermo, Jack Rushing, Johnny Robertson, Russ Campbell, Red Walters, Lowery Moak, John T. Lincecum, Elbert Rachal, Eugene Marshall, Glenn Lee, Clyde Thompson, Clyde Harrison, Johnny Warren, Randall Ewing, Ryan Lemoine, L. D. Laborde, Danny Lively, Chuck Easterling, Duke Yates, Mark Johnson, Bill Spangler, David Henslee, Gene Wilson, Ronny McMurry, Jay Duprato, Jason Pike, Shannon Anderson, William Hatton, John Tarver, Len Bennett, Rodney Bennett, Jerry Farrar, Clifford "*Cliff*" Williams, Huey Sanders, Marvin Deason, Rowland Vernon, Bubba Parker, David Hayden, Cliff Sonnier, Tommy Bruhl, Robert Magee, Jerry Wagnon, Bruce Knight, Calvin Waskom, Jason Childress, Scott Durham, Keith Hemsteter, Kate Hasapas, John Hanks, Jeff Johnson, Leslie Johnson, Seth Miller, Jimmy Butcher, Jarrod Hughes, Christian Winslow, Mike Perot, Bradley Breland, Jimmy Ernst, Jill Day, Forest Burks, Wendell Smith, Larry Herrington, Eric Stokes, Mike Berg, C. M. Johnson, Paul Jackson, Bill Burns, Ben Holten, Jewell Sawyer, Czerny Newland, David Breithaupt, James C. Davis, Dr. Jim LaCour, Dr. Rusty Berry, Col. Joey Broussard, Harry Cook, Charlie Booth, Todd Bridges, Richard McMullen, Kensey Martin, Charles Smith, Levi McCullin, Steve Hebert, James Brooks, Jim Taylor, John Haygood, Robert Kimble, Todd Buffington, H. C. Beasley, Larry Weldon, Dave Taylor, Cliff Dailey, Brad Kennon, Judith Heintze, and Johnny Berry. Many more LDWF staff not listed assisted with habitat improvements and other complimentary tasks. A special thanks to LDWF enforcement officers that enforced turkey laws and protected turkeys through the critical restocking years until today. Some enforcement agents assisted biologists in restocking efforts, at least one even allowing turkeys to be trapped and moved from his own lands. Five present or former LDWF biologists, David Moreland, Larry Savage, Dr. Jim LaCour, Dr. Jeff Duguay, and Cody Cedotal, deserve a special thanks for their wise council, review, and comments during the writing of this book.

The National Wild Turkey Federation (NWTF) has also played an important role in the wild turkey recovery within Louisiana. From its start in 1973, the organization has sought to promote management, conservation, and hunting of wild turkeys. The recently unveiled "*Save the Habitat-Save the Hunt*" initiative focuses on restoring habitat to improve turkey hunting and hunter recruitment. There are some 6,000 active NWTF members in Louisiana who work tirelessly each year to hold events and raise funds for wild turkeys and are the backbone of this organization. Some 25 years ago with a small group of local turkey conservationists, the author like many others across the state, helped start an NWTF chapter in southeast Louisiana. This small chapter from an economically depressed corner of the state, has to date raised more than a million dollars to help wild turkeys. This kind of local effort duplicated in numerous communities across the state, has made Louisiana one of the most successful states in the nation at raising dollars for wild turkeys. In addition to fund raising, local Louisiana chapters sponsor and participate in public land youth hunts, JAKES (Juniors Acquiring Knowledge Ethics and Sportsmanship) events, Women in the Outdoors events, Wheelin' Sportsman handicap hunts, Wounded Warrior hunts, and LDWF Hunting Heritage (mentored) hunts for new hunters. Within this state, the NWTF has been an invaluable support of turkey restoration, management, research, and conservation. To date the NWTF has provided more than $3,090,206 to help turkeys in Louisiana. These dollars have helped improve turkey habitat on some 84,824 acres (NWTF 2016). The Louisiana Chapter of the NWTF is actively engaged with the LDWF and offers financial support each year to accomplish common goals. The NWTF has supported habitat projects on Wildlife Management Areas, National Wildlife Refuges, Corp of Engineers land, Kisatchie National Forest, and other public lands. NWTF also supports 4-H shooting sports, LDWF Louisiana Archery in the Schools program, LDWF Operation Game Thief, and has helped publish for public use, various educational writings regarding wild turkeys. Thanks to the members of the LA NWTF board of directors, Luke Lewis, regional and national NWTF staff, and special thanks to NWTF former Chief Conservation Officer, now Development Advisor, James Earl Kennamer Ph.D.

Another group that is unknown to most, but so important to wild turkeys across the southeast United States, is the Southeast Wild Turkey Working Group commonly called the Southeast Technical Committee. This group is composed of each southeastern state's top wild turkey biologist and meets at least once each year for a multi-day meeting. At these meetings, each state program leader shares information regarding their state's wild turkey status, issues of concern, and research activities. Between each day's meetings and well into each night, turkey discussions continue between state turkey program leaders making this annual gathering most informative. Members stay in contact throughout the year sharing information critical to successful wild turkey programs in each state. Top university wild turkey researchers are also included in the technical committee meetings, which keeps the group on the cutting edge of research findings. I thank the members of this committee for their friendship and efforts during the 6 years that I served as the Louisiana technical committee representative.

I especially thank the private landowners across the state that have graciously allowed LDWF staff to trap and move from their lands, wild turkeys for the purpose of restocking other parts of the state. These courageous and forward thinking individuals gave sacrificially so that others could enjoy wild turkeys. Certain corporate entities and timber companies also allowed trapping of turkeys from their land holdings further advancing restoration efforts. Other governmental agencies in addition to the LDWF allowed access and trapping of turkeys for restocking from lands under their authority. Each deserves thanks for their generous contribution to turkey restoration. Incomplete records, and in some cases a desire to remain anonymous, prevents proper acknowledgment of all that have contributed to this monumental effort. Nonetheless their gift to the people of this state (wild turkeys) lives on throughout Louisiana.

There are many notable Louisiana citizens like J. C. *"Sonny"* Gilbert, H. B. Fairchild, John Kean, Jerry Antley, Dr. James *"Jim"* Dickson, Kenny Morgan and so many other local wild turkey enthusiasts that deserve recognition. One that stands out in this group is the late John Barton, Sr. Mr. Barton was not only a wild turkey enthusiast and National NWTF leader, but he made vital contributions to the turkey restoration effort during the critical early years in Louisiana when he acquired part of the Terzia Wildlife Refuge in Morehouse parish (later Georgia-Pacific WMA). John agreed to donate several hundred wild turkeys over a period of years for the state's fledgling wild turkey restocking program. This generous donation formed the nucleus of many new flocks across Louisiana. *"His leadership as a member of the national NWTF board of directors was a major contributor to the early direction of the NWTF to help the organization mature to what it is today"* commented former NWTF Chief Conservation Officer James Earl Kennamer, Ph.D. Barton worked at the state and national level to further wild turkey conservation until his death in 2012. His children and grandchildren continue his tradition of wildlife conservation leadership.

The dedicated staff of Kisatchie National Forest who through the years have offered KNF lands as a source for turkeys used in restocking and research are sincerely thanked. So too are the U. S. Fish and Wildlife Service

(USFWS), Natural Resource Conservation Service (NRCS), Farm Service Agency (FSA), U. S. Department of Defense, and U. S. Army Corps of Engineers (USACE)' each having worked to protect and restore much needed wild turkey habitat and ensure that the tradition of turkey hunting continues.

Numerous universities have conducted research in Louisiana and provided vital information used in this text. More recent work has been conducted by Michael Chamberlain, Ph.D. (Univ. of Georgia), Bret Collier, Ph.D. (Louisiana State Univ.), Jim Dickson, Ph.D. (Louisiana Tech Univ.), Mike Byrne, Ph.D. (Nova Southeastern Univ.), and their various graduate students who have greatly advanced the understanding of wild turkeys in Louisiana. I offer a special thanks to Michael Chamberlain and Bret Collier for their review of this text and insightful comments during its writing.

I have had the privilege to hunt wild turkeys with the late Kenny Morgan, talk turkey with Lovett Williams, Jr., Ben Rogers Lee, George Wright, John Lewis, George Hurst, James Earl Kennamer, Allen Jenkins, John Barton, Sr., Preston Pittman, Michael Waddell, and so many other well-known wild turkey legends. Through the years I have had the opportunity to compare notes with dozens of nationally renowned wild turkey experts. These experiences have been tremendously rewarding, however, time spent hunting with close friends, my wife Tina, sons David and Brandon, dad James, and mom Lillian have been most memorable. My dad introduced me to turkey hunting and taught me that sharing the sport with others brings the greatest reward. I have since had the joy of introducing several to the sport of turkey hunting, but still relish most time hunting with a select few family members and close friends. A great friend that I hunted with most often was the late James Arthur. From the age of 6 we chased any form of game and fish we could find, but grew to love most the pursuit of wild turkeys. *"Leroy"* as I called him and *"Hobo"* as he nicknamed me, were evenly skilled self-described *"turkey assassins"*. So equal that if alive today he would likely not even read this book as he would probably tell me that he taught me everything in it anyway. Such a statement would not be that far from the truth.

I owe more than can ever be repaid to my wife Tina who has tolerated much from a husband and two sons completely obsessed with wild turkey hunting. From the start, she understood this passion and graciously supported vacations with the kids to hunt turkeys rather than trips to Disneyland. To our two son's David and Brandon, I am thankful for all of the fun times we have had together. It has been a joy to see them mature into young men of conviction to do what is right. Both now pursue careers in wildlife habitat conservation. To the rest of my family and all of those I failed to properly acknowledge, I apologize but know that you too are much appreciated.

Last but surely not least, I would like to thank God for giving us the beauty of nature and the wild turkey to enjoy. Also for blessing this author, a person of limited intellect, the privilege of spending a lifetime in the company of so many gifted people, a myriad of unique experiences, and an opportunity to share with others. *"What no eye has seen, nor ear heard, nor the heart imagined, what God has prepared for those who love him"* (1 Corinthians 2: 9 ESV *Holy Bible*).

Sons Brandon and David a few years back after a great afternoon hunt in Tangipahoa parish (T. Stafford)

History of Wild Turkeys in Louisiana

Dr. Lyle St. Amant recorded in the 1959 *Louisiana Wildlife Inventory and Management Plan* that DuPratz (1758), Shultz (1810), and Joutel (1846) documented wild turkeys ranging over the entire state in considerable numbers. They also indicated that it was a choice food of the early settlers and in great demand in the open market. Evidence across the wild turkey's range indicates that Native Americans relied heavily on their meat for food (Dickson 1992). It is speculated, based on numerous historical reports, that wild turkeys were less wary when pursued by Native Americans and early European settlers than they are today. St. Amant (1959) reported that turkeys were probably plentiful in Louisiana until about 1880. It was believed by early researchers, that the range of Louisiana's original wild turkeys included the upland Florida Parishes from the cypress/tupelo swamps northward and east to Mississippi. The turkey's range also occurred north of an irregular line starting at the Texas line (Sabine River) mid-Calcasieu Parish extending to lower Concordia Parish. There is some documentation suggesting that wild turkeys may have occurred near New Orleans, Avery Island, and St. Mary parish when these areas were first explored by Europeans, but corroborating information is limited. Since no geological barrier existed to preclude expansion south of the assumed range line, it is possible turkeys historically could be found on riverine ridges where suitable habitats occurred.

The first Louisiana turkey hunting season was established by the state legislature in 1902 extending from November through March (Hollis 1950). No daily or season bag limits were set and turkeys of either sex could be harvested. Baiting, the use of dogs, and selling of harvested game was common practice during this time. My dad reported that his grandfather, Hollis Lindsey, Sr., used dogs in St. Helena and Tangipahoa parishes to flush young turkeys into trees in the fall for easy harvests. It is commonly believed that during the early years turkeys were more readily approached by man. Early LDWF biologists were told that on occasion shooting turkeys from horse drawn buggies could be done (pers. comm. J. Haygood). By 1905 the turkey hunting season was reduced by one month, restricted to males only, and a daily bag limit of 25 was set. This was a rather insignificant adjustment to an already rapidly declining population. Even so, President Theodore Roosevelt, Jr. and hunting party pursued wild turkeys in Louisiana during their famous bear hunts (pers. comm. Theodore Roosevelt, IV). President Roosevelt was instrumental in spurring a nationwide conservation movement that in Louisiana led to the establishment of the Board of Commissioners for the Protection of Birds, Game, and Fish. In 1912, Act 127 of the legislature consolidated activities regarding wildlife, fish, forestry, and mineral resources under the Conservation Commission of Louisiana. In 1918 this act was amended creating the Department of Conservation. Later by vote of the people in 1944, the Louisiana Wildlife and Fisheries Commission (later called Department) was created (Adkins 1988). Early turkey harvest numbers are scarce but it was reported that despite very liberal regulations only 2,219 turkeys were bagged during the 1909 – 10 season (McIlhenny 1914).

In 1912 Edward A. McIlhenny, founder of the well-known Tabasco company located on Avery Island, completed one of the nation's earliest books about wild turkeys, titled *The Wild Turkey and Its Hunting* (McIlhenny 1914), that featured information provided by his friend Charles L. Jordan. Jordan was an accomplished turkey hunter, call maker, and manager of the 10,000 acre Morris Game Preserve (now locally known as Zemurray Park) in Tangipahoa parish. While working on his planned book, Jordan was tragically killed by a poacher in 1909. His notes and photographs were used by McIlhenny to write the book. Assistant Secretary of the Louisiana Department of Conservation, Captain John K. Renaud, a confederate veteran, was a personal friend and hunting companion of Jordan (Cope 1932). The site that Jordan managed and studied wild turkeys on was first owned by Nathan Joiner in the 1790s according to William E. Perrin Jr.'s 1971 thesis. It was later acquired by John A. Morris who created the game preserve. Samuel Zemurray, Sr., a Russian immigrant who made his fortune in the Central American banana trade, purchased the property in 1928. The site quickly became known for its beautiful lakes and azalea gardens. The property was then acquired by Fred Reimers in 1974 and is still managed for wildlife including wild turkeys by his heirs today. Zemurray Park served as a WMA from the 1950s through early 1970s. As a young biologist in southeast Louisiana, I had the privilege of spending many hours working on various wildlife management projects with Zemurray Park managers.

In the late 1800s, with the clearing of vast areas of virgin forests and unrestricted hunting, wild turkey numbers began to plummet. By 1920 wild turkeys had completely disappeared from 18 of the original 39 states where turkeys once occurred (Mosby and Handley 1943). In 1905 the first daily bag limits were instituted in Louisiana. Hunting restrictions gradually increased over the next 27 years until the season was closed in 1933 for lack of turkeys (Hollis 1950).

It was during this time that efforts of early conservationists like Caroline Dorman helped spur the establishment of the Kisatchie National Forest (KNF) in 1930. Caroline, a self-made naturalist, was alarmed by the destruction of massive areas of forest by the *"cut out and get out"* policies of early logging companies. Caroline would ride a horse pulled wagon through great forests of longleaf pine. She noticed the many plant and animal species that inhabited the longleaf forest and she spent considerable time exploring the forest and inventorying the plants and birds. Previously the Weeks Act of 1911 had authorized the purchase of lands for national forest purposes. The act carried a provision that each state legislature had to pass an *"enabling act"* to allow the federal government to purchase land within its boundaries. Because of the tireless efforts of Ms. Dorman, the Louisiana legislature passed the enabling legislation which made the Kisatchie National Forest possible. The first block of the Kisatchie proclaimed by congress was the Catahoula District in 1930.

Despite wild turkey declines, state forester V. H. Sonderegger reported in 1932 seeing turkeys during his work across Louisiana (Sonderegger 1932). At that time, there were still areas of uncut virgin pine in proximity to areas recently cut where turkeys could be found. Sonderegger, who once lived in Winn parish, reported *"There is no question that the wild turkey of Louisiana has been rather ruthlessly destroyed by hunters who did not appreciate the sport..."*. As overseer of state forests Sonderegger (1932) gave detailed reports from his field staff. *"Ranger E. M. Thorton in charge of the area of Union and Morehouse parishes reports that eight wild turkeys were killed during the past season. From information obtained from Mr. Thorton, there are, at least fifty known turkeys to be found in the forests of his region. In addition to the piney wood areas mentioned above, the region constituting Madison, Richland, and the two Carroll parishes are reported to have more turkeys than any other section of the state. In the Northwest section of Louisiana, Assistant Ranger J. A. Frazier, reports about fifty head of turkey in the woods, and further states that this year none of these birds have been killed. In southwest Louisiana wild turkeys are grouped in areas protected against fire, particularly in the branch bottoms that feed into the Calcasieu River and those bottoms that feed into Sabine River. Turkeys are not propagating well in this area, due to being extensively hunted, and there is no question that they will be gradually killed out..." "...the Florida Parishes ... contains the largest number of turkeys in the state for its size. Wild turkeys are found in the rough woods and bottoms of St. Helena and Livingston parishes... Turkeys are also found in the dense hardwood bottoms bordering the lake and on the rivers that enter Lake Ponchartrain in St. Tammany and Tangipahoa parishes."*

During 1941 – 42 a turkey population census was conducted by Dr. George H. Bick that found only 1,738 wild turkeys statewide. The survey was meant to continue but was abandoned due to World War II. The turkey hunting season was opened again *"without justification in 1945, despite vigorous protests of the Department of Wild Life and Fisheries "*(Hollis 1950). Even in those days' politicians were known to ignore advice from professional wildlife biologists. Sometime around 1946 it is believed that Louisiana's turkey population hit its lowest point. A similar survey as that done by Bick was conducted by F. D. Hollis during 1946 and estimated that only 1,463 wild turkeys remained in Louisiana (Hollis 1950). Figure 2 illustrates the few isolated pockets within the state where turkeys existed in 1946.

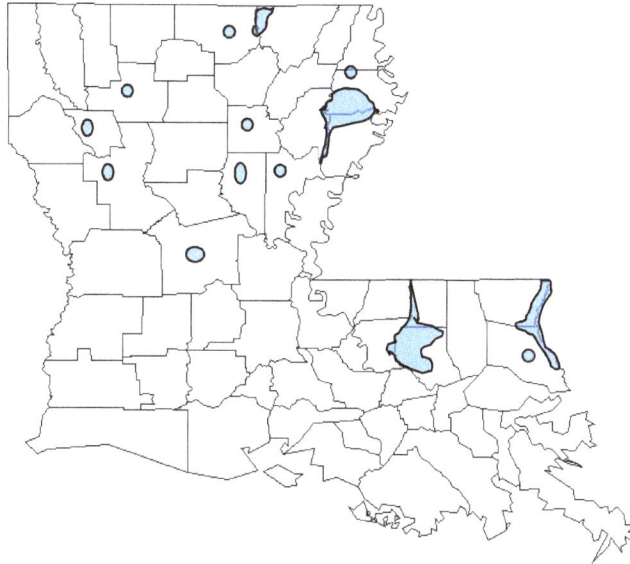

Figure 2: Habitat occupied by wild turkeys in 1946 (Hollis 1950)

The area occupied represented only 5% of the wild turkey's original range in Louisiana (Bick 1947). Most of the turkeys were found in Livingston, Madison, St. Tammany, Morehouse, St. Helena, Tensas, and Washington parishes, in descending order. Forty-six percent of the population was found on the Singer-Ayer Wildlife Refuge and Morehouse Game Refuge (Hollis 1950). These areas offered isolation and some level of protection against poaching. Approximately 78% of the total population was restricted to hardwood bottomlands (Bick 1947). Each area where turkeys persisted was typically composed of large remnant contiguous forest, sparsely populated, and often had numerous waterways that limited human access. Many of the more proficient turkey hunters today hail from these 7 parishes due to institutional hunting skills passed down from hunters of this lean period. In the 1940 census Louisiana averaged 30 persons per square mile, yet parishes occupied by wild turkeys averaged only 18 persons per square mile. Livingston Parish, where the greatest turkey population occurred in 1950, was heavily forested. Eighty-two percent of the parish was forested, with 38% being hardwoods, 24% mixed pine-hardwoods and 38% pure pine (Hollis 1950). Based on personal conversations with Livingston residents, fire was a common practice of the time used to encourage grasses for free ranging cattle. Hollis (1950) stated that *"Many citizens of Livingston Parish showed a pronounced interest in the wild turkey and its requirements. However, it was from this area that the most startling reports of flagrant violations were received."* Bick (1947) stated regarding this parish that *"every indication is that an illegal kill has always been high"*. Not to discriminate, he went on to report that *"every indication is that poaching has always been extensive"* in the Pearl River bottomlands of St. Tammany and Washington Parishes where this author's family has its roots.

In 1942 the Singer-Ayer Wildlife Refuge was some 125,000 acres of bottomland forest in Madison and northern Tensas Parishes. By 1946 the Singer-Ayer Wildlife Refuge had been reduced in size to 81,000 acres (Hollis 1950). It was described as having a large variety of mature mast producing trees that in many areas had a lush green ground cover which gave it a *"parklike"* appearance. However, even this refuge was heavily logged during the war years (Hollis 1950). The Morehouse Game Refuge, in Morehouse Parish was approximately 113,000 acres in 1942 but was reduced to 81,000 acres by the end of World War II. This refuge also offered both vast bottomland hardwoods and mixed pine/hardwood areas for turkeys. The Morehouse Refuge experienced frequent flooding in portions of the refuge that created open understory conditions. Both areas were considered to be well protected from poaching unlike the Honey Island/Pearl River/Bogue Chitto River area which was considered less protected.

The dramatic decline of turkeys during the early 1900s caused many to fear total extirpation of wild turkeys from the state. In 1932, E. B. Cope reported in the *Louisiana Conservation Review, "today the turkey is facing extinction"*. Near this same period the Pittman-Robertson Act of 1937 was passed which used an excise tax on sporting goods and ammunition to fund conservation efforts in each state. As concern grew, and with these new funding resources, wildlife managers earnestly began work to reverse the decline in turkeys. From 1948 to 1950 some 2,203 game farm turkeys were stocked throughout the state (St. Amant 1950). This was an expensive operation that put more pen-raised turkeys afield than were estimated to exist naturally in the wild. A handful of these turkeys were wild trapped but most were pen-reared. Some were hatched from eggs of wild origin birds while most were raised from captive wild stock. Some 5,000 pen-raised turkeys were released from 1949 – 1953. Of these, 2,144 were released on newly created refuges and wildlife management areas (WMAs) and 2,400 released at other sites in various parishes across the state. These turkeys were purchased from farms in Alabama, Maryland, Pennsylvania and West Virginia (Duffy 1974). Turkeys released were fitted with blue celluloid leg bands to help identify these birds from any native birds in the area. A total of 568 pen-raised turkeys were released on Red Dirt, Catahoula, and Union Game Management Areas from 1949 – 53 but by 1953 only 95 remained (Fifth Biennial Report 1953). It was reported that the birds survived for a period of time at 3 sites but after 11 years failed to produce huntable numbers (Murry 1963). By the early 1950s the practice of using pen raised wild turkeys was abandoned in Louisiana due to expense and lack of success. Many other states also experimented with pen-raised wild turkey releases and experienced the same lack of success.

Considerable effort was expended during the Bick and Hollis studies to survey statewide turkey numbers of the time period and to document the date of the last known wild turkey sighting in parishes where they had already disappeared (Hollis 1950). Both researchers recruited hundreds of observers that included conservation agents, state forestry staff, local Louisiana Wildlife Federations members, and certain local officials selected at random across the state to document turkey sightings.

Table 1 is a compilation of dates and parishes where wild turkeys were considered extant (geographically extinct), it includes the year of the last turkey sighting and the observer where available.

Table 1

Last Known Record of Turkeys in 20 Parishes (Hollis 1950 and St. Amant 1959)

Parish	Date	Observer
Avoyelles	?	No Records Available
Beauregard	1940	Chuyler Gill
Bossier	1935	G. H. Lowery
Caddo	?	No Records Available
Calcasieu	1939	Dr. W. A. K. Seale
Claiborne	1911	J. N. Brown
Concordia	1916	T. H. Forman, Jr.
DeSoto	1936	C. H. Harris, Jr.
Evangeline	1941	E. A. Butler
-	1940	W. R. Vailot
Grant	1937	B. H. Lemoine
Jackson	1941	T. H. Kilpatrick
Lincoln	1941	Jos. Singer
Ouachita	1940	J. L. Frost
Richland	1940	Mark B. Cooper
Sabine	1939	W. D. Davis, Jr.
Tangipahoa	1940	Recy Husser
Vernon	1938	H. B. Marcus
Webster	1925	J. E. Long
West Carroll	1936	Allen Hawsey
West Feliciana	1938	T. H. Martin

Again during 1948 to 1950 intensive field investigations were conducted to estimate the numbers of native wild turkeys in each parish where turkeys existed. During the same period of time large numbers of pen-raised wild turkeys were stocked throughout the state. It is interesting to note that the number of stocked pen-raised turkeys exceeded the estimated population of 1,507 native wild turkeys in Louisiana.

The following table contains the list of parishes and estimated wild turkeys present as well as pen-raised turkey releases from 1948 – 1950 (St. Amant 1959) (Table 2).

Table 2

Louisiana Turkeys in 1950 (St. Amant 1959)

Parish	Estimated Native Turkeys	Stocked Turkeys 1948 - 50
Allen	0	365
Beauregard	0	91
Bienville	11	11
Caldwell	11	226
Catahoula	11	0
East Baton Rouge	11	0
East Feliciana	0	8
Evangeline	0	20
Franklin	44	16
LaSalle	33	0
Livingston	341	99
Madison	286	318
Morehouse	143	166
Natchitoches	11	124
Rapides	11	44
Red River	33	0
Sabine	0	99
St. Helena	132	0
St. Tammany	154	0
Tensas	110	268
Union	55	106
Vernon	0	162
Washington	99	0
Webster	0	8
West Feliciana	0	8
Winn	0	75
Totals	**1,507**	**2,203**

*All other parishes assumed to have no turkeys present.

Prior to the 1960s, the few native wild turkeys live captured for restocking purposes were usually taken via wooden/wire walk-in coral type traps (Figure 3). Turkey injuries were common with this method and trapping success was very low, as most wild turkeys would simply not walk into such a confined space.

Figure 3: Stationary coral "trap door" type turkey trap (L. Williams, Jr.)

There were many different wire coral type trap designs used during the early years of turkey trapping. Traps used funnel entrances, shallow ditch entrances, or trap doors and were still being used by some until about 1965 (Pellerin 1965). However, by 1963 Louisiana biologists began to increasingly use a new trapping method successfully used by waterfowl biologists for several years prior. This method employed the use of "*cannon nets*". Cannon nets used black-powder at the base of tubes to propel projectiles attached to a folded net. Cannon nets were soon replaced by more advanced "*rocket nets*" that used electronically detonated howitzer propellant explosive charges, placed within small metal rockets containing exhaust ports at the rear to propel an attached net. Nets and rockets were highly mobile and easy to hide from the wary eyes of wild turkeys (Figure 4). This advancement allowed the rapid deployment of a large net over a group of pre-baited wild turkeys before they had time to escape. Entire flocks could now be captured, greatly increasing efficiency and ease of acquiring free ranging wild turkeys. Year 1962 marked this new modern era of turkey restocking in Louisiana that initiated the turning point for restoration of wild turkeys in the state.

Even with this advancement in trapping technology, old fashion turkey scouting skills and woodsmanship were required to regularly capture turkeys. Those most skilled at locating turkeys, baiting sites, setting nets without disturbance, and spending countless hours in frigid blinds saw the greatest results. Efforts to capturing a single flock of turkeys could take a few days, several weeks, or not be accomplished at all following weeks of effort. Those LDWF biologists and wildlife technicians that participated in turkey trapping remained committed to the task even if it took multiple years to complete a specific release.

Figure 4: Rocket net being set by LDWF Ferriday biologist Reggie Wycoff and crew (L. Savage)

The peak of the first phase of modern restocking using wild trapped turkeys came during the late 1960s to the mid-1970s. Prior to and during this early restoration period, turkey project leadership was a shared part-time responsibility led by various other game division program biologists. Later Dan Dennett, Jr. would be selected to serve as the state's first full time turkey program (study) leader. Louisiana supplemented in-state trapping efforts with wild trapped turkeys received from other states. Based on conversations with LDWF staff of that era it is believed that most, if not all, of the turkeys used from the state of Florida were of the subspecies *Meleagris gallopavo osceola* commonly referred to as the Florida wild turkey. LDWF biologist James Taylor reported in his 1969 thesis that 18 *M. g. osceola* subspecies turkeys were received from Florida in exchange for two Louisiana deer per turkey. The turkeys were released on Jackson-Bienville WMA (Taylor 1969). Noted Florida wild turkey researcher Lovett E. Williams, Jr. assisted Louisiana biologists during this restocking effort (Joe Herring per. comm.). Florida turkeys were released in Claiborne, Webster, Bossier, Bienville, Natchitoches, Vernon, Allen, St. Landry, and Concordia parishes. Some of these stocked areas saw early reproduction, but by 1970 areas such as Bodcau Wildlife Management Area (WMA), Fort Polk-Vernon WMA, Jackson-Bienville WMA, and Red Dirt WMA each reported Florida turkey stockings to be a failure (14th Biennial Report 1970 – 71). Former LDWF District Supervisor John Haygood suspected that failures may have been due in part to earlier nesting chronology of Florida turkeys (pers. comm. J. Haygood).

Louisiana hunters and some biologists have speculated that the Florida subspecies may have been native to Louisiana especially in the easternmost portion of the state. In 1955 a range map was created that described an area extending from southern South Carolina to southeast Louisiana as occupied by an *"intergrade"* mixture of both *osceola "Florida"* and *silvestris "Eastern"* subspecies (Aldrich and Duvall 1955). Today this area continues to contain turkeys that exhibit physical characteristics of both but looked exactly like neither. This author personally spoke to Lovett Williams, Jr. regarding the possibility of some original Louisiana turkeys being *"Florida"* subspecies. Williams expressed doubt of this occurring outside of the original Florida birds released during the 1960s and 70s. However, it is possible, and I believe likely, that certain Louisiana populations maintain characteristics somewhat similar to the *osceola* subspecies. Considering the influence of birds relocated from northern states, and releases of birds from other coastal states, turkeys in some sites may no longer be as genetically *"pure"* as the original Louisiana wild turkey.

Hunters of old, including this author, will testify that adult *"native"* gobblers harvested during the early years in southeast Louisiana would seldom weigh more than 16 pounds. Hunters of that time who reported harvesting an adult weighing 18 or more pounds were considered liars or worse yet turkey baiters. I have witnessed many adult gobblers weighing between 12 to 15 pounds. In very low populations this may have been a product of limited genetic variability or some environmental influence of the time. Today, adult gobblers in these same areas where low weights were once common now often weigh 18 to 20 pounds or more. Early records from north Louisiana parishes such as Tensas, Madison, Franklin, Union, and Morehouse, reported greater weights during the early 1960s (Newsom 1962). An interesting observation in Newsom's article was that most hunters posed their trophy gobblers by holding the wings outward to show the large wingspan. Wingspans ranging from 56 to 62 inches were noted under the photographs illustrated in Newsom's report. Today most hunters pose their harvested turkeys breast down and tail fans displayed.

By 1970 wild turkeys could be found in 26 parishes (Olinde and Timmer 1997). A second peak in restocking came during the early to mid-1980s under Dennett's leadership. Turkey numbers began to rapidly grow during this period especially in the Florida Parishes where most of the state's turkey hunters and harvests occurred. The next even larger peak of restocking came during the late 1980s through the 1990s under the leadership of turkey program leader Danny Timmer. This phase of restocking focused on moving turkeys from areas of high concentration to areas of good habitat primarily in central, northcentral, and southwest Louisiana. During this period of restoration, turkey numbers greatly increased in newly stocked areas and subsequently more areas were opened to turkey hunting (Figure 5). By 1996 wild turkeys could be found in about 50 parishes (Olinde and Timmer 1997) all the more evidence of what a monumental success restoration efforts achieved.

Figure 5: Red indicates areas open to turkey hunting each decade from 1963 – 2013 (La. Hunting Regs.)

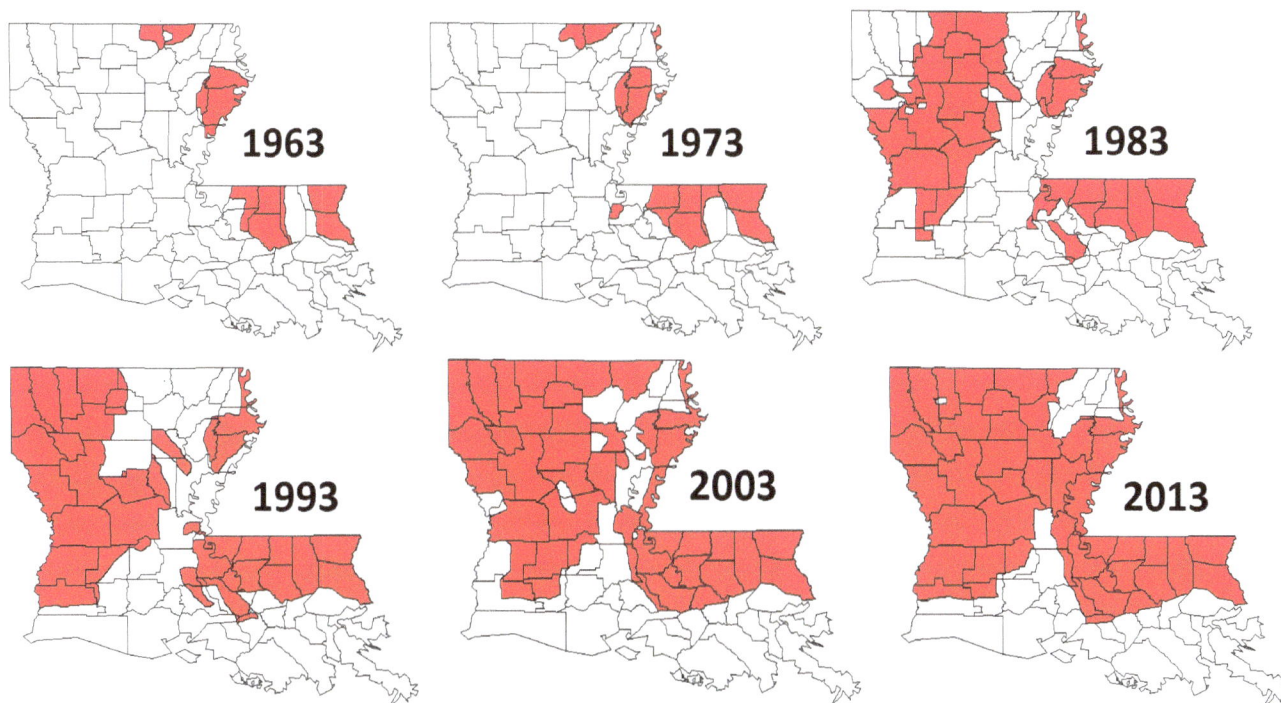

Occasionally, interstate "*horse trading*" would occur involving wild turkeys. Former LDWF biologist, wildlife division chief, and agency Secretary Joe Herring reported to this author that Louisiana swapped marsh deer for Florida wild turkeys. Louisiana river otters were traded for Missouri wild turkeys (Olinde and Timmer 1997). Other swaps occurred, one trading Louisiana turkeys for pheasants. Since many surrounding states like Louisiana were working hard to restore various species, they worked together to achieve individual state wildlife restoration goals.

From 1962 through 2016 some 3,913 wild turkeys have been translocated in Louisiana. Most (3,160) were wild captured in Louisiana then moved to other sites within the state. Some 753 wild trapped turkeys came from outside of Louisiana from states including Mississippi, Alabama, Florida, Arkansas, South Carolina, Missouri, Wisconsin, Connecticut, and Iowa. Many of these out-of-state turkeys, 427 in total, were secured as part of the NWTF "*Target 2000*" program. This program paid donor states $500 per turkey to advance ongoing state restocking programs. Appendix A lists the number of wild turkeys stocked and states of origin during 1962 through 2016.

x‑-

Restocking Years

Wild turkeys being captured by use of a rocket net (J. C. Davis)

Over time, LDWF biologists and wildlife technicians trapping turkeys became more skilled in rocket net trapping techniques and success rates climbed. A few wild turkeys were captured in Louisiana using bait laced with oral tranquilizing drugs such as alpha-cloralose and tribromoethanol. This method worked well in certain other states with more open habitats, but in Louisiana's thick habitats, intoxicated turkeys could easily wander away from the view of biologists hiding in blinds, never to be found. On occasion this author participated in such efforts and found it very entertaining to watch as turkeys became *"drunk"* to the point where they could easily be captured with dip nets. One problem associated with oral drugs was that some turkeys ate too much treated bait while others did not eat enough. This resulted in different turkeys wandering off in multiple directions in various stages of intoxication. On at least one occasion an intoxicated hen was killed by a non-intoxicated gobbler during an LDWF capture attempt (pers. comm. H. Cook). This author once rescued a gobbler so relaxed that his head fell into a water puddle and was seconds from drowning. On another occasion I witness an intoxicated crow fly at full speed into a pine tree. Neighboring researchers in Mississippi once observed a pair of small birds fly in and become intoxicated then minutes later 3 gobblers arrived only to eat the two small birds (pers. comm. D. Godwin). It is such unpredictability of outcomes that eventually steered LDWF biologists away from using drugged baits.

Rocket nets proved by far the best method of wild turkey capture in Louisiana. With increased capture success came more stocked sites. Early releases received a 10/5 stocking, meaning 10 females and 5 males. Obviously, trapping seldom followed this precise script and releases would be whatever combination that could be captured, understanding that both sexes were required for success. Later releases were increased to 20/5 stockings. Twenty hens and 5 gobblers meant fewer releases but promised a greater chance of restoration success. After stocking, hunting was usually prohibited by Louisiana Wildlife and Fisheries Commission action for a period of three to five years within a larger surrounding area. This period allowed turkeys time and room to expand. If things went well, a group of 15 turkeys could expand in numbers by 50 – 60% annually (Dennett & Duffy 1982) within areas where turkeys had been absent for decades. Certain areas that this author observed responded exceptionally by nearly doubling in number each year. Sometime between 7 to 15 years after restocking new populations would often reach their zenith. Much to the disappointment of hunters, turkeys would begin to decline then stabilize at a more modest level. This phenomenon, expected by biologists, was often hard to explain to the average hunter now hearing half the gobblers he did just a few years earlier. Many biologists believe such declines are caused by *"density dependent"* factors. Density dependent factors are variables in the environment that limit population growth as the population increases in density. These factors are not as limiting when turkeys are new to an area, but as time goes on can become an ever increasing population constraint as the turkey density increases. Normal limiting factors such as quality nesting and brood rearing habitats are abundant when turkeys are first released into a new site. Also predators at these new release sites have not yet become proficient turkey eaters. This results in a few years of high production and survival that continues until density dependent factors catch up and become more apparent. As time elapses post-release, these density dependent factors become more restrictive to a population until a natural more sustainable population-habitat balance is reached.

F. D. Hollis (1950) suggested that optimal turkey habitats might require 10,000 to 50,000 acres of forest to be considered suitable. Early in the restocking years 10,000 acres of forested habitat was the minimum benchmark desired for consideration of a new release site. This minimum acreage for restocking was reduced over time as biologists saw that well managed smaller tracts could sustain substantial turkey numbers. Four thousand acres of good habitat is now considered the minimum contiguous forest size to qualify for a release of wild turkeys. Regardless of this somewhat arbitrary number, there exists an acreage minimum for each site where turkeys cease to thrive.

Sites considered for restocking are usually devoid of turkeys before stocking. If even a few birds are present biologists believe that if conditions were favorable for expansion these few birds should have increased in number. In such situations an evaluation of the factors constraining this population is essential. Factors constraining a population from growing are known as limiting factors. Density dependent factors are one category of limiting factors. The other category of limiting factors is known as density independent factors. Density independent factors can limit a population regardless of its population size. For example, a hurricane or flood may diminish a certain percentage of a population regardless of its size.

Sites selected for restocking should also have a strong potential to benefit the public. Restocking is a significant sportsman funded expense. The LDWF avoids releases on single landowner tracts where expansion to other lands is not likely due to habitat barriers. Almost every year the LDWF receives requests, particularly from south Louisiana, to stock turkeys in areas dominated by cypress/tupelo swamps. Although a few such trees are an asset to good turkey habitat, they must be accompanied by a preponderance of dryer mast producing (oak type) bottomland forests. History has proven that releases done on marginal habitat sites within Louisiana fail to produce sustainable turkey numbers.

Protection is essential for a new turkey release to succeed. As a new biologist during the early 1980s I participated in the restocking of south Livingston parish. At this time you could hardly find a deer track, much less a turkey track, in the areas that were being considered for restocking. As we released the first wild turkeys, having heard the parish reputation as poaching capitol of Louisiana, I predicted total failure in reestablishing turkeys there. I could not have been more wrong. As we released turkeys on several Livingston parish hunting clubs, I quickly saw that the local people were determined to protect these cherished turkeys. Some even threatening bodily harm to anyone caught killing one of these newly released turkeys. Within a few short years turkeys were thriving in south Livingston parish and I couldn't help recalling the Bible verse to *"Judge not lest ye be judged."* (Mathew 7: 1 KJV *Holy Bible*)

In most cases protection of newly stocked areas also included a period of *"closed season"*. During the first peak of restocking that occurred during the 1960s and 1970s hunting was not allowed by LDWF regulation for a minimum period of 3 years (pers. comm. L. Savage). This may not have been long enough for some areas and was later changed to a minimum of 5 years that seemed to be more successful in protecting newly established populations. In some cases, longer periods are warranted before hunting is justified.

Owners/land managers at each site that received restocked turkeys would be required to sign a 10-year agreement that would allow the LDWF, once turkey numbers grew, to trap from their site for other releases. This wise policy ensured continued trap sites and a continuous return on the state's initial investment of turkeys.

The following graph shows the wild turkey restocking numbers from 1962 through 2016 (Figure 6).

Figure 6: Louisiana Wild Turkey Restocking 1962 – 2016

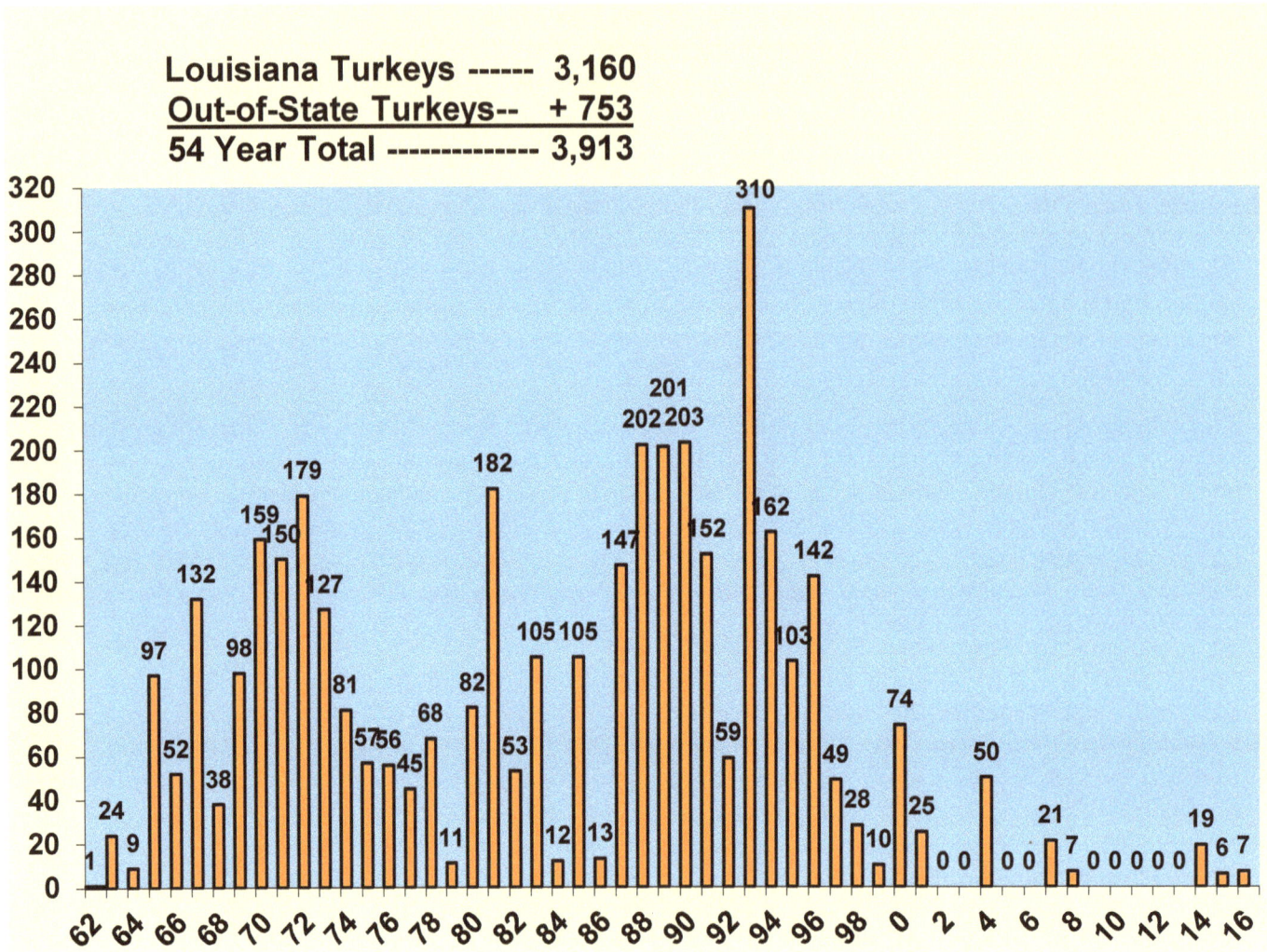

In 1997 the LDWF published a detailed record of capture/release locations and numbers of wild turkeys stocked in Louisiana. This publication, titled *Louisiana's Wild Turkey Restoration Program 1962 – 1997* authored by Mike Olinde and Danny Timmer, gives parish by parish capture and release information in considerable detail.

Louisiana has been the beneficiary of several out-of-state donations of turkeys and has participated in three transfers of turkeys to neighboring Texas. One donation of 12 turkeys during the 1980s, one during the mid-2000s of 12 turkeys, and one transfer of 12 turkeys in 2014 as part of a multistate effort to reestablish eastern wild turkeys in east Texas. There is an unsubstantiated report of 8 turkeys captured and moved in-state from Pearl River WMA during the 1970s. Outside of these reports, current records are believed complete for the period of 1962 - 2016. If other turkeys were moved during this period no record was found nor was any such undocumented activity divulged to this author during his 33 years with LDWF. Figure 7 shows the number of turkeys stocked in each parish from 1962 – 2016.

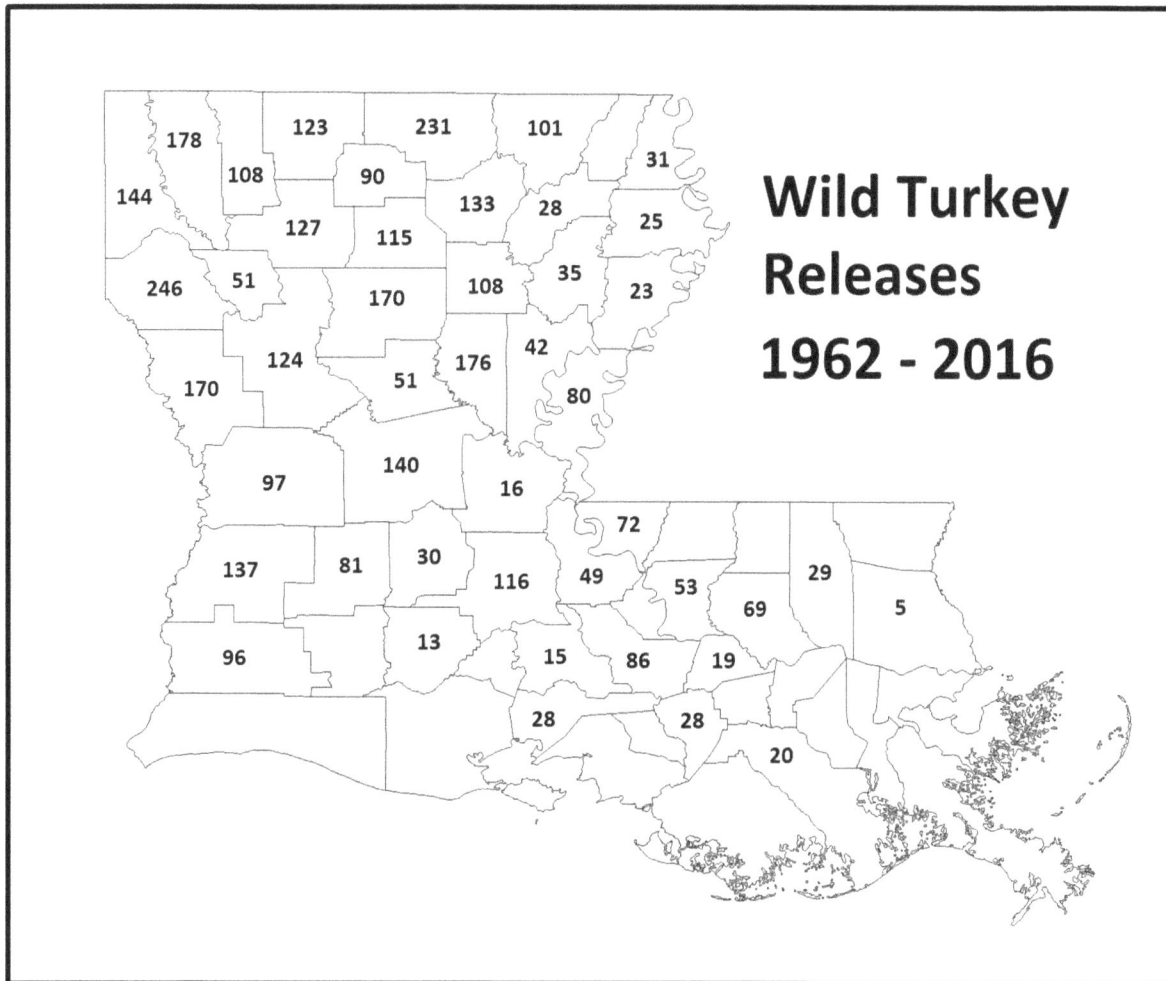

Figure 7: Number of wild trapped turkeys released in each parish 1962 - 2016. (LDWF)

Eight sites within Louisiana were extremely important as sources for wild turkeys. These sites contributed some 2,070 turkeys for use in restocking efforts. The managers and LDWF staff that worked so diligently on these areas during this multiyear effort greatly expanded turkey numbers throughout the state. These areas include Fort Polk-Vernon WMA (427 turkeys), Georgia-Pacific WMA (369 turkeys), Sicily Island Hills WMA renamed J. C. Sonny Gilbert WMA (304 turkeys), Lookout Point (280 turkeys), Gulf States Utility now Entergy (197 turkeys), Peason Ridge WMA (184 turkeys), and Red River WMA renamed Richard K. Yancey WMA (155 turkeys). Most of these capture sites were WMAs but two were corporate owned lands of Gulf States Utilities (now Entergy) in West Feliciana Parish and Lookout Point owned by International Paper Company in East Carroll Parish.

Additional turkeys were captured on other WMAs, U. S. Forest Service lands, and other public and private lands where permission was granted. Turkey trappers, including the author, have at one time or another received verbal chastisement from hunters for moving turkeys out of their hunting area. Turkey trappers have on occasion faced protest fliers erected to encourage local people to oppose trapping efforts (Figure 8). Turkey trapping equipment has been vandalized, burned, sabotaged, and stolen by those that objected. Little did protestors know that many of us working at LDWF moved turkeys from our own favorite hunting grounds during this period to advance the cause of statewide restoration. It is such sacrifice that expanded wild turkeys across this state. With few exceptions, nearly every turkey hunter in Louisiana today can trace the origin of turkeys in his or her favorite hunting spot to these restocking efforts.

The flier in figure 8 was distributed by those who objected to LDWF capturing turkeys from their area for restocking. A small number of turkeys were moved from this particular area during the 1960s and early 1970s, yet the turkey population still increased in the area from that time until the 1990s. Not all hunters of this area agreed with those who erected such fliers.

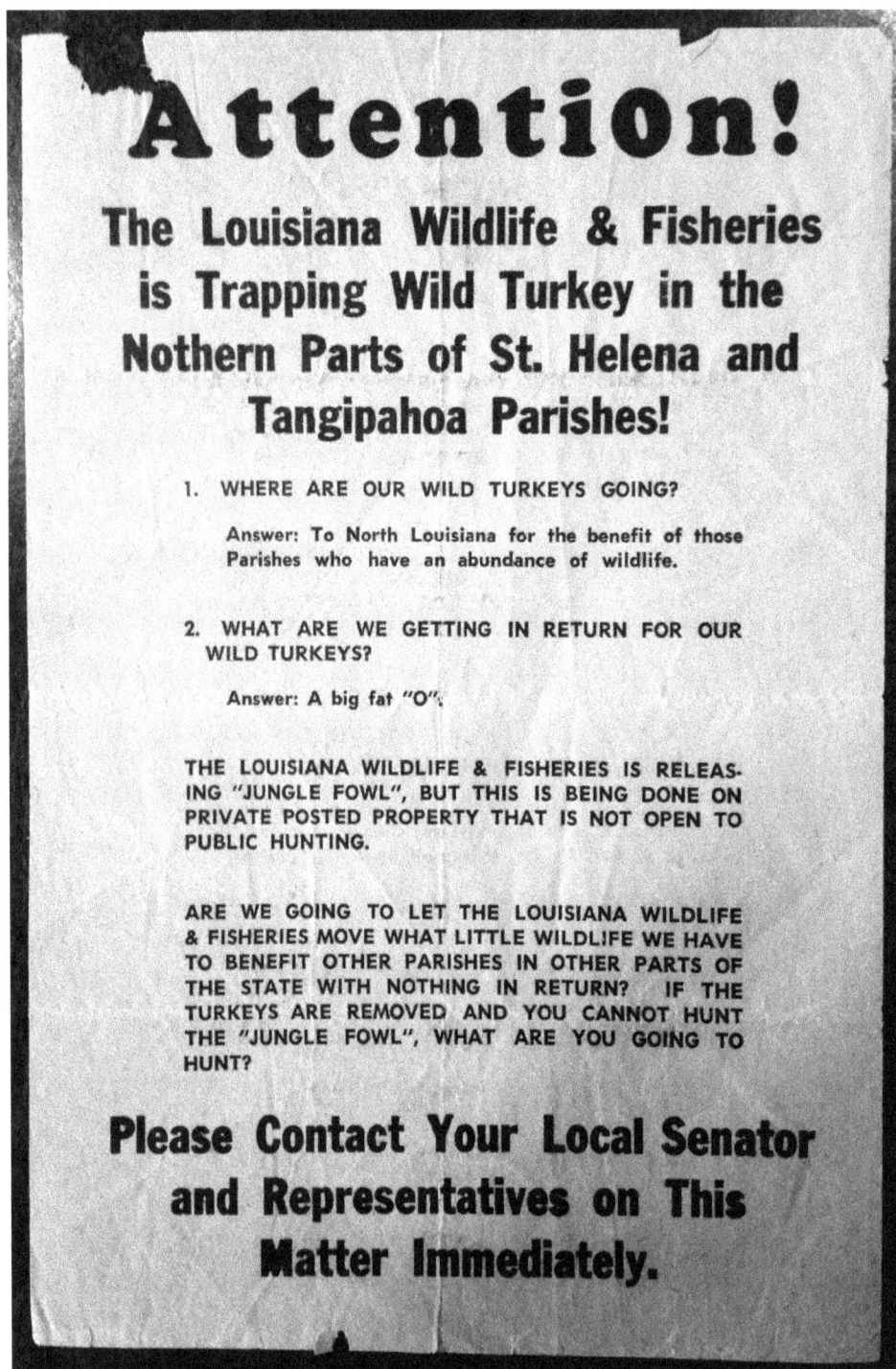

Figure 8

LDWF turkey trapper Curtis Parker releasing a wild turkey in north-central Louisiana. (LDWF file photo)

By the early 2000s most of the state's suitable habitat had been stocked with wild turkeys and restocking efforts were winding down. Larry Savage assumed leadership as turkey program leader in 2004. During this time the wild turkey program emphasis was on habitat management, research, and staff training. With the exception of a few isolated sites, the state was deemed stocked by the LDWF. This did not mean that turkeys occurred on every acre of suitable habitat, but it was decided that most of the suitable areas where turkeys did not occur were within 10 miles of existing turkeys. It was thought that time would naturally facilitate turkeys moving into such habitats if suitable travel corridors existed. The importance of managing lands where turkeys occurred and improving lands nearby where they did not occur became a priority. The LDWF restructured its wildlife division biological staff during this time to accomplish this goal and emphasized private landowner technical assistance. These efforts continued as the author assumed leadership of the resident small game and wild turkey program in 2010. Working with WMA staff, U. S. Forest Service managers, and other partners, significant gains to increase youth opportunities were accomplished. These priorities continue under the leadership of current resident small game and Wild Turkey Program Leader Cody Cedotal.

Ongoing Louisiana research continues to help LDWF turkey managers refine habitat and wild turkey management efforts. With new technology using backpack mounted micro GPS (Global Positional System) satellite tracked telemetry units, turkeys can be tracked 24/7 without disturbance. Rather than traditional VHF telemetry tracking that required laborious field tracking and triangulation to manually estimate location points, accurate GPS points can be easily downloaded from great distances. This technology allows precise mapping of each bird's daily movements, giving researchers more detailed habitat usage data than ever before. Based on GPS monitored restocked wild turkeys in Caddo parish in 2014, large movements (mean 3.6 miles) from the release sites were documented between 60 – 80 days after release (Cohen 2016). It was speculated that these large movements put birds at increased predation risks as they travel far from the optimal habitats where released. Today researchers are using GPS telemetry units to monitor early season released turkeys in the same area to compare findings.

LDWF biologist David W. Moreland releasing a young tagged gobbler in Southeast Louisiana. (D. Moreland)

<u>Population</u>

Wild turkey numbers in Louisiana pre-European settlement are not well documented. Two articles in the *Louisiana Conservationist* magazine reported differing numbers from sources unknown. McFadden Duffy (1974) reported pre-European settlement populations of 450,000 turkeys while Cliff Williams (1967) estimated 1,000,000 turkeys. No one really knows, but the odds are turkeys were quite plentiful. The population of Louisiana wild turkeys in more recent times has been much lower and quite dynamic. From F. D. Hollis' (1950) state population estimate of 1,463 turkeys in 1946 to today's turkey program estimate of 60,000 turkeys in Louisiana, these numbers represent best informed guesses for the time. Bick and Hollis (1950) went to great effort to count every Louisiana flock during the 1940s. Turkey flocks were rare and this task was more achievable then, as opposed to today when turkeys are far more abundant. Accurately estimating wild turkey numbers is problematic for any state. At a small scale, *"mark-recapture"* studies can be conducted and achieve somewhat accurate estimates for a given location. However, such surveys are expensive, require the capture of large numbers of turkeys, and only give an estimate for the area studied. Gobbler banding studies have been conducted at various sites across the state but such surveys primarily examine males and generally focus on harvest rates rather than abundance estimation. Mail surveys of hunters are used to estimate statewide harvests and have been considered to produce a good tracking index of turkey harvest over time. However, mail surveys only consider gobblers since hens are not legal to harvest. Annual turkey production surveys consist of opportunistically recording all gobblers, hens, and poults encountered from July 1 to August 31. By examining the ratio of poults to hens biologists can get an idea of annual poult production across the state, these surveys have been conducted since 1994. Examining long-term trend data indicates that poult production has been declining. Although this type of information provides a good index of production, it is not designed to provide population estimates. For years many states, including Louisiana, have simply relied on a population estimation formula that uses the statewide average annual gobbler harvest obtained by annual mail out harvest surveys. Studies have indicated that gobbler harvests can represent approximately 10% of a turkey population including both sexes. Therefore, multiplying the reported gobbler harvest by 10 provides a crude population estimate. Obviously this method has many deficiencies but is an inexpensive index that can be tracked over time. Based on this method Louisiana probably achieved its highest wild turkey population from 1990 to 2002 when the population may have exceeded 100,000, but has general experienced a declining trend since that time.

The July/August issue of the 1962 *Louisiana Conservationist* reported a statewide harvest of 239 turkeys while the 1974 March/April issue reported only a modest harvest gain in 1973 averaging 250 – 300 turkeys. This leads one to believe that the real breakthrough in population growth did not occur until the second peak of restocking during the late 1980s and 1990s.

Many believe that restricted public access, increased wildlife management associated with the leasing of private timber company lands for hunting clubs, and increased protection and management allowed turkeys on public wildlife areas to begin a phase of rapid expansion in many areas. The LDWF and USFWS also expanded its acquisition and management of wildlife lands during the 1980s. It was during the 1980s and 1990s when most industrial forestlands, formerly open for hunting to all, became leased for private hunting clubs. Deer hunting was the primary purpose of these leases. Many bottomland areas along the Mississippi, Red, and Atchafalaya rivers and upland hardwoods in the Felicianas historically prized deer hunting areas had already been leased some years earlier. By the end of the 1990s most upland pine timber company lands across the state were under hunting club lease. Turkey population increases appeared to correspond to these changes in user access and to the second peak of wild turkey restocking.

The following map shows the latest LDWF estimated turkey densities (figure 9).

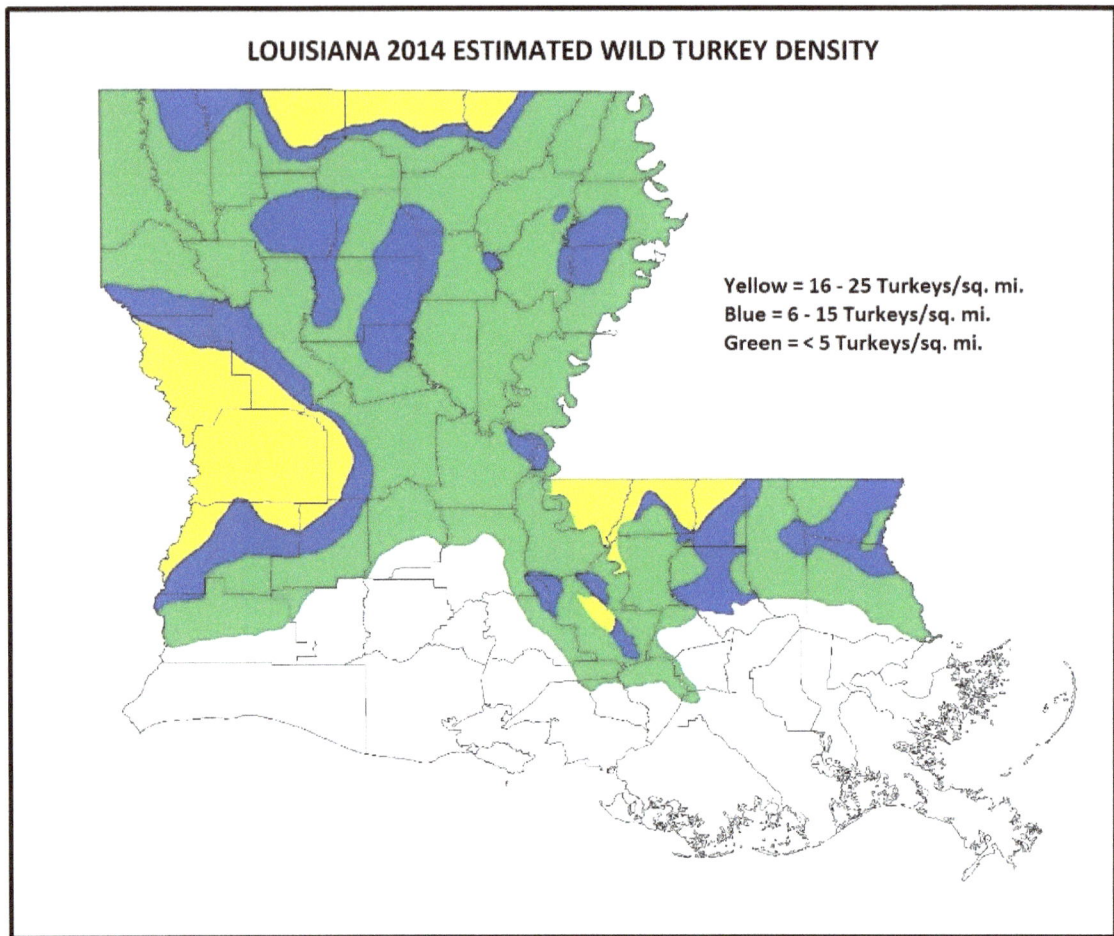

LOUISIANA 2014 ESTIMATED WILD TURKEY DENSITY

Yellow = 16 - 25 Turkeys/sq. mi.
Blue = 6 - 15 Turkeys/sq. mi.
Green = < 5 Turkeys/sq. mi.

Figure 9 (LDWF)

Wild turkey densities have shifted over time from certain sections of the state to others, much the result of restocking efforts, public access changes, and habitat degradation. The following maps illustrate how, with time, harvest rates shifted away from southeast Louisiana to west and North Louisiana (Figure 10). Much of this harvest shift was due to expanding turkey populations in west and northern parishes of the state. At the same time southeast Louisiana was experiencing rapid habitat degradation due to increased clearcutting caused by increased timber prices, decreasing use of prescribed burning, and human population expansion into turkey habitats.

Figure 10: The Percent of Statewide Harvest by Parish Over Time (LDWF)

| 1991 – 1994 | 1999 – 2003 | 2012 – 2015 |

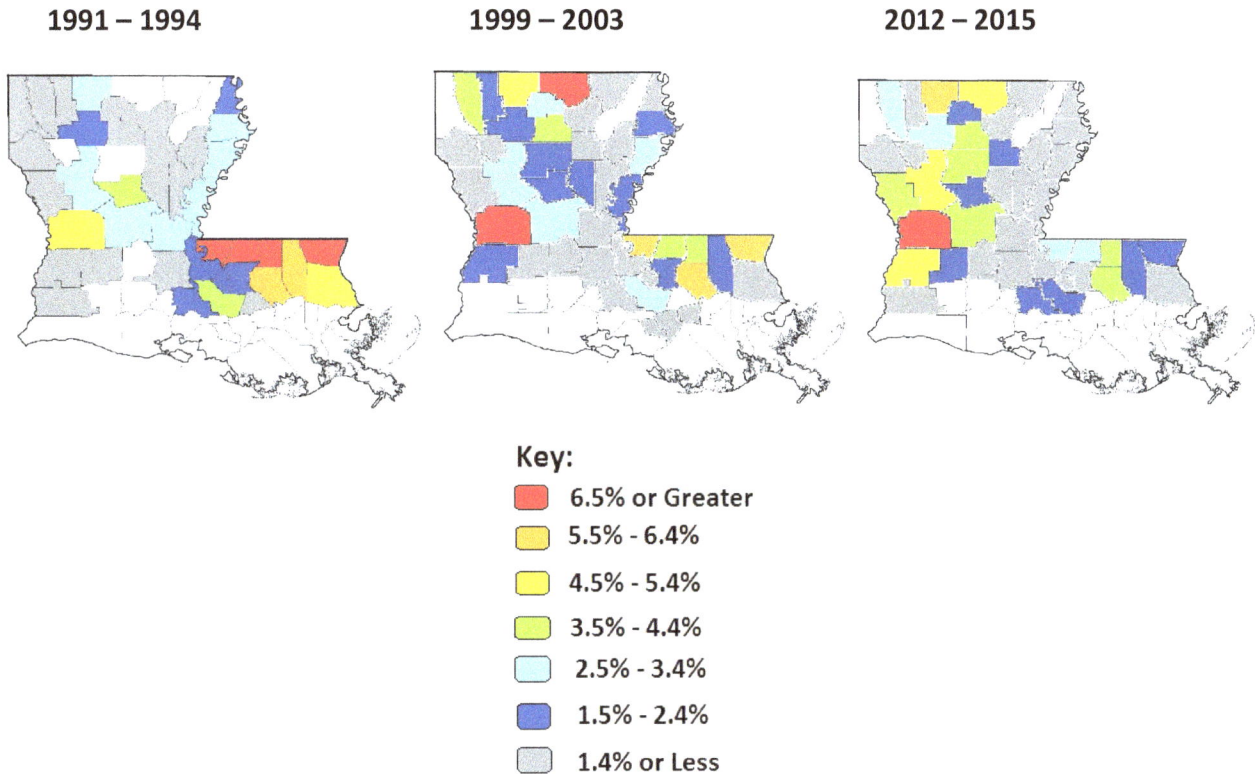

Key:
- 6.5% or Greater
- 5.5% - 6.4%
- 4.5% - 5.4%
- 3.5% - 4.4%
- 2.5% - 3.4%
- 1.5% - 2.4%
- 1.4% or Less

Across the southeastern United States wild turkey productivity (reproductive success) has declined concomitant with increasing or stabilizing population sizes (Byrne et al. 2016). This productivity decline has been observed in Louisiana as well. Starting just a few years after the second peak of restocking in the state, productivity documented by annual poult surveys began to decline. Each southeastern state studied in Byrne's research demonstrated a reduction of the number of poults per hen observed over time during brood surveys. This same research found a growing number of hens without poults. Based on telemetry studies across the southeast U. S., adult hen survival was found to be increasing over time. With each decade from the 1980s forward, hens were found to be living longer (Byrne 2016). The question then became *"why?"*. It was speculated that *"density dependent"* factors were the cause. Density dependent limitations occur when populations reach a point where needed resources become finite in relation to the population size. The primary finite resource speculated in this study was quality nesting habitat. It is assumed that *"nesting habitat"* in this case includes quality brood habitat. This density dependence resulted in many hens being forced to nest in less than quality habitat which in turn resulted in a higher percentage of failed nests and therefore more hens without poults.

Recent research conducted in Louisiana has documented reproductive success to be lower than many other southeastern states. More research is needed in Louisiana to examine these complex population issues to determine what management actions are best to mitigate declining production trends.

Large numbers of jakes indicate good production. West Feliciana parish jakes (D. Moreland)

Biology and Habits

There are many books that cover in great detail the biology of wild turkeys. One of the most complete books is *The Wild Turkey Biology and Management* (Dickson 1992). This book, edited and compiled by Louisiana's very own Dr. James G. *"Jim"* Dickson, is a compilation of information from numerous wild turkey experts across the country. A good friend once told me that after reading Dickson's book he was convinced that he could build a turkey from scratch. Therefore, this writing will not attempt to retrace all of the many facets of wild turkey biology in great detail. However, it will cover basic biological factors important for Louisiana turkey hunters and managers to understand. It will also discuss various habits of wild turkeys; some habits never having been published. Established facts, research both new and old as well as expert opinions will be shared. As with all opinions, even those of this author, time and sound research will illuminate their accuracy or lack thereof.

Wildness of Wild Turkeys

Any chapter about wild turkey biology would be incomplete without discussing the *"wild"* in wild turkeys. During the 1940s and early 1950s the LDWF tried to reestablish wild turkeys using pen-raised wild strain turkeys. These turkeys were from eggs taken from the wild then incubated by domestic poultry or subsequent generation pen-reared *"game farm"* wild turkeys. Wayne Bailey and D. J. Putnam (1979) conducted a survey from 36 states that examined the success of pen-raised (or game farm) *"wild"* turkeys and wild trapped wild turkeys. They determined that more than 330,000 pen-raised turkeys were released on almost 800 sites resulting in 760 site failures. While 30,000 wild trapped turkeys were released on 968 sites producing 808 established populations (Dickson 1992). Although the physical appearance and genetic components of pen-raised wild turkeys are nearly identical to wild trapped turkeys, something is woefully lacking in those raised by man. Wildness, is that something.

Most offspring from first generation wild birds cannot survive confinement. They die from stress, trying to escape (Dickson 1992). The few more docile survivors propagate future generations. Turkeys raised in the presence of man simply do not have the fear needed to survive long-term. They have not learned essential skills in predator avoidance and food search habits that growing up with wild turkeys produce. LDWF biologist John Haygood, who was involved with early pen raised turkey releases, reported that some of the birds would live for a while but quickly died out as they failed to successfully reproduce (pers. comm. J. Haygood). Despite wildlife agencies abandoning the use of pen-raised turkeys in the 1950s, well-meaning turkey enthusiast continue to illegally raise and release pen-raised birds within Louisiana in futile hopes of establishing turkey populations. Time has demonstrated that there are no shortcuts to establishing sustainable wild turkey populations.

Wildness is the trait that maintained the remnant native wild turkey population that took refuge in remote Louisiana swamps during the 1930s through the 1950s. Wildness is a survival response that must be present for the species to thrive. I have observed wild turkeys that allow relatively close approach outside of hunting season then fly at first sight weeks later during the hunting season. Wildness promotes the ability to quickly assess danger then adapt to survive. Once during the 1980s while conducting a poult survey in north Livingston parish, I noticed that nearly all of the adult turkeys witnessed from my truck during the summer survey would immediately take flight, some even when observed at distances of greater than 500 yards. This perplexed me until told by locals that this site had been open land for years and outlaws regularly used high powered rifles to shoot turkeys all year long. These turkeys had adapted to survive by taking flight at first sight of humans. In the same way that turkeys can become exceptionally wary when pursued by man, in the absence of hunting over an extended period of time the opposite effect can occur. Human-turkey conflicts can then be the result as witnessed in many states to the north where hunting is limited.

Out of caution, wildness sometimes causes a gobbler to circle behind a hunter's calling. Just this past season on a heavily hunted public area in north Louisiana, my son David witnessed a gobbler roosting in a dead beech tree in the middle of a cutover to elude the relentless pursuit of hunters in nearby traditional roosting sites. This ability to quickly adapt for survival is of paramount importance and key to the survival of the species. Wildness causes a hen to avoid taking her young near a thicket where a bobcat is likely to have the upper hand. These traits are perpetuated by those individuals that survive each year. Anything that alters the promotion of wildness into subsequent generations is detrimental to the species as a whole. It is also this wildness that intrigues and challenges us most as hunters.

Physical Characteristics

Eastern wild turkeys are taller and much more streamline than their domestic cousins. The male of the species is called a "*gobbler*" and the female a "*hen*". An adult male is sometimes called a "*Tom*" and a juvenile male "*Jake*". A juvenile hen is sometimes called a "*Jenny*". From hatching until 4 weeks of age turkeys are called "poults". However, most biologists refer to older young as poults until they become indistinguishable in size from adult hens. Adult males (usually 14 – 22 lbs.) are about twice the weight of adult hens (usually 7 to 12 lbs.). In a southeast Louisiana study, hunter measured jakes (n=30) [note that "*n*" is the number sampled] averaged 11.4 lbs., 2 year olds (n=94) averaged 16.3 lbs., >3 year olds (n=24) averaged 17.4 lbs., >4 year olds (n=11) averaged 18.3 lbs., >5 year olds (n=3) averaged 20.3 lbs., and >6 year olds (n=1) averaged 16.0 lbs. Hens tend to be more drab in color which is a protective adaptation useful to ground nesting birds. The feathers of a hen's neck, back, and breast have cream color tips, while the adult gobbler has black tipped feathers on the lower breast, back, and sides. The head of turkeys is generally featherless except for a few hairs (which are actually modified feathers) and a thin line of small feathers running up the back of the neck. Feathers throughout the body are maintained by regular self-grooming with oil produced from a gland near the base of the tail. Figure 11 labels the external anatomy of a male wild turkey.

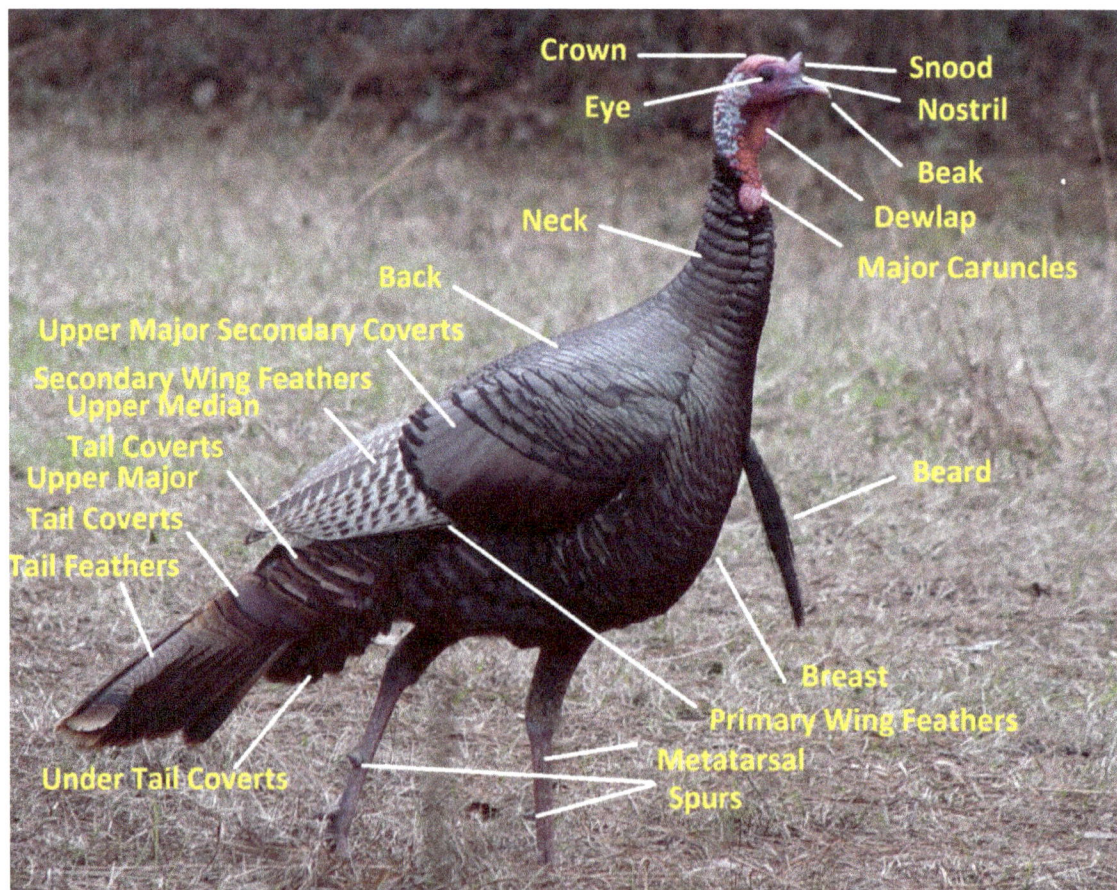

Figure 11: External anatomy of a male wild turkey (J. C. Davis)

Adult gobbler heads generally have more areas of bright red, white, and blue colors than adult hens. A mature male turkey crown is often white in more dominant gobblers but can readily change in color to red when excited as in Figure 11. The skin near the eye is most often colored a deep purplish blue but it too can turn red as illustrated. Major caruncles and minor caruncles can be white, pink, or red depending on the mood of a gobbler. The author has witnessed caruncles change in color like a chameleon from near white to bright red in less than 10 seconds. These colors, regulated by blood flow, can change when gobblers wish to frighten rival males or challenge predators. I once watched three adult gobbler heads turn instantly bright red when approached by a bobcat in East Feliciana Parish. Once the heads turned red the bobcat realized its element of surprise was lost, then simply walked away. The more excited a gobbler becomes, the redder its head will appear. If multiple males are present brighter reds often occur on the more dominant males. During the cold of winter or when frightened, the male turkey's head will appear pale blue. Hens may also display a few red caruncles, but much smaller in size and their heads appear more blueish grey. Being able to accurately sex and age turkeys while looking only at the head is an asset to any turkey hunter.

Males have stiff black keratinous filaments protruding from their breast called beards. They arise from a raised oval of skin called a papilla (Lucas and Stettenheim 1972). The beard begins to be visible in males at about 6 to 8 months of age. By a jake's first hunting season, at about 11 months, his beard will be between 3 to 5 inches long. By his second hunting season, his beard will generally be between 7 to 10 inches long. In a southeast Louisiana gobbler study conducted by the author, hunter measured turkeys averaged 3.47 inch beards (n=30) as jakes, 8.87 inch beards (n=94) as 2 year olds, 10.01 inch beards (n=24) at $\geq$3, 9.73 inch beards (n=10) at $\geq$4, 10.42 inch beards (n=3) at $\geq$5, and 9.75 inch beards (n=1) at $\geq$6. At about 10 inches long, a turkey's beard is long enough to be stepped on while feeding. I have observed long bearded gobblers repeatedly stepping on their beards pulling them taut. It is speculated that this constant wear causes the tips to break off at about 10 ½ to 11 inches in length. Beards continue to grow throughout the life of a gobbler and it is this author's opinion that this daily abrasion limits the beard from extreme lengths. Nutrition may be an important factor in beard strand quality. It is speculated that the overall health of the bird is reflected in the quality of its feathers and may influence the degree of beard wear. Another hypothesis is that longer legged gobblers have longer beards, but after measuring a few legs of males possessing 12 inch beards and those with 9 inch beards, I found no discernable difference in leg lengths. The number of bristles contained in a beard also seems to influence length, with thin beards often wearing more than thicker ones after reaching about 10 inches. Occasionally, adult gobblers are found with very short beards that appear to have rotted along a line partially across or completely across the width of the beard. This condition called *"beard rot"* by some, appears in the form of a horizontal line of light brown colored bristles. In northern states this condition can be caused by ice forming on the beard. Lovett Williams speculated to this author that in the south the condition likely resulted from a lack of melanin production in that section of the beard. It may also be the result of the turkey going through an extended period of unusual physical stress. After beards break off with this condition and health returns, bristles continue growing from the base of the papilla. On rare occasions males may completely lack a beard while hens on the other hand can be sometimes be found with beards as illustrated in Figure 12.

Figure 12: A GPS radio monitored bearded hen captured at Red Dirt Wildlife Management Preserve (Kisatchie National Forest) held by US Forest Service wildlife technician Charles Boles. (J. Stafford)

It has been my experience that about 1 in 25 Louisiana wild turkey hens will sport a beard. However, I have trapped in certain areas that produced bearded hens at a higher rate. The beards of hens are usually very thin, about the diameter of a pencil compared to males that have beards about the diameter of a quarter. I have witnessed exceptions in thickness of beards with each sex. Gobblers may also have multiple beards. Based on a review of capture records of some 906 juvenile and adult gobblers trapped in Louisiana, about 3% of males were found to have multiple beards. A review of the southeast Louisiana capture data revealed a 5.2% (n=466) occurrence of multiple beards in males. It is believed that these rates are minimums since many of the birds examined were juveniles. It is difficult to determine multiple beards in young birds and some multiple beards are not visible until later in life when birds become adults. As many as 8 multiple beards have been reported from turkeys harvested in Louisiana. Figure 13 is a photograph of a turkey with multiple beards harvested in southwest Louisiana by Dustin Pole in 2013.

Figure 13: *A multiple bearded gobbler killed in Allen parish. (D. Pole)*

Very short beards can be a good field indicator of juvenile birds. To a lesser extent beards can help identify 2-year-old males when beards of 7 to 9 inches in length are observed. However, such aging by beards of 2-year-old birds may only be accurate about 60% of the time, since many birds 3 years and older will sport beards of similar size. In general, based on known aged gobblers captured as jakes, it has been this author's experience that most turkeys sporting beards greater than 10 inches are 3 years or older, but again this may only be accurate 60 – 70% of the time since some 2 year olds do grow beards reaching 10 or more inches, especially in higher quality habitats. Using a combination of both beard length and spur characteristics gives a more accurate estimate of age.

Most male turkeys will grow a metatarsal spur on each leg. The spur of adult gobblers will have a bony core covered with a keratin surface. Spurs can be black, pink, white, or any combination thereof. Occasionally, some will be missing one or both spurs (Figure 14). Males with more than one spur on a single leg have been reported in Louisiana as well as hens with spurs, but these occurrences are very rare. I have also witnessed certain areas within Louisiana with a higher incidence of spurless or gobblers missing a single spur. It is speculated that genetics plays a large part in spur characteristics.

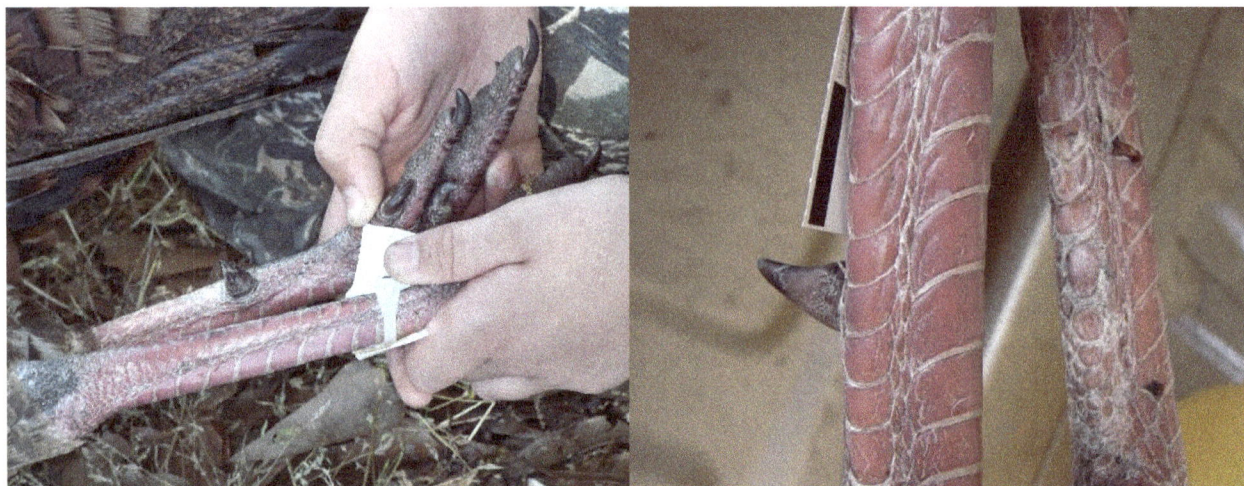

Figure 14: Left is a gobbler from West Feliciana Parish missing one spur, the right is another taken from the same area by the same hunter also missing a spur. (J. Stafford)

Jakes will usually have rounded *"bump"* spurs from 1/8 to 3/8 inches in length during the first season hunted, with the average being ¼ inches long. While 2 year or older adult gobblers will have spurs from ½ inch to 1 ½ inches long, with 3/4 to 1 inch being common. In more than 30 years of trapping, collecting harvest data from known aged juvenile captured birds, and examining known aged recaptured gobblers, I have observed one particular spur characteristic to always indicate a 2-year-old bird. This characteristic is identified by a pointed but blunt tipped spur, commonly referred to as a *"candy corn"* spur, has always been confirmed as a 2-year-old turkey in the banding studies that I participated in (see Figure 15).

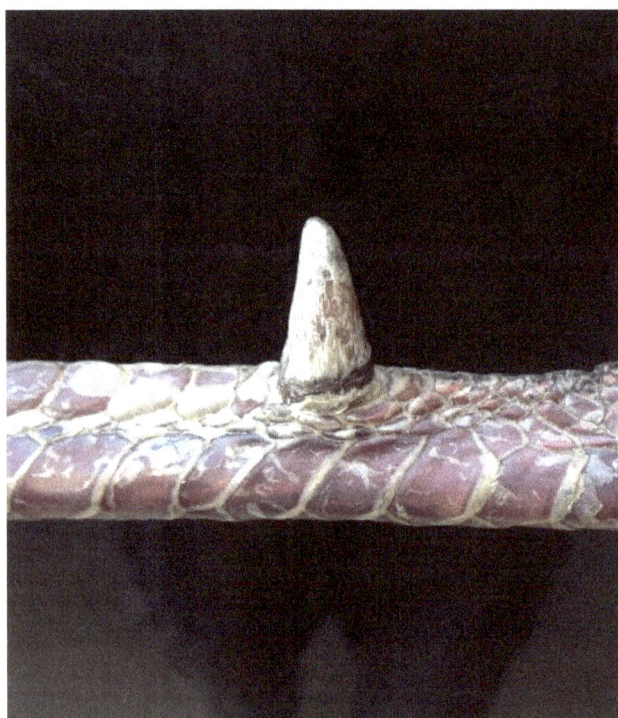

Figure 15: Known 2-year-old "candy corn" spur characteristic (J. Stafford)

Unfortunately, as many as half of all 2 year olds have well-developed, sharp pointed spurs by their second hunting season, confounding attempts to age the entire age class accurately. It was reported in 1975, that spur length was the least variable age determinant (Kelly 1975). Males could accurately be separated by spur length from age 1 to 2 and from age 2 to 3. Kelly determined that 2 year olds in Missouri averaged spurs 7/8 inches long, 3 year olds averaged 1 inch, and 4 year olds averaged 1 3/16 inches long. A more detailed study was conducted nearby in Mississippi where spur lengths and spur apex length (distance from the spur bone to keratinous spur tip) of known aged males was done (Steffen 1990). Researcher David Steffen found spurs less than 12.4 mm (0.49 inches) were 100% accurate in separating 1-year-old from $\geq$ 2 years old age classes. 24.5 mm (0.96 inches) was determined to separate 2 year olds from $\geq$3 year olds but had an error rate of 20 to 25%. Steffen found that using a radiograph (x-ray) to measure the spur apex produced only a 5.4% error rate. From 1989 – 2007, LDWF staff measured spurs of known aged gobblers from southeast Louisiana and found that some 60% did not conform to Kelly's age classification and 30% did not conform to Steffen's external spur age classification determinations (Stafford 2007). The Louisiana study found that known aged 2-year-old male spurs averaged 0.90 inches (n=38), $\geq$3 year olds had spurs 1 inch (n=13), $\geq$4 year olds had spurs 1.03 inches (n=4), $\geq$5 year olds had spurs 1.04 inches (n=3), and $\geq$6 year olds had spurs 1 inch (n=1). Hunter measured gobblers during the same study, of known aged 2-year-old gobbler spur lengths averaged 0.89 inches (n=89), $\geq$3 year olds averaged 1.03 inches (n=22), $\geq$4 year olds averaged 1.09 inches (n=10), $\geq$5 year olds averaged 1.08 inches (n=3), and $\geq$6 year olds averaged 1.25 inches (n=1). Although some age group sample sizes were very small, these results indicate that accurately aging adult gobblers by spur length is not an exact science. Based on this author's experience, aging of gobblers with sharp spurs based solely on length is likely more often correct for 2 year old gobblers, but far less accurate for gobblers 3 year olds and older in Louisiana.

The southeast Louisiana study also demonstrated that the odds of harvesting an "*old*" gobbler are slim. Based on known aged gobblers, 69% (n=127) of hunter killed males were 2 years old. Only 19% (n=35) of hunter killed gobblers were $\geq$3 years old, 8% (n=14) were $\geq$4 years old, 3% (n=6) were $\geq$5 years old, and 1% (n=2) were $\geq$6 years old. Gobbler harvest studies conducted on Kisatchie, Southwest Louisiana, Atchafalaya, Tensas, West Feliciana, and North Central Louisiana found lower overall harvest rates than the southeast Louisiana study, but somewhat similar proportions of each age class in the harvest.

With few exceptions, feather colorations throughout the state are consistent with eastern subspecies wild turkeys. Color anomalies can occur in any turkey population. One determining characteristic of the "*Florida*" wild turkey found in wing feather barring, can be similar to turkey wing barring in certain Louisiana locations. Florida turkeys have a greater percentage of black within the black-white barring of primary wing feathers. The white barring is often intermittent rather than in solid lines. This characteristic is sometimes observed in Louisiana, especially in southeast Louisiana. I once observed 2 jakes from the Pearl River WMA with solid black primaries and I regularly see intermittent barring in southeast Louisiana. However, these characteristics alone are likely insufficient to qualify as being Osceola subspecies. To quote Lovett Williams, "*Far too much attention is given to sub specific differences among wild turkeys. A subspecies is nothing more than a population that has some physical characteristic, such as color or size, that can be used to distinguish it from other populations of the same species. Until other differences are discovered, designation of a population as a separate subspecies implies nothing else.*" (Williams 1991)

Color Anomalies

Color anomalies that occur with animals usually are the result of recessive alleles. This deviation from normal is a natural occurrence that over time gives species the ability to adapt to changes in their environment. These rare but reoccurring "*imperfections*" can, with some species, become their perfect salvation.

Most are familiar with the large white domestic turkey raised in mass to provide our Thanksgiving meal. However, even this unsightly creature traces its roots to the wild turkey. The original "*tame*" turkeys thought to have been domesticated by the Aztecs were of wild turkey origin. These turkeys were thought to be from the now extinct Mexican turkey (*Meleagris gallopavo gallopavo*) and appeared similar to today's Merriam and Gould's subspecies. By the early 1500s turkeys were brought to Europe by Spanish explorers and scattered across the continent by the mid-1500s (A. H. Wright 1914). Eventually, domestic breeders began to select for natural color aberrations. Common domestic colorations of white found in breeds such as *"White Broad Breasted"* or *"Narragansett"*, red typical of the *"Bourbon Red"*, and black common to *"Spanish Black Turkeys"*, all trace their roots to color variations of native American wild turkeys.

On occasion, red-tinted wild turkeys are observed or harvested. A slight erythritic (red) color abnormality is a fairly common color deviation from normal. These birds possess secondary wing feathers that appear more red than normal. Primary wing feathers may have reddish shafts and red (rust) colored barring rather than black. The lower side of breast, neck, and back feathers can appear mottled like that of a woodcock or quail as compared to the normal blackish gray (Figures 16). Erythritic wild turkeys can range in color from slightly more red than normal, to nearly solid red with more whitish wing feathers, with the latter description being very uncommon in the wild.

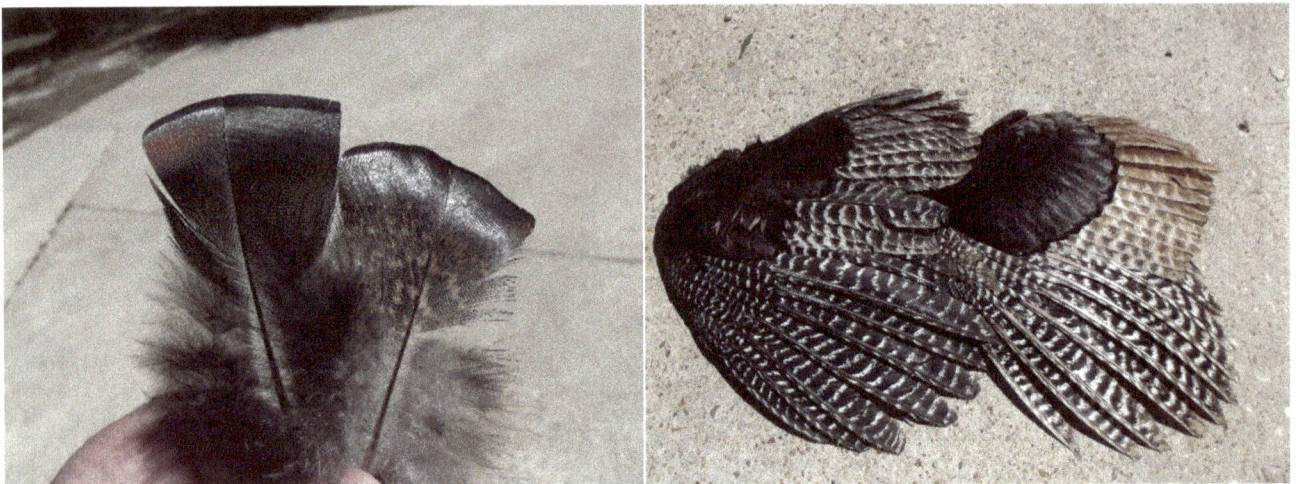

Figure 16: The right breast feather of the left photo and right wing feathers of the right photo demonstrate slight erythritic coloration. (J. Stafford)

The next most common color aberration is albinotic (white) coloration. True albino wild turkeys with pink eyes are extremely rare. However, the lighter *"smoke color"*, an incomplete albino (Dickson 1992), is more common but still rare. In Louisiana this author has captured approximately 1 white phased turkey per 250 turkeys captured. Certain areas in Louisiana seem to have a higher incidence of white (smoke phase) turkeys which suggests a more prevalent genetic influence in some populations. Sometimes multiple white turkeys will hatch from the single clutch again indicating a genetic link. More white color phase turkeys likely hatch each year, but due to their lighter coloration, mortality rates are suspected higher compared to darker/normal colored poults that are better able to hide from predators.

As with erythritic turkeys, white turkeys come in a wide range of shades. Some, and what many believe are the most beautiful, are those that blend a mixture of white with more normal colorations similar to the Narragansett domestic variety. In 2015 the author's son Brandon harvested such a unique wild bird in Jackson Parish (Figure 17).

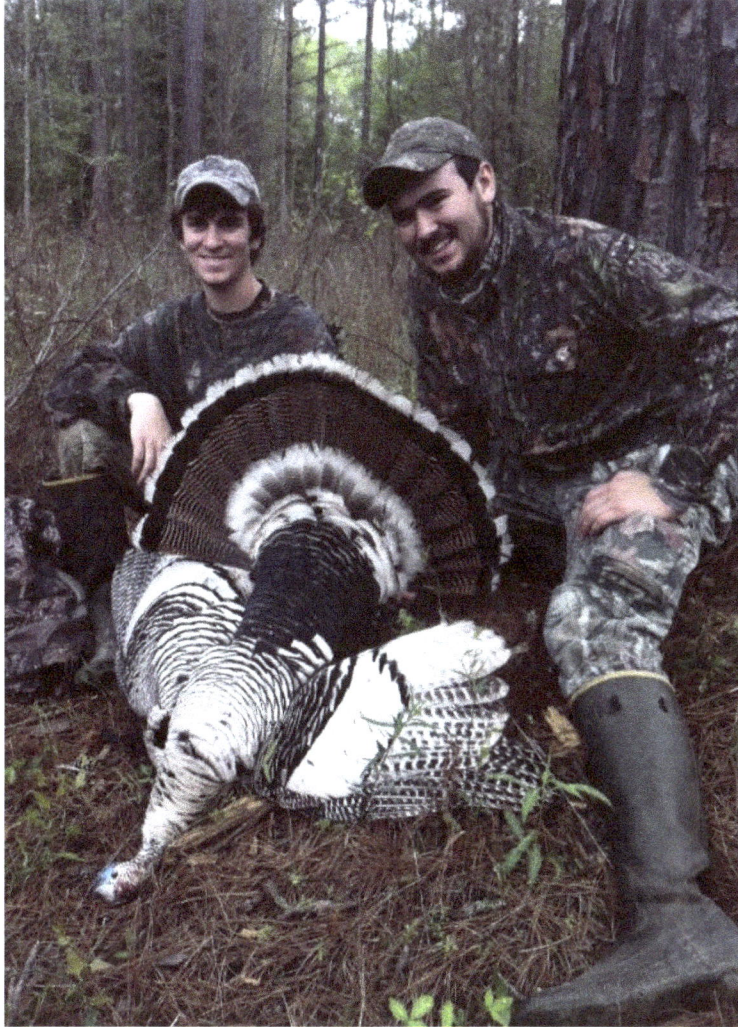

Figure 17: A white "smoke" phased wild turkey harvested by David and Brandon Stafford in 2015 on the former Jackson-Bienville WMA. (J. Stafford)

Occasionally, adult gobblers are harvested with light (cream) colored tail feather tips and cream tipped tail coverts. Jake tail feathers tips are normally lighter than older birds. With subsequent annual feather molts, tail feather tips will usually grow darker. However, light tail feather tips can be an indication of cross breeding with domestic turkeys or the influence of pen-raised "*wild*" turkey releases and is an undesirable trait to most hunters. Domestic and pen-raised influence can also lead to solid white patches on primary wing feathers. Another occurrence indicating domestication is that pen-raised wild turkeys will often stay in mixed sex flocks during the winter which does not normally occur in true wild flocks except when numbers are critically low. Winter flocks of wild turkeys will on occasion mingle with opposite sex flocks but spend most of the time separated until spring.

Black (Melanistic) phase turkeys are the least common color aberration. Short of 2 jakes observed in St. Tammany parish during the 1980s with solid black primary wing feathers and all other feathers appearing normal, this author knows of very few occurrences of partial melanism and no occurrences of complete melanistic wild turkeys within Louisiana. However, this lack of personal knowledge does not mean that it has never occurred.

Tail feathers are considered by some to be the wild turkey's most beautiful asset. These feathers, collectively called a "*fan*", are displayed in the upright position when males strut for the attention of females. Females will on occasion posture with their fan in the upright position, but this is rare and usually associated with assertion of dominance toward other hens. In recent years this author has begun closely examining fans of individual wild turkeys and suspects that like human finger prints, no two fans are identical. Figure 18 shows 3 points where differences are most often observed, but there are additional fan points where differences can be found. With advances in computerized imaging, this hypothesis might better be tested following multiple molts to see if individual birds maintain such patterns and can be identified over time using this method.

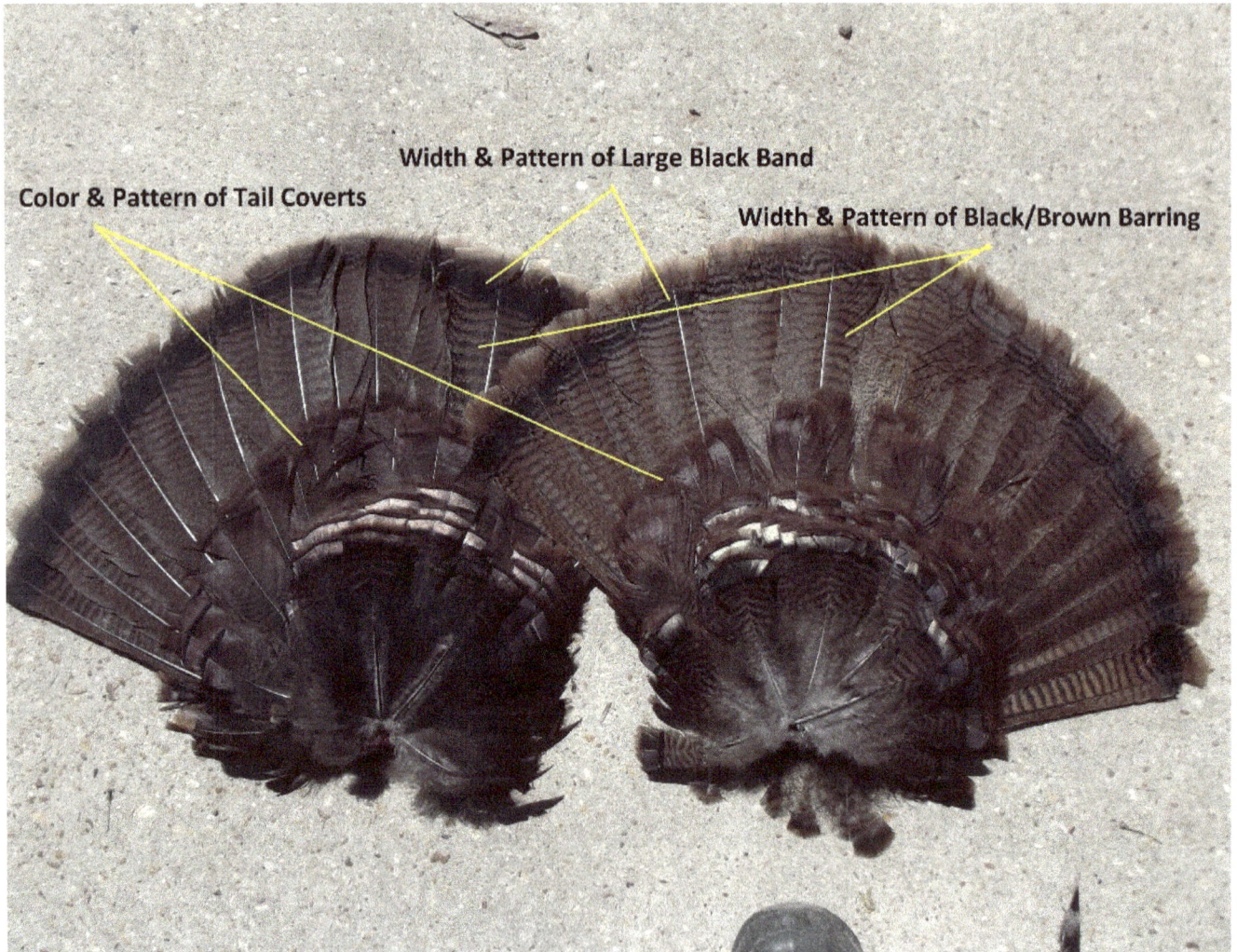

Width & Pattern of Large Black Band

Color & Pattern of Tail Coverts

Width & Pattern of Black/Brown Barring

Figure 18: The fans above demonstrate sites where differences can be observed. (J. Stafford)

Everything in nature has a purpose, irrespective of man's ability to figure out what that purpose is. Many believe the one characteristic that gives the wild turkey its greatest beauty is its iridescent feathering. This iridescence of turkey feathers also likely serves a survival purpose. It has been this author's experience that turkeys are very difficult to see from the ground when in a tree, especially when facing away from the observer. One can often more easily see the turkey's two legs, head, and neck, but the larger body is far less noticeable against the sky than one would expect. Like being cloaked in hundreds of tiny mirrors, iridescent feathers seem to reflect the color of the sky when observed from below and behind which may reduce its detection by predators. The following photograph shows the iridescent feathers of an adult gobbler harvested in Vernon parish.

Iridescent feathering on a Vernon parish gobbler (J. Stafford)

Breeding, Nesting, and Brood Rearing

Prior to breeding considerable flock social behavior occurs. During the fall and winter, hens often separate into large same sex groups that may exceed 30 birds. Noted turkey trapper Curtis Parker reported to this author seeing one winter flock with 225 turkeys in East Carroll parish during the 1980s (Parker hired by LDWF in 1966 was one of the state's most successful turkey trappers). During winter other hens may remain with late hatched juvenile males, but once these males become boisterous, jakes usually separate from hen groups. Males also form groups after the breeding season and into the fall and winter, but due to their lower numbers within the population, seldom exceed groups of more than 10 to 15 birds. Smaller groups of males are more common and are often made up of siblings or males raised together from different hens within the same group (Williams 1991). Competition for food generally limits the size of groups. Large groups can periodically occur during winter when smaller groups may converge in more open habitats due to weather or food availability. Figure 19 shows a group of males that the author photographed on a very cold winter day during 2003 in Washington Parish. During cold weather males tolerate other male groups quite well, but during warmer days they become far less tolerant of same sex company.

Figure 19: The photograph above taken in Washington Parish shows 43 males and one female leading the flock. (J. Stafford)

Breakup of larger flocks occurs during the late winter and early spring as days become longer and temperatures rise. Breeding behavior (gobbling and strutting) in males may occur weeks or months prior to actual breeding. This prompts turkey hunters each year to wonder why biologists delay the opening of hunting season. Photoperiod is a proximate cue for initiation of breeding activity, whereas growing season phenology is an ultimate cause of timing of breeding (Gill 1994). After the vernal equinox, March 21st, the length of time that the sun shines each day (photoperiod) increases. Plants also sense this change and respond as conditions for growth improve. Simply put, the gradually longer hours of daylight in the spring stimulate hormones that bring on breeding (Latham 1956). In 2004 a range-wide study was conducted and it was determined that various factors influenced breeding but photoperiod, latitude, and time since stocked each made a difference (Whitaker et al. 2004). Whitaker also determined that on average peak gobbling occurred 24 days prior to mean nest incubation starts. Other factors affecting the onset of breeding are food scarcity, drought, rain, and lack of nesting cover. In Louisiana, poor body condition may be the greatest factor resulting in delayed nesting (and assumed breeding). In studies conducted by Louisiana State University on Sherburne WMA and one conducted by The University of Georgia on Kisatchie National Forest, nesting/breeding of radio marked hens was delayed due to poor acorn mast crops the previous fall combined with harsh winters that delayed spring vegetation. Studies of wild turkeys in Arkansas found similar results with poor conditioned hens nesting later and producing smaller clutch sizes (Thogmartin and Johnson 1999). Hens in the Sherburne WMA study had a mean first nest initiation date of April 2 during years 2008 and 2009 but in year 2010, when acorn mast was scarce, that mean date shifted some 3 weeks later to April 23. In Natchitoches, Winn, and Vernon parishes a similar shift was noted in mean nest initiation dates on Kisatchie National Forest. The Kisatchie incubation start mean was April 16 in 2015 (a more normal weather year) but May 7 in 2014 (a harsh winter-late spring year). This fluctuation in breeding/nesting occurs somewhat frequently and is yet one more reason to ensure that hunting seasons do not start too early.

In Louisiana gobblers have been heard gobbling every month of the year, but they significantly increase gobbling just prior to winter flock breakup. This period of increased gobbling, usually from late February to mid-March in much of the state, causes many hunters to desire an earlier season opening. During this time males are often still in large flocks and begin mingling with large hen groups. Flocks break into smaller groups as temperatures rise, but may regroup during cold days. As days grow longer, hormone stimulation increases, causing disharmony in both hen and male groups. Jakes may be completely banned from some adult male groups by mid-March while other groups may allow well behaved jakes to tag along throughout the season. Based on experiences observed in the field, it is this author's opinion that male dominance is determined more by the weight of individual birds than any other factor. This is believed due to the fact that males fight by locking necks then pushing one another around like two sumo wrestlers. Tactics are important, but weight usually wins the day. The author has observed this being true as individuals within small gobbler groups are harvested in succession during a single hunting season. The primary strutter killed from such a small group is often the heaviest. When the next one assuming dominance is killed, it is most often smaller than the first, but larger than the next. Other factors such as group numbers, long spurs, and age can also influence the dynamics of male dominance, but most often weight is believed a primary influence. Dominance also influences gobbling activity. It can determine which male gobbles the most, at what time during the morning he gobbles, and at what volume birds gobble. The author once monitored gobbling of two adult males for a 4-week period. Both birds gobbled voraciously for 2 weeks prior to the hunting season then continuing one week into the season. One morning as both birds gobbled as loud as ever, in the presence of several hens a fight erupted between the two males lasting about 5 minutes. From that day forward, the defeated gobbler reduced his gobbling rate by about 90% and the volume of gobbling he produced was reduced by more than half.

By late March gobbler groups are small, often 1 to 3 adults, and hen harems are commonly 4 to 10 birds. Late March thru the first 2 weeks of April are when most turkeys breed/nest in Louisiana (Stafford 2004 and Savage 2008). Data from a southeast Louisiana study illustrating nest initiation dates (date of first egg laid) are found in Appendix C. Below is a graph that illustrates the southeast Louisiana results obtained from 1990 – 2004 (Figure 20)

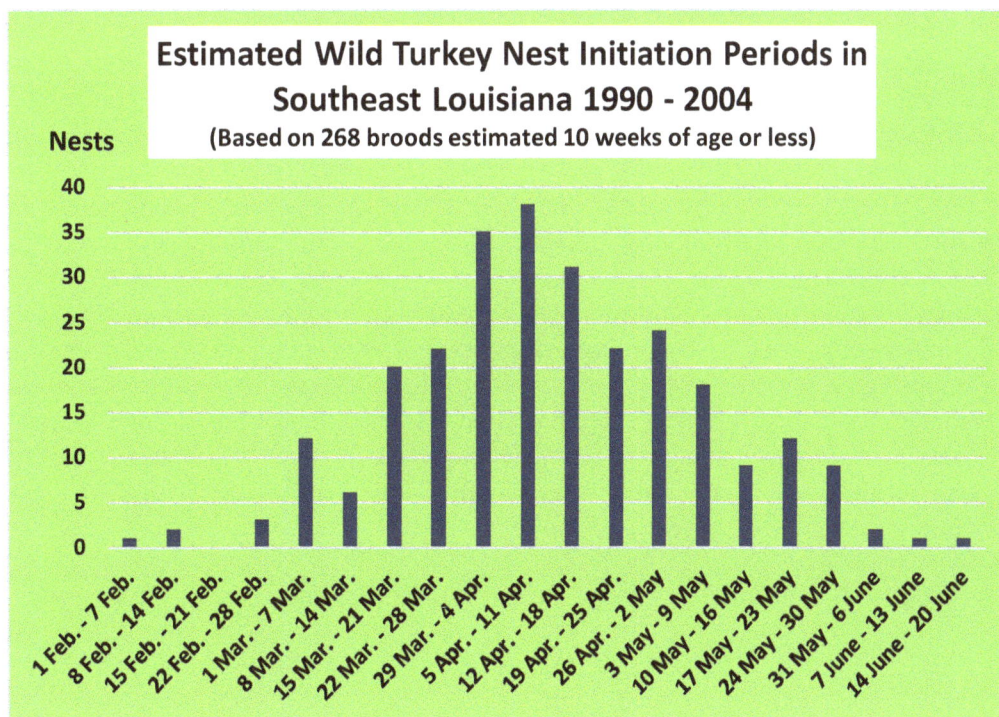

Estimated Wild Turkey Nest Initiation Periods in Southeast Louisiana 1990 - 2004
(Based on 268 broods estimated 10 weeks of age or less)

Figure 20 (J. Stafford 2004)

45

These dates represent averages over multiple years that do not account for annual fluctuations but are important when setting the opening of turkey season. Based on domestic poultry findings, it is speculated that wild turkey breeding takes place about 25 to 30 hours before the first egg is laid. This means that peak breeding for the area represented in figure 20 likely occurred March 27 through April 16. Since the wild turkey breeding peak is so concise and important, turkeys must be allowed time to breed for optimal reproduction to be maintained. Since dead gobblers do not breed, managers must ensure that hunting seasons do not open well before this period, especially where low turkey populations occur.

There is debate among some whether or not there is a significant difference in when breeding occurs from north to south Louisiana. There is evidence to support both sides of this argument. Photoperiods are relatively the same in both north and south Louisiana, which has been demonstrated to stimulate the hormones responsible for breeding activity. Based on average dates of embryo aged young, telemetry studies, and brood sightings, similar hatching dates have been observed, yet individual nesting studies such as those conducted on Sherburne WMA (Byrne et al. 2010) and Kisatchie (Yeldell 2016) have shown differences at the same sites of about 2 weeks in mean incubation dates in subsequent years. Other studies conducted in neighboring Texas have shown that turkeys will delay breeding/nesting in dry years when vegetation is not well-suited for nesting. This suggests that turkeys use visual stimuli of vegetative conditions in addition to photoperiod. Therefore, it is this authors opinion that in years of similar *"green up/bud break"* there is likely little difference in breeding/nesting, but in years where there is a substantial difference from north to south in plant growth, breeding/nesting is likely delayed in north Louisiana by 1 to 2 weeks.

Besides increased gobbling, strutting is another important behavior that may help induce hens to become receptive. Strutting (Figure 21) is the raising of tail and body feathers while wing feathers extend toward the ground. With its head tucked in and feathers out, the bird appears much larger to hens and rival males. Strutting gobblers emit unique sounds while strutting. Often in the process of taking a couple of quick steps the gobbler will make a *"chump"* sound commonly called *"spitting"* followed by a drawn out *"hum"*, called *"drumming"*. At close range one can sometimes hear the gobblers wing feathers dragging the ground during the hum sound. The chump sound can be heard sometimes before dawn as roosted gobblers begin to awaken during the spring. The hum is a much more intriguing sound. Some have speculated that the hum comes from the shaking of feathers. Yet it is more likely that the sound comes from deep within the male's body as it exhales. This belief was confirmed to the author while hunting in Allen parish as I listened to a gobbler that I harvested make this same *"hum"* sound as it exhaled its last breath. The hum is a low frequency sound that seems to wrap around you at close range, making it nearly impossible to course the direction of its origin. I have long hypothesized that drumming has a greater ecological purpose than we know. In 2004 it was reported by National Geographic News (Maynell 2004) that researcher Michael Garstang determined elephants communicate with low frequency rumbles inaudible to humans beyond a few meters away. These *"infrasonic"* sounds, ranging from 1 – 20 Hertz, can be heard up to 6 miles away by other elephants. The hard to hear low frequency sounds of drumming, like elephant rumbles, are sometimes felt by humans as well as heard. I believe that drumming sounds can be heard by other turkeys at much greater distances than humans and other wildlife species can hear. I believe it is an important and near continuous form of turkey communication in the spring that attracts hens from afar and reduces predator detection compared to more audible gobbling. An even wilder hypothesis is that the drumming sounds at close range may even elicit fear and confusion in a predator. Such feelings have been experienced by this author when drumming was heard at very close range.

Figure 21: Strutting East Feliciana Toms (D. Moreland)

Breeding behavior is one of the least researched and understood behaviors of wild turkeys. As a hunter and turkey biologist I have witnessed the act of wild turkey breeding only 4 times in more than 50 years. Breeding is required for hens to produce fertile eggs. From a single breeding event, the hen can store sperm in the upper oviduct for 56 days (Grigg 1957). This means that bred once, a hen may nest again during the same season without subsequent breeding. Hens in Louisiana commonly nest up to three times if the earlier two nests are destroyed. However, in 2015 researchers from the University of Georgia found one hen on Kisatchie National Forest that made 4 nesting attempts (Yeldell 2016). Such very late nesting likely requires post-hunting season breeding encounters emphasizing the importance of some gobblers surviving the hunting season.

An old turkey hunter once told me that turkeys breed at the peak of the flowering dogwood bloom. The idea of using plants to determine the peak of breeding may not be very scientific but experience demonstrates that it does have some merit. Both turkeys and plants depend on photoperiods and other environmental conditions to breed, bud, or bloom. Both can be affected by weather extremes. Louisiana hunters understand that slight differences in spring *"bud break"* can occur from one area to the next. With this in mind, a chart has been developed based on anecdotal Louisiana observations that generally correspond to spring turkey behavior and plant bud-blooms (Table 3).

Table 1

Normal Date Range	Turkey Activity	Plant Status
January - February	Large male and female groups	Most plants are dormant
Late February to early March	Large male and female groups begin to mingle	Elms, red maple, plums, May haws, huckleberries, redbuds, and some oak species flower; black willows begin to leaf out
Mid-March	Males and females begin to break into smaller groups; gobbling increases some breeding occurs	Pines, wild azaleas, and most oak species flower; leaves begin to form on trees
Late March to early April	Peak of breeding occurs; nest initiations peak; gobbling may wain slightly	Crabapples, fringe trees, and black locust flower; dogwood blooms peak; most hardwood trees have well developed leaves
Mid- to late-April	Hens are laying/incubating nests and gobbling increases as males are seeking the few remaining hens not yet nesting	Pecans flower-leaf, pines are growing new needles, and most hardwoods have mature size leaves; huckleberries are large but green and dewberries are becoming ripe

Weather conditions some years can cause spring not to follow the above described gradual progression. In such years the flowering, bud break, and turkey social behavior time sequence becomes much more concise.

Breeding is often culminated only after a drawn out and complex series of social behaviors occur. The following is a description of one such breeding event witnessed and documented by the author:

On March 20, 2013 about 3 pm I witnessed a rarely seen event at a food plot on the Tunica Hills WMA. Without being seen, I approached to within 25 yards of a flock of turkeys containing 3 adult gobblers (2 strutters and 1 non-strutter), 8 jakes, and 3 hens. The non-strutting adult tom's job appeared to be keeping the jakes away from the hens. At times he had some success, at other times not. After about 20 minutes of two adults strutting near the hens, one of the hens took several quick steps and squatted. She quickly did this two more times and settled between the two strutters within 5 feet of both. The sub-dominant strutter immediately froze in his tracks with the hen 5 feet to his side. This bird apparently did not want to be seen making an advance on the crouched hen, but continued in his strut pose without movement. The dominant tom slowly moved to within 2 feet of the back side of the hen, seemed to be in no hurry, and continued to strut on both sides of her for about 3 more minutes. He then mounted her and began to tread on her back for the next 8 minutes. Copulation appeared to occur briefly (for a few seconds) two times during the 8 minutes. The co-dominant Tom never moved and the jakes dared not come within 20 yards, but were aware of what was going on. The two other hens appeared non-receptive and ignored the activity. When the dominant Tom dismounted, the hen stood up shaking her feather several times and walked away but did not leave the food plot. No sounds were uttered by the hen or gobblers during this time and no more breeding took place for the next 30 minutes. Immediately following breeding, both strutting males again returned to walking and strutting among the hens. Eventually all of the birds quietly left the food plot.

Three years earlier on the same WMA, biologist James C. Davis photographed a gobbler and hen breeding on a gravel road right in front of his truck. The following photograph was taken through his truck window (Figure 22).

Figure 22 (J. C. Davis)

Once bred, hens soon leave gobblers to nest. They sometimes return for subsequent breeding, but are primarily involved with seeking a nest site and foraging voraciously to prepare for the extended incubation period when time spent feeding is greatly reduced. It was once thought that hens preselected their nest site well prior to nesting, however new research, much conducted in Louisiana, strongly suggests that preselection of nest sites does not regularly occur (Conley et al. 2016). Since hens choose similar habitat characteristics, it is believed that hens are instinctively programmed to seek certain vegetative structure and nest access conditions but may have never seen their nest site prior to laying. Hens often nest within 25 yards of a road, trail, or open area. Often such sites provide good poult foraging habitat or quick access to other areas of good brood habitat nearby.

Hens generally lay between 9 to 12 eggs in a clutch. Larger numbers of 13 to 15 are also common. In 1983 the author observed one nest on Pearl River WMA with 22 eggs. Turkeys nest in shallow depressions on the ground 1 – 3 inches deep. On occasion, hens will be triggered to lay a *"dump"* egg on a road, levee, or other open place due to stress, lack of suitable nesting habitat, or predator harassment. Laying the average size clutch takes about 2 weeks. During this laying period hens spend little time on the nest, then cover the eggs with leaves to reduce the chance of predators finding the eggs. Incubation is the period when a hen sits on the eggs both day and night. The near continuous heat from the hen during incubation synchronizes development of embryos laid at separate times during the two weeks prior. Hens also softly call to eggs just before they hatch, which stimulates activity of pre-hatched chicks so that all hatch within 12 - 24 hours of one another. Using Louisiana telemetry study data and egg embryo aging, Savage (2008) determined peak nest initiation for Louisiana to be April 8 which is directly in line with southeast Louisiana findings (Stafford 2004). The start of peak nest incubation occurs April 21 and peak hatch is May 20 (Savage 2008) (Figure 23). While, Nathan Yeldell found the average first nest incubation start date of 39 nests to be 7 days later than Savage (Yeldell 2016).

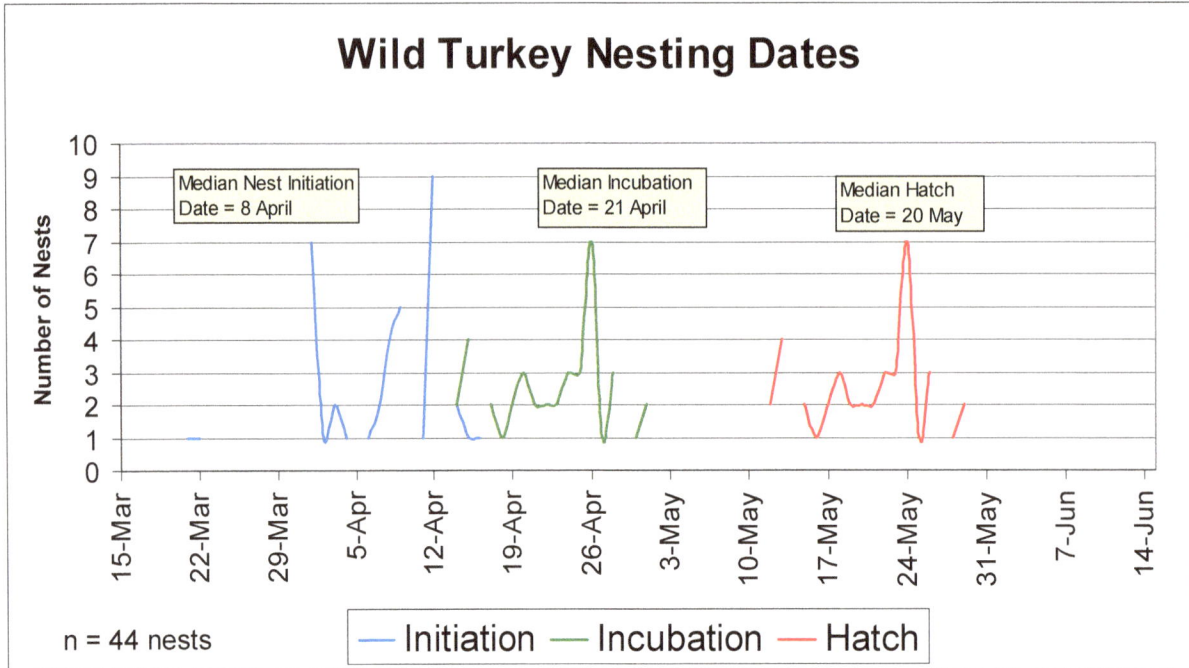

Figure 23 (L. Savage)

During hot weather hens regulate the temperature of the eggs by alternating sitting on and standing over the eggs. Hens regulate their own body temperatures by opening their feathers to allow cooler air in. The following are game camera photographs placed on a turkey nest in Washington Parish (Figure 24).

Figure 24: Left is a hen regulating body heat by opening feathers and right is the hen encouraging hatching poults. (J. Stafford)

Nesting and early brood rearing puts hens, eggs, and poults at their greatest risk of predation. Young hens (1-year-old) are usually unsuccessful nesters and contribute little to fall population recruitment. For about 2 weeks before poults fly well enough to roost in trees, they are at great risk. Various studies have shown that about 10 - 40% of turkey nests survive and of that, only about 25% of hatched poults survive to 4 weeks. By the fall only a few will have survived to be recruited into the population. Several Louisiana studies have shown much lower recruitment rates than other neighboring states. Maximizing production and poult survival into fall is the key to having good turkey numbers.

Most turkey biologists are convinced that when it comes to wild turkeys, timing is everything. The timing of hunting season and how it influences peak breeding, the timing of egg laying and its relationship to predation rates, and the timing of hatching and its relationship to weather events. If most gobblers are harvested before they breed, problems with egg infertility may occur (Exum et al. 1987). If laying starts later in the spring, studies in Arkansas and Louisiana indicate higher rates of nest predation by snakes. And multiple studies have documented the negative effects of heavy rain periods during peak hatching.

Hatching chicks use an *"egg tooth"* on the top of their beak to crack the egg open from the inside. Successfully hatched egg shells look as if they were purposely opened at the large end of the egg while predated egg shells will often be crushed or opened from the side (Figure 25). Eggs that disappear from a nest leaving no egg shell particles have often been consumed whole by snakes.

Figure 25: The photo on the left is a successful hatch and the right a predated nest which also resulted in the loss of the hen. (J. Stafford)

Despite the odds being stacked against eggs lasting long enough to hatch, some nests succeed. Within the first month of a poult's life insects are their primary diet. Access to good brood habitat that produces plenty of insects is critical for poult survival. As the summer progresses juvenile turkeys eat more green vegetation, seeds, berries, and other soft mast (Healy 1981) but even into maturity they never lose their love of insects.

Young poults can also be vulnerable to extended rain events although probably to a lesser degree than most think. Poults less than 10 days old can usually be protected from rain by the wings of a brooding hen (Dickson 1992). If rains inundate large flat terrain areas isolating flightless poults, mortalities can occur. Poults reaching two weeks of age may experience increased rain related mortality since hens may not be able to effectively brood the larger young. As poults grow just a few weeks older they quickly become more immune to rain caused deaths with the growth of additional protective feathering.

Poult survival is improved if there is greater availability of quality brood habitat. Poults not required to repeatedly use the same foraging sites each day have decreased predation risks. Grassy fields, woodland savannas, riparian woodlands, and other sunlit openings are important brood rearing sites. Good brood cover will most often be near trees for escape cover. Trees also provide thermal cover on hot days and some protection from heavy rains. Hens with poults often select *"parklike"* forests with near continuous grass-forb cover and overhead cover of only 10 – 50% (Dickson 1992).

Within just a few weeks of life poults become highly mobile and will travel great distances with the hen. Often hens with young will join other hens with poults to form larger groups. Such associations may improve predator detection and avoidance. As summer progresses movements become more a product of preferred foraging opportunities and predator avoidance. As different grass species mature to produce seeds and various plants produce fruit, this will greatly influence daily movements. By the early fall young are near equal in appearance to adult hens and very familiar with food source locations. They are now quite aware of most predation risks and are very adept at avoiding death.

Figure 26 shows a very young < 1 week old poult (left photo) who's only defense from predators is to hide and sit motionless. While the older poult > 2 weeks old (right photo) accompanied by an adult hen is capable of extended travel and flight into nearby trees to escape predators.

Figure 26: (J. Stafford & J. C. Davis)

Predation

Predation of nests and young is the primary mortality factor for wild turkeys. Predation is the leading cause of death in poults, hens, and yearling wild turkeys (Hughes et al. 2005). Man (hunting) is the leading cause of adult gobbler mortalities.

It has been speculated that predator numbers have grown due to increasing fragmentation of habitats. However, wild turkeys have faced predation since the first turkey walked the earth. The key to overcoming negative impacts of predators is to provide turkeys with quality habitat. Top researchers and many wildlife biologists believe that the whole process of increasing turkey numbers centers around mitigating predation losses through the creation and/or maintenance of high quality habitat. Increasing the survival of the youngest cohort of the population increases annual recruitment into the population. In plain terms, improving survival odds of the very young results in more turkeys to hunt later on.

The list of predators is long: raccoons, opossums, coyotes, foxes, dogs, skunks, bobcats, weasels, hogs, crows, hawks, eagles, feral cats, owls, and snakes. As eggs, the threat is primarily from raccoons, opossums, snakes, skunks, hogs, and crows. Common poult and adult turkey predators (excluding man) include bobcats, coyotes, foxes, and dogs, but each of these will readily search out and consume eggs also. Hawks, owls, and the occasional eagle continue to be a threat to turkeys throughout their lives.

For years raccoons have been credited as the primary culprit of egg losses (Hughes et al. 2005). Multiple studies have documented that raccoons continue to be a major wild turkey nest predator. From 2007 – 2010, 48 raccoons were radio monitored in the Atchafalaya River basin to determine if they actively sought out turkey nests. The results indicated that raccoons spent most of their time searching wet areas for invertebrates (primarily crawfish) rather than searching more upland hardwood sites where most turkeys nested (Byrne et al. 2016). Therefore, this study suggests that raccoon depredation of turkey nests is more likely incidental rather than targeted. Nonetheless, raccoons are very adept at finding eggs and remain a major influence on turkey nesting success. New multi-state research shows that turkey production has declined in all southeastern states, demonstrating that some environmental constraint restricting higher poult production of the past is at play, the symptom of which is manifested in higher predation losses (Byrne et al. 2016).

Snakes may be a greater influence on nest success rates than once believed. Snakes primarily predate nests by simply swallowing turkey eggs whole. They may consume some or all of the eggs in a nest. A study conducted in Arkansas of 246 radio tagged wild turkey hens found increased snake depredation on nests occurring later in the nesting season (Schaeffer 2002). It is speculated that as temperatures warm snakes become more active and more successful at finding turkey eggs. Schaffer found that snakes predated 17% of first nesting attempts and 44% of second nesting attempts. It is speculated that the Louisiana nest start peak in early April is after excessively cold weather but still cool enough to reduce snake effectiveness at finding eggs. This reinforces the importance of hens nesting on time and being successful early in the nesting process. A GPS telemetry study done by the University of Georgia on Kisatchie National Forest (Natchitoches, Winn, and Vernon parishes) found higher than expected snake depredation (33.3%) of nests studied (Yeldell 2016). Most snakes recovered at nest sites were rat snakes (Figure 27).

Figure 27: Above is a rat snake captured on Kisatchie in the act of predating a turkey nest. (N. Yeldell)

Free ranging dogs (including family pets) may also be a greater threat than many believe. Dogs, like other predators, instinctively chase after and sometimes catch hens that fake injuries to protect their young. If the hen dies, her entire brood is lost. Dogs should be kept out of turkey woods from April through June for this reason.

Turkeys are most vulnerable when very young. Survival begins to increase at about 2 weeks of age when poults begin to roost in trees. Most mortalities will occur prior to 3 weeks of age. With each proceeding week of a poult's life, predator avoidance skills increase.

Many Louisiana private game managers engage in "*feeding*" animals. Feeders and the feeds placed in them are a growing concern in Louisiana. When looking specifically at wild turkeys the risks of feeders far outweigh any gains. Feeding increases predator occurrence within a given habitat by luring more predators to an area. Managers concerned with production of wild turkeys and other ground nesting birds should avoid placing feeders in nesting habitat or avoid supplemental feeding during the nesting season (Cooper and Ginnett 2000). Feeders also increase the risks of disease transmission, parasite transmission, and aflatoxin poisoning. Feeders become easy kill zones for predators. Anyone that has spent time looking at pictures from game cameras set near feeders will see predators concentrated at such artificial feeding sites. What is seen is only a fraction of what is lying in wait near feeders. The following is a photo of a feeder in Grant Parish that deer and turkeys heavily used, so did a red-tailed hawk (Figures 28).

Figure 28: The left photo is of juvenile turkeys and deer using a feeder in Grant parish and the right photo minutes later of a red-tailed hawk holding a dead turkey. (LDWF file)

Feeders tend to increase the presence of feral hogs. Hogs are rapidly expanding across Louisiana. Wildlife biologists have warned about the perils of expanding hog numbers for decades and tried to encourage laws to reduce their expansion. This expansion, now exponentially growing, is due in part to state governing entities that have failed to work together to take much needed action and special interest group influence that has thwarted efforts to control their expansion. The uncontrolled movements and stocking of feral hogs across Louisiana by those ignorant or indifferent to the ecological damage they cause, is a threat to turkeys and other wildlife in this state. As long as it continues to be legal to transport live feral hogs that often end up released in new areas, their range and numbers will continue to expand in Louisiana

It is important to keep abreast of feral hog numbers while intensive removal efforts are being attempted in order to determine their local effectiveness. Accurately monitoring hog populations can be difficult for most game managers. New research from Louisiana Tech University using game cameras offers promise in monitoring hog numbers. Pre-baited sites and the placing of 1 game camera per 100 acres was used to assess feral hog numbers on the former Jackson-Bienville WMA (D. Stafford 2016). Their method used spotted hog return visits to baited sites during a seven day period to create an observation probability ratio (OPR). For example, if 10 different unique spotted hogs were seen on camera 150 times, the OPR is 15. If 1,000 images of non-spotted hogs were captured on camera during the same period dividing by 15 provides an estimate of 67 non-spotted hogs in the population. Adding the 10 spotted hogs brings the total population estimate to 77. For more details regarding specific techniques of this survey method one can contact study author David Stafford at **David.stafford@hughes.net**.

Today only the gun, dogs, disease, and natural predators limit their numbers, which has to this point in time has proven insufficient. The following is a photo taken on Pearl River WMA of one of the feral hog's few natural predators (Figure 29). These new revelations regarding coyote-feral hog interactions has many rethinking coyote control practices in areas with high hog numbers. Regarding coyotes, former LDWF wildlife biologist and avid northwest Louisiana turkey hunter Richard McMullen reported that some turkey hunters unknowingly encourage coyote predation of turkeys by discarding turkey carcasses within turkey habitats. To avoid getting predators accustom to the taste of turkey flesh, he recommended disposing of harvested turkey remains in ways that make predator contact unlikely.

Figure 29: There is growing evidence that coyotes are adapting to predate increasing feral hog populations. (M. Perot)

Can attempts to control predator numbers be effective in improving turkey numbers? Maybe, maybe not. Some predators, such as feral hogs, are a non-native species that cause extensive damage to habitats of a plethora of wildlife species. Managers must be diligent to seek and use any effective means to reduce hog numbers. Other native predators are a more natural product of the land that usually occur in numbers reflective of natural prey numbers and habitat conditions. Yes, each individual predator removed will no longer be a threat to turkeys, but the constant replenishment of their kind through annual reproduction and habitat expansion will near always outnumber those removed except where intensive and sustained removal efforts are employed. The most effective predator control continues to be altering habitats to reduce predator effectiveness at capturing turkeys. These techniques will be discussed in later chapters.

Disease

There are numerous diseases, toxins, and parasites that can affect wild turkeys. This section will briefly examine some that can pose a threat to wild turkeys in the state. The most common reported by hunters and often most easily diagnosed illness is **Avian Pox**. Commonly called *"wart head"*, this disease is most unattractive resulting in enlarged gray scabs on the head and feet of turkeys (Figure 30). Avian pox is transmitted by blood feeding arthropods, especially mosquitoes. In local areas throughout the south high morbidity and mortality rates have been attributed to avian pox (Davidson 2006). Birds can survive for extended periods with avian pox but as lesions become debilitating or block vision, predators have an easy time catching them. The avian pox virus can remain active for long periods in sluffed scabs or remains, further increasing risks to healthy turkeys. Avian pox can also be spread via direct contact when foraging close to one another at concentrated feeding sites such as feeders. This disease has no reported human effects.

Figure 30: The left photograph is of a gobbler at an East Feliciana parish feeder and right one from Washington parish both with Avian Pox. (J. LaCour & J. Stafford)

Lymphoroliferative Neoplasms are transmissible tumors caused by retroviruses. Two types affect wild turkeys, *reticuloendotheliosis* (RE) *virus* and **lymphoproliferative disease (LPD) virus**. Until 2009 LPD had not been found in wild turkeys, since then it has rapidly spread across the southeast. RE has not been diagnosed in Louisiana but LPD exposure was diagnosed in 61% of harvested gobblers tested from across the state during 2013. Similar testing was conducted during 2014 and resulted in only 14% testing positive for LPD antibodies. Clinical signs of RE and LPD are often nondescript and include ruffled feathers, anorexia, diarrhea, and reduced activity (Davidson 2006). Transmission mechanisms of the diseases are unclear but likely include direct contact, eggs, and mosquitoes. Mortality rates from these diseases in the wild are unknown. However, anecdotally the first years that LPD was diagnosed in Louisiana many people were reporting unexplained turkey declines in areas that traditionally had good numbers. To date, no clinical link to observed declines has been confirmed as being caused by LPD.

Infectious Sinusitis is caused by *Mycoplasma gallisepticum* (MG). MG is a much feared wild turkey disease due to the impact it can have and the difficulty in field diagnosis. Turkeys with MG may have swollen nasal sinuses, have respiratory difficulty, or show no outward symptoms. MG has been devastating to the domestic poultry industry and has been shown to be associated with population crashes in wild turkeys. Within Louisiana few cases have been diagnosed. Two such MG positive cases came in 1987 from pen raised wild turkeys in south Livingston

Parish. Pen raised birds from this same source were rumored to have been released illegally in Washington parish. Extensive MG testing was done by LDWF staff via rapid plate agglutination (RPG) tests during the 1990s gobbler study in Washington Parish. This testing found no evidence of the disease (Figure 31). There are no reported human implications from this disease (Davidson 2006).

Figure 31: Above, the author takes blood samples during the early 1990s from wild trapped Washington Parish turkeys for MG testing. (R. Magee)

Histomoniasis commonly called "**blackhead disease**" is caused by the protozoan parasite *Histomonas meleagridis.* Turkeys with *histomoniasis* are listless, depressed, and often stand with drooped wings and ruffled feathers. Infected turkeys often pass sulfur-yellow feces (Davidson 2006). Turkeys experience high mortality rates (75%) while other host species such as ring-neck pheasant and chickens have very low mortality rates when infected. These last two species can act as reservoirs of the disease. *Histomonads* are often passed via cecal worms (*Heterakis gallinarum*) after ingested as food. Cecal worm larvae and earth worms that carry *histomonads* may then be eaten by wild turkeys exposing them to blackhead disease. In Louisiana, the LDWF periodically monitors hunting preserves that release pheasants within wild turkey range. Biologists test for *Heterakis* within pheasant feces. If infections are found, the pheasants must be wormed and later retested before further releases. Wild turkey feces from woodlands across the state are occasionally tested and have been found to have *Heterakis* larvae at higher rates than expected. However, the presence of *Heterakis* does not necessarily mean these larvae are contaminated with *Histomonads* that carry the blackhead disease. Since this disease is passed through feces, wild turkeys can be exposed through chicken manure used for fertilizer or feeding sites where turkeys congregate. No human health implications have been reported (Davidson 2006).

There are various **internal worms** that may infest wild turkeys to the point of death or cause debilitations resulting in death. These infestations may affect the trachea, intestines, lungs, and other organs. Some include *Syngamus trachea*, *Ascardia dissmilis*, *Metroliasthes lucida*, *Raillietina williamsi*, and *R. ransomi*. Wild turkeys also harbor **external parasites** such as ticks, mites, lice, and louse flies. Occasionally, Louisiana hunters will harvest gobblers with dozens of very small insect bites on the head and neck caused by biting gnats. To reduce such external parasites turkeys regularly partake in dusting. A turkey will scratch a bare spot of dry ground, then it vigorously flaps its wings next to its body, while rolling about in the loose dirt which allows dust to be distributed over its body. The dust acts similar to talcum powder by preventing feathers from sticking together and aids in reducing parasites.

Aflatoxicosis may affect turkeys and is the result of mycotoxins produced by fungi. There are many *aflatoxins,* the most significant to turkey managers being *"aflatoxin B"*. It is often found in spoiled grains such as corn contaminated with *Aspergillus* (Davidson 2006). With so many people using corn across the state to feed deer, hogs, and other wildlife, this threat is very real to wild turkeys. While deer and other mammals can consume considerable amounts of tainted grain with little effect, birds are susceptible to aflatoxins at very low amounts. Feeders can provide the perfect dark and humid environment for aflatoxin development. Aflatoxins were found to be at dangerous levels at several locations across Louisiana when LDWF biologists collected 206 corn samples placed in the wild for wildlife during the late 1990s. The FDA recommends that humans not consume corn containing aflatoxin at more than 20 parts per billion (ppb) and adult poultry more than 100 ppb. The LDWF study found 28% were greater than 20 ppb, 17% were greater than 100 ppb, and 7% greater than 300 ppb (Savage 1999). Commercial grain producers have since become more aware of aflatoxin poisoning and taken some steps to improve the quality of their products, however, most turkey experts continue to strongly discourage feeders within wild turkey inhabited areas.

In the mid-1980s, LDWF biologist David Moreland began to notice several harvested gobblers from the Pearl River WMA with badly damaged tail feathers (Figure 32). At the same time the author was finding birds from more upland parishes such as Washington and St. Helena with lesser but similar tail feather damage. Moreland sent some of the tail fans to William R. Davidson, Ph.D. with the Southeastern Cooperative Wildlife Disease Study at the University of Georgia where it was determined that the tail feather shafts and retrices had been invaded by a greenish gray fungus that weakened the feathers to the point of breakage. This condition was diagnosed as ***Mycotic Infection*** (Davidson et al. 1989). It was speculated that turkeys wading in water during flooding at Pearl River WMA or in wet pastures in more upland parishes, exacerbated this condition. Mycotic infection is still occasionally observed at several Louisiana sites causing varying degrees of feather damage today.

Figure 32: Damaged tail feathers found in St. Tammany parish due to feather shaft fungus and wet conditions (D. Moreland)

Food Habits

Food habits of wild turkeys in Louisiana are very diverse and change through the seasons of summer, fall, winter, and spring based often on food availability. Like people, wild turkeys eat a tremendous variety of foods, but appear to have preferences for certain items. Food habit studies are most often done by field observations of feeding turkeys, fecal examination, or crop/gizzard content analysis.

Dr. George A. Hurst, former professor at Mississippi State University conducted numerous studies of Mississippi wild turkeys in habitats very similar to Louisiana. Hurst and assorted graduate students studied turkey feeding habits throughout their life cycle. He determined that in mature pine forests poults consumed an animal (insects) to plant ratio of 60 to 40 from 4 to 7 days old and 37 to 63 from 8 to 14 days old. While poults that feed in fields had an animal to plant ratio of 79 to 21 from 3 to 7 days and 72 to 28 from 8 to 14 days (Owen 1976). Since insects provide poults with considerably more protein than plants, fields or similar openings are extremely important. B. D. Stringer (1977) determined that week old poults filled their crops to capacity with insects in about 30 minutes when feeding in clover patches. Poult survival was found to be directly related to the type of brood habitat selected by successful hens (Everett et al. 1980). The general assumption is the less time poults and hens spend foraging for food, the greater their survival odds. High quality brood habitat should result in increased turkey survival. This rather simple but important point should not be overlooked by those seeking to increase turkey numbers.

By 6 weeks of age turkeys began stripping seed heads of grasses (Healy et al. 1975). Turkeys strip seeds with their beaks much like a person can strip seeds from grass with thumb and forefinger. Seeds provide valuable carbohydrates for growing turkeys. Grass seeds and soft mast are arguably the two most important summer food groups for turkeys.

Two early Louisiana studies using fecal samples were conducted (Savage 1977 and Bittner 1973) during poor acorn crop years (pers. comm. L. Savage), one in the Atchafalaya basin and the other in the Mississippi River batture. Bittner (1973) documented turkeys consuming 97% green vegetation and 3% other items (dewberry, hawthorn, poison ivy, grass and weed seeds, sweet pecan, and insects) during the spring. In the summer turkeys consumed 98% green vegetation and 2% other items (hackberry, blackberry, poison ivy, grass and weed seeds, sweet pecan, and insects). He reported in the fall turkeys consumed 95% green vegetation and 5% other items (poison ivy, hackberry, swamp dogwood, grass and weed seeds, sweet pecan, and insects). In winter turkeys used 92% green vegetation, and 8% other items (sweet pecan, poison ivy, hawthorn, hackberry, grass and weed seeds, and insects). Savage (1977) found somewhat different food consumption rates. During the summer, he documented turkeys consuming 9% green vegetation, 75% grass and weed seeds, 9% insects, and 4% soft mast (grape, swamp dogwood, poison ivy, and hackberry). In the fall they used 18% green vegetation, 37% grass and weed seeds, 9% insects, and 34% soft mast (grape, poison ivy, hackberry, and swamp dogwood). In the winter he documented 61% green vegetation, only a trace of grass and weed seeds, <1% insects, and 36% soft mast (grape, swamp dogwood, poison ivy, and hackberry). Kenneth M. Hyde and John D. Newsom (1973) examined droppings in the Atchafalaya basin and reported turkeys feeding on hackberry, acorns, pecan, swamp dogwood, pepper vine, poison ivy, blackberry, grasses, green forage (oats, wheat, & ryegrass), and corn.

Another food habits study examining turkey crops (the enlarged area in the esophagus where food is held prior to digestion) was conducted during the early 1980s in the batture lands of East Carroll and Madison parishes by International Paper company and the LDWF. During the winter this study found pawpaw, sweet pecan, and hackberry to be important food sources. In the fall, it found pawpaw and nearby agricultural wheat and soybean crops were utilized for food. While in June the researchers found mulberries and dewberries comprising 25% of wild turkey diets and grasshoppers and crickets 66% of their diet. Other important foods were chervil, grasses, false (Indian) strawberry, Virginia creeper fruit, poison ivy fruit, and cranefly larvae. During severe Mississippi River flooding in 1983, turkeys living in trees consumed female cottonwood and sycamore flowers as well as elm seeds. An important implication was that turkeys need habitats composed of very diverse plant species.

The left shows a compacted full crop of an adult male from St. Martin Parish and right is its partially sorted contents during examination. (J. Stafford)

In more recent times, 159 wild turkey crops were examined from 1998 – 2015 (Stafford 2015). Some 87 different food items were identified as being used by turkeys during the spring. Most of the turkeys were hunter harvested males. The food utilized by more turkeys (65%) than any other food item was insects. It was somewhat a surprise to some to find that even as adults turkeys continue to heavily consume insects. Beetles, especially June bugs, were most common in crops followed by crickets, lady bugs, stink bugs, and caterpillars. The next food category found in 60% of turkeys examined was grasses and grass seed heads. Native panic grass seed heads and blades were by far the most used grass. About 57% of turkeys used the seed, fruit, or other parts of woody plants. An unusual favorite of turkeys was American elm seed which was consumed by 29 turkeys. Poison ivy seed was also a favorite within bottomland hardwood areas. Some 47% of turkeys used cultivated crops such as clover, wheat, oats, ryegrass, and chufa generally planted in food plots to attract game. Clover was the most utilized specific food item of all food categories used by some 51 turkeys. Clover also represented the greatest volume found in crops. Green ryegrass and wheat seed heads also seemed to be favored by turkeys. Forbs were used by 42% of turkeys. Vetch seed pods were the most common type of forb found in crops. About 19% of turkey crops had "*other items*" such as rocks, mud balls, wood, crawfish, snakes, and fungi. Acorns were found in only 16% of crops, with water oak being the most common. Based on past observations of turkey crops of the 1970s and 1980s this author believes that the acorn use percentage is trending downward in many areas due to competition for this important food source from growing feral hog numbers. Lastly, 8% were found to have consumed "*placed grains*" commonly used for bait such as corn, sorghum, soybeans, oats, and livestock feed. Food availability is an important factor in the selection of items consumed and evidence supports that turkeys will eat a wide variety of items; however specific items seem to be selectively sought out. This indicates a feeding preference for particular items. It also reinforces the need for habitats to be composed of a rich diversity of plant species.

The following photographs depict common turkey food items (Figure 33).

Figure 33

Left: Acorns, panic grass, privet seed, stink bugs, larva, fern, ryegrass, etc. [W. Feliciana] Right: Blackberry.

Left: American Beech nuts. Right: Panic grass seeds. [Natchitoches]

Left: American elm seeds. [Concordia] Right: Clover, vetch, American elm seeds and poison ivy seeds. [St. Martin]

Left: Flower heads, crawfish, acorns, clover, beetles, & etc. [Bienville] Right: June bugs. [St. Helena]

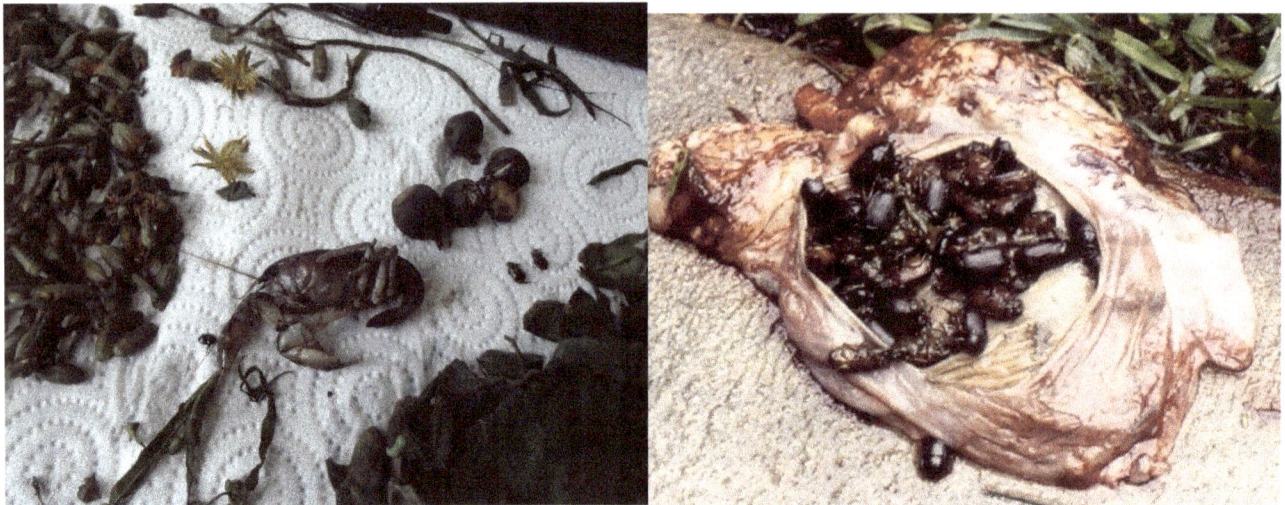

Left: Lady bugs, snails, cricket, & grass seed. [Tensas] Right: Pecan, poison ivy seed, chervil, & etc. [E. Carroll]

Habitat and Management

Louisiana Habitat Regions

Louisiana has 6 physiographic ecological regions (ecoregions) with unique habitats and plant communities. These ecoregion designations extend into neighboring states with similar habitats. Within Louisiana, wild turkeys occur in all but the Gulf Coast Prairie and Marshes ecoregion.

The following map shows Louisiana ecoregions and the southernmost turkey range line (Figure 34). Turkeys generally do not occur south of the range line due to the limited size of non-flooded forests available. Nearly all areas of higher ground south of the range line now unoccupied by turkeys have been cleared for human habitation, farming, or were part of Louisiana's original prairie. Attempts to stock wild turkeys below this line have been unsuccessful at producing viable populations. Remaining small islands or linear strips of habitat simply do not offer turkeys adequate resources to sustain turkey populations.

Figure 34: Louisiana Ecoregion Map (LDWF)

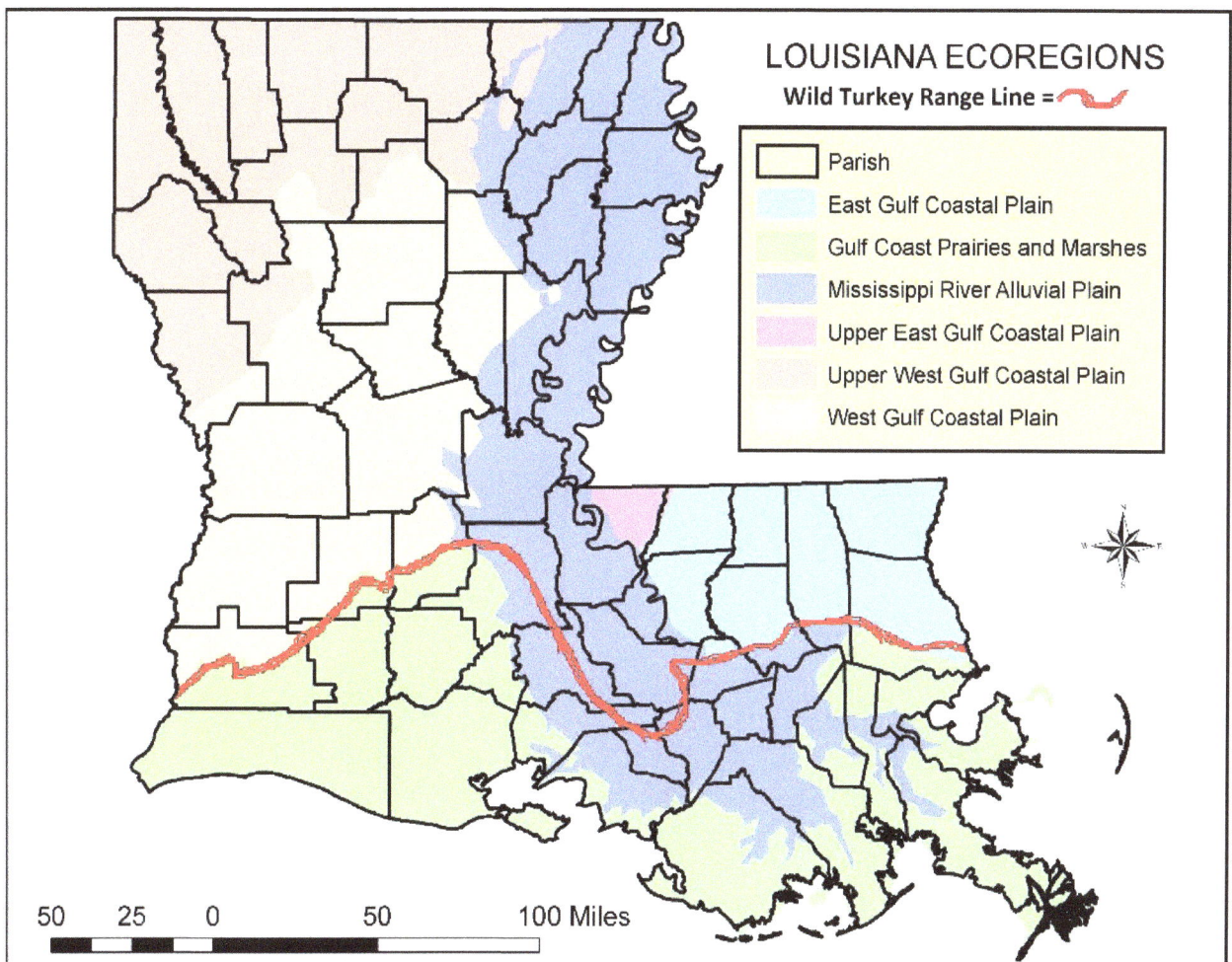

Less than 50% of the state's land base is forested. Nearly all of the Red River and Mississippi River alluvial plains or "*Mississippi alluvial valley*" (MAV) have been cleared for agriculture and are no longer inhabited by turkeys. Of the remaining upland forested areas of the east gulf coastal plain (EGCP), upper east gulf coastal plain (UEGCP), west gulf coastal plain (WGCP), and upper west gulf coastal plain (UWGCP), much has become too fragmented or urbanized to be used by wild turkeys. Wild turkeys require substantial areas of relatively unbroken forest to thrive. These large forested areas capable of sustaining a turkey population over time are sometimes referred to as a "*forest base*". "***Fragmentation***" occurs as such large areas of contiguous forested habitat become converted from forest to open land, often for the purpose of human and farm expansion (Figure 35). Fragmentation is most often a product of land ownership patterns. As more numerous ownerships occur within a given area, fragmentation increases. Small scale fragmentation for agriculture and livestock which occurs within large forest base blocks can be of benefit to turkeys. However, when fragmentation exceeds about 30% of intact forestlands, wild turkey numbers can begin to decline. A recent study revealed that when it comes to improving turkey habitat, "*management strategies to maintain a diversity of habitat types, yet lead to less fragmented, more contiguous habitat patches, should be considered*" (Byrne 2016). It has been this author's experience that over time as large forest blocks become fragmented to the point at which more than 50% is open/developed, the habitat is usually of little value to turkeys. Some exceptions to this rule of thumb occur along riparian forest corridors that connect to larger forests and within habitats with extreme topography.

Figure 35

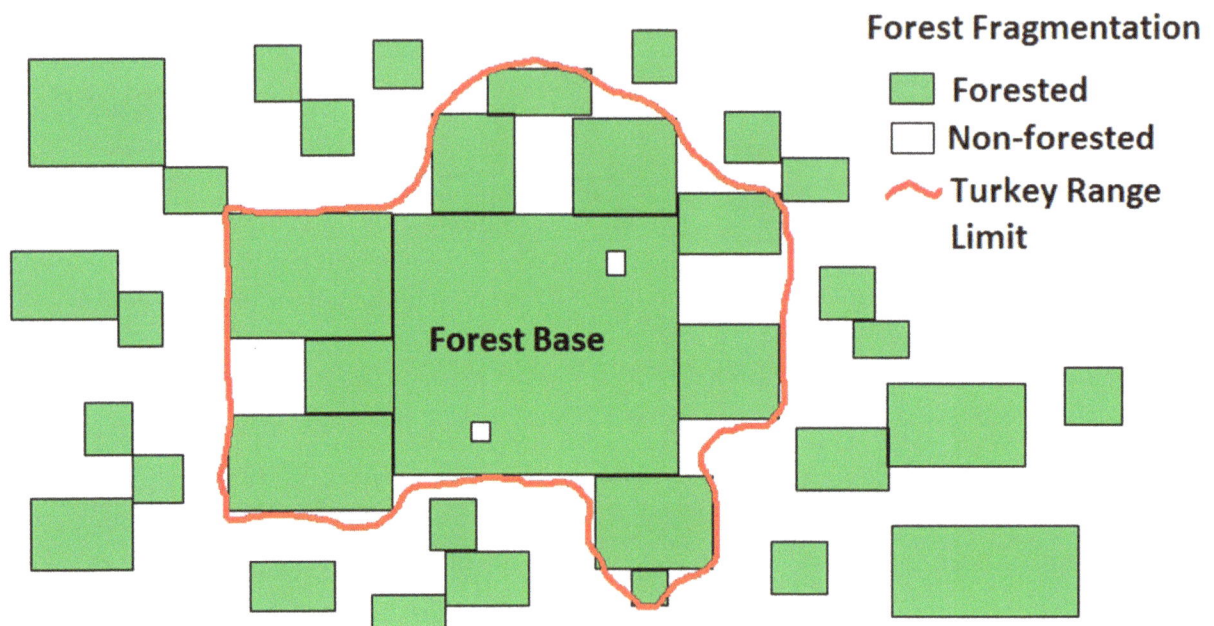

"***Urbanization***" is a similar form of habitat fragmentation but is identified by the presence of more people, more structures per acre, and more human activity. Urbanized areas often find themselves devoid of turkeys much quicker than do more rural fragmented areas. The added disturbance of the presence of people hastens turkey abandonment of otherwise suitable habitats. According to retired north Louisiana LDWF biologist Harry Cook, "*The added increase in free ranging dogs associated with somewhat rural urbanizing areas is likely a major factor causing increased nest and poult predation*". In addition to nesting and brood rearing difficulties near populated areas, wild turkeys have a limit to their tolerance of human activity. The following photographs (Figure 36) are of a field and surrounding forest in southeast Louisiana where the author harvested multiple turkeys in years prior to Hurricane Katrina. The photograph on the top is prior to Hurricane Katrina and the bottom is the same field a few years after Katrina when new residents seeking higher ground moved to the area. Today turkeys no longer inhabit the area after some 25 new homes were built. This migration of people to more rural areas seeking higher ground has been repeated in many areas throughout Louisiana due to hurricanes and recent devastating floods. One can only expect this threat to turkey habitats to increase.

Figure 36: Urbanization before and after Hurricane Katrina (Google earth-U.S. Geological Survey)

This steady decrease of usable habitat across the state will continue to limit Louisiana's turkey population. This makes it ever more important to manage current turkey habitats to their full potential and ensure that large forested corridors between such habitats are maintained in a useful condition for turkeys.

Approximately 43% of Louisiana's land base is forested. In addition, some 88% of the state is privately owned. Of the land in private ownership, 28% is industrial ownership and 60% non-industrial. Much of the non-industrial land has become too fragmented for wild turkeys, but much of the industrial owned land is in substantial blocks throughout the state. This fact makes industrial forestlands of extreme importance to wild turkeys. Some believe that due to the lack of fragmentation and urbanization on industrial forests, these lands have the greatest long-term potential for improved turkey numbers through increased turkey habitat management. 12% of Louisiana is in public land, with much of it already managed for good turkey habitat. Even so, these lands with greater management emphasis for turkeys could see improved numbers. Of these public lands, 36% is Kisatchie National Forest, 28% LDWF, 13% National Wildlife Refuges, 13% in other state lands, and 10% in other Federal lands.

During the last 60 years there has been considerable change occurring on timberland acreage within Louisiana uplands. When discussing wild turkey declines with former Chief of the LDWF Wildlife Division, Hugh Bateman, he pointed to the loss of hardwoods within pine/hardwood forests as a major factor limiting the carrying capacity of turkeys today (sites with higher carrying capacity support more turkeys). Bateman replied that *"our gray has been replaced by green"*, meaning that when looking at aerial photographs, hardwood areas appear gray while pine areas appear dark green. Over time, much of the historically *"gray"* (hardwood) areas have been converted to *"green"* (pine) wherever there was a reasonable expectation that pines would grow on such sites. Additionally, many mixed pine/hardwood forests have also been converted to pure pine. This widespread tree species conversion was also referred to by former LDWF Turkey Study Leader Dan Dennett (1982) as a *"serious problem"* for turkeys. Where this has occurred in excess within southeast, west, central, and northwest Louisiana, the habitat has greatly diminished in value for wild turkeys, much of the tree species conversion being done for commercial forest management purposes. The wildlife benefits that hardwoods previously added were, at the time of these conversions, considered less important than commercial gains if replaced by pines. Ironically, today mature hardwoods bring a higher commercial timber price than do pines.

Without a doubt, mature hardwood forests (Figure 37) are the backbone of any turkey habitat and cannot be overemphasized. Any forest management prescription that reduces the area in mature hardwoods will reduce an area's turkey carrying capacity. In upland pine dominant sites hardwood bottoms, provide a multitude of high quality foods and also have the added benefit of being several degrees cooler during hot summer days which aids in turkey thermoregulation.

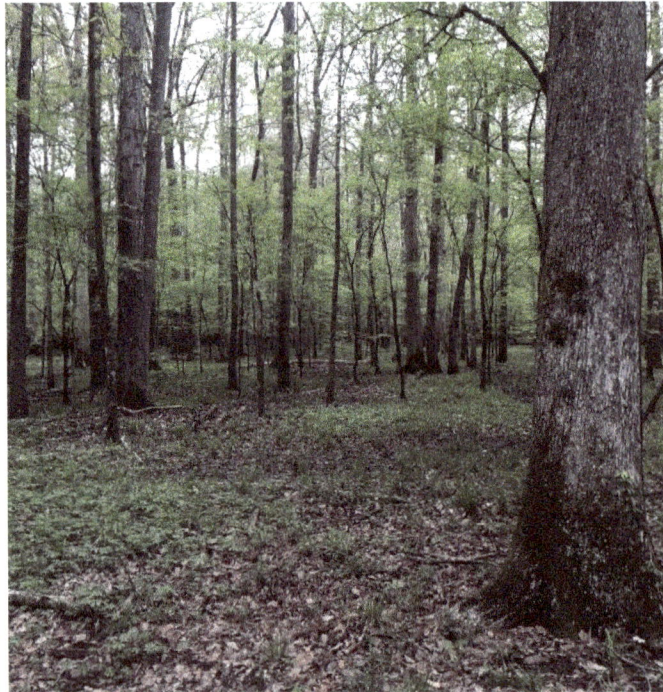

Figure 37 (J. Stafford)

Most turkeys in Louisiana are found in those parishes composed of greater than 51% forests. When forested areas within each parish are reduced, so does the potential to maintain turkeys. Figure 38 illustrates the percent of forested area by parish/county for Louisiana and surrounding states (USDA Forest Inventory 2009). The areas shaded in the two darker shades of green are where the largest contiguous forest blocks occur and where turkeys have the greatest potential to be maintained over time barring local urbanization, fragmentation, and hydrology factors.

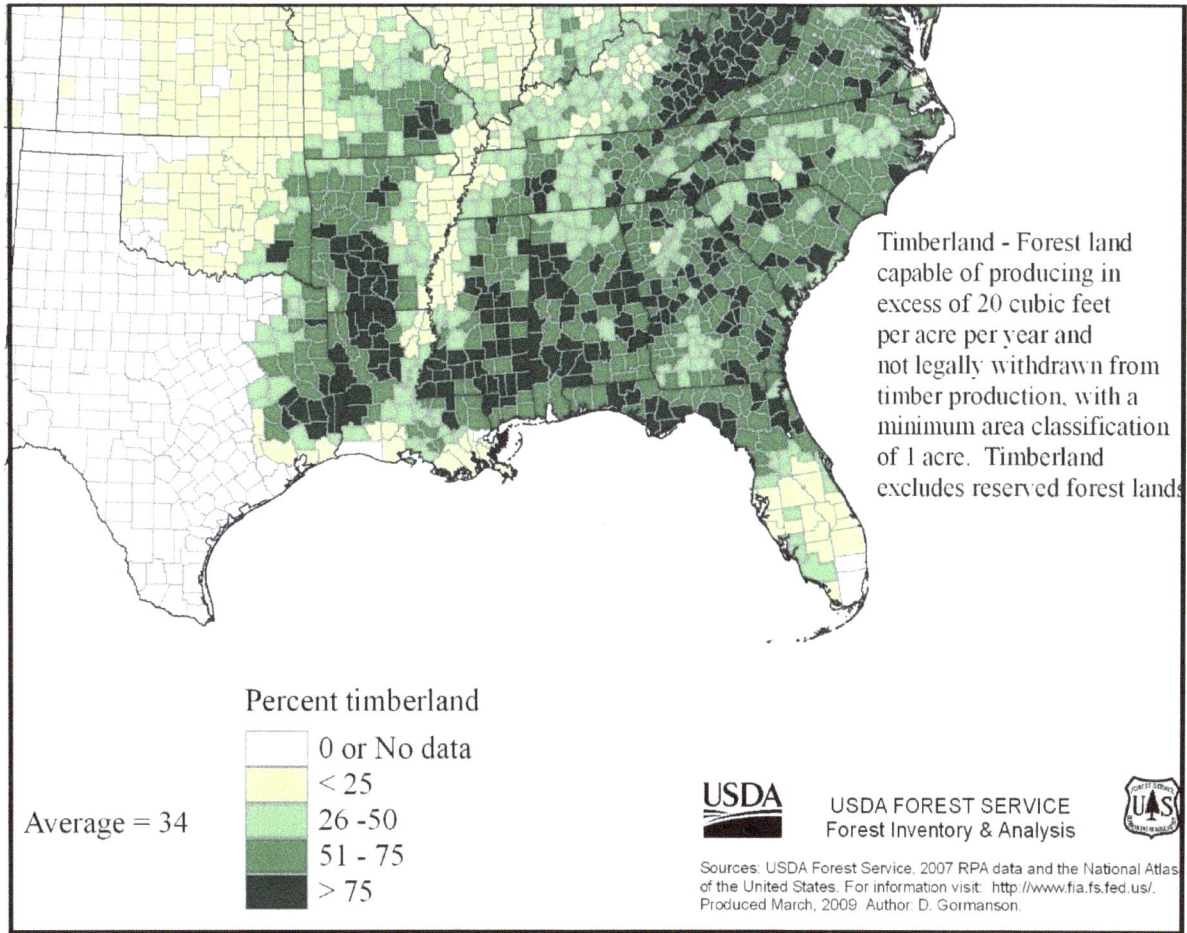

Timberland - Forest land capable of producing in excess of 20 cubic feet per acre per year and not legally withdrawn from timber production, with a minimum area classification of 1 acre. Timberland excludes reserved forest lands

Percent timberland

Average = 34

0 or No data
< 25
26 -50
51 - 75
> 75

USDA FOREST SERVICE
Forest Inventory & Analysis

Sources: USDA Forest Service. 2007 RPA data and the National Atlas of the United States. For information visit: http://www.fia.fs.fed.us/. Produced March, 2009. Author: D. Gormanson.

Figure 38: Percent forested by parish/county (U. S. Forest Service)

The next sections will examine each Louisiana ecoregion where turkeys exist. Ecoregion assets and wild turkey population limiting factors will be examined for each.

East Gulf Coastal Plain Ecoregion

The east gulf coastal plain ecoregion (EGCP) in southeast Louisiana once contained the state's highest population of wild turkeys. In decades past the EGCP had a vast expanse of forests. East St. Tammany to Livingston Parish, now referred to as the EGCP "*Near Coastal Pine Flatwoods*", was sparsely populated and burned in many areas annually for cattle grazing and timber management. These large forested areas, kept intact by timber companies, were pine dominant but had numerous hardwood "*flats*" scattered throughout. These hardwood flats were often a few inches lower in elevation than adjacent pine areas and were wet much of the year yet provided an exceptionally food-rich environment for turkeys. These hardwood flats combined with the large expanse of regularly burned pinelands, offered turkeys good habitat and relative seclusion. Today, conditions have drastically changed within this area that once held considerable numbers of wild turkeys. Many hardwood flats have been drained by man-made canals, numerous hardwood areas have been replaced with pines, and once common prescribed fire is now nearly gone. More upland EGCP parishes of Washington, North Tangipahoa, and St. Helena today maintain significant timber company owned acreage managed primarily for loblolly pine. Turkeys have persisted in many of these upland areas where suitable habitat remains but in lower numbers than in previous years when prescribed fire was common. Smaller privately owned mixed pine hardwood tracts abound across the Florida parishes, the larger of these often containing turkeys. Several rivers traverse EGCP parishes, generally from north to south. The larger contiguous forested blocks along these rivers often contain turkeys. Hardwoods such as water oak, cow oak, cherrybark oak, white oak, overcup oak, magnolia, American beech, yellow poplar, sweetgum, black gum, red maple, tupelo, and American elm are common along these rivers and streams. Some of the larger river basins, such as the Amite and Bogue Chitto rivers, have become degraded for turkeys where sand and gravel mining activities are extensive and no reclamation efforts were made.

From the 1960s through the early 1990s, the ECGP combined with the upper east gulf coastal plain (West Feliciana and Thompson Creek uplands), had the highest harvest of turkeys in the state. Following Hurricane Katrina, the EGCP experienced significant human population growth as people moved from flood prone areas to the south. This greatly accelerated the fragmentation and urbanization of turkey habitats. Also, just prior to that time industrial forest companies were abandoning the use of prescribed fire as a management tool. Fire was replaced by the widespread use of herbicides, generally producing a lower quality brood habitat compared to burning. Turkey harvests in this area have continued in a declining trend to this date. The following satellite photograph shows the urbanization and fragmentation of this ecoregion (Figure 39). Open areas appear as lighter colors compared to larger, dark green areas where turkeys still occur. In areas where lighter colors dominate, wild turkeys are generally absent.

Figure 39: The following satellite photograph includes the east gulf coastal plain (outlined in yellow) and upper east gulf coastal plain (outlined in green) ecoregions. About half of the EGCP is now unsuited for wild turkeys. (Esri, DigitalGlobe, GeoEye, Earthstar, Geographics, CNES/Airous, DS, USDA, USGS, AEX, Geimapping, Aerogrid, IGN, swisstopo, and the GIS User Community)

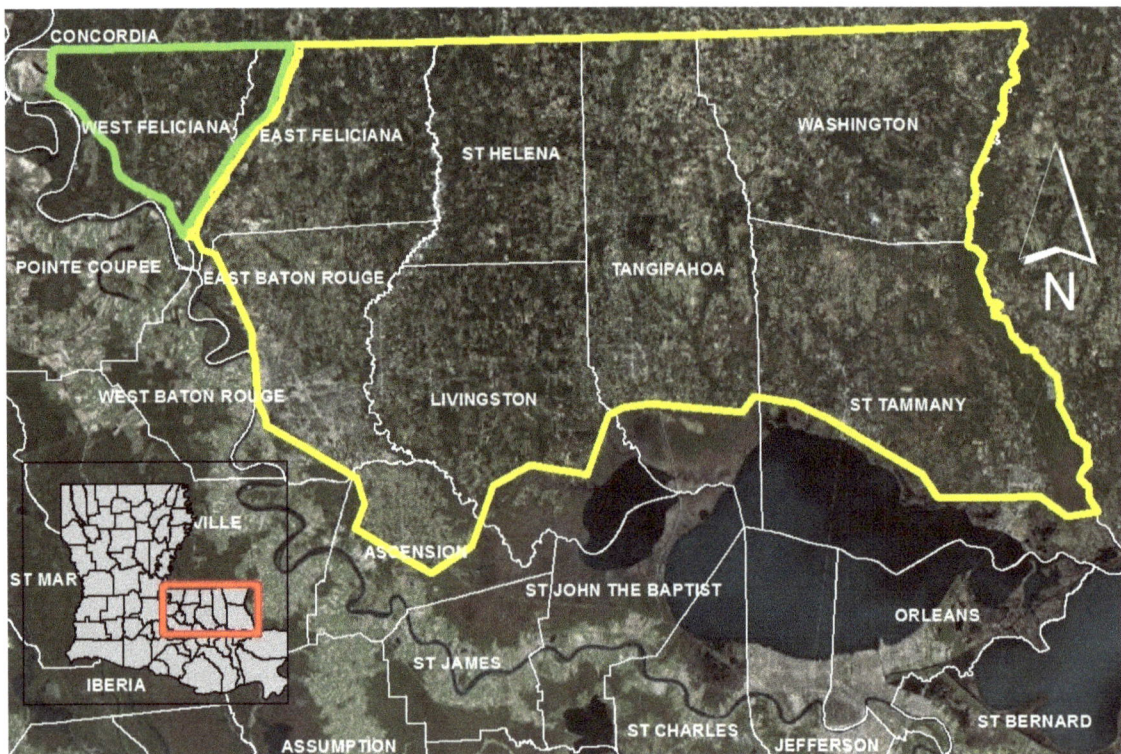

Assets of the EGCP ecoregion include a long tradition of turkey hunting and concern for wild turkeys. This ecoregion has reasonably large blocks of industrial forestland not likely to be developed as residential areas in the near future. It also has two public hunting areas (Pearl River WMA and Bogue Chitto NWR) on the eastern side encompassing a significant landscape where wild turkeys occur. In years past the interspersion of dairy farms within large forested blocks helped maintain strong turkey numbers. Researchers found that turkeys heavily used dairy fields and would concentrate home ranges in association with such farms (Smith et al. 1986). Market changes and government sponsored Conservation Reserve Program (CRP) incentives within the region resulted in most dairy farms converting to pine plantations or other purposes less useful to wild turkeys. On a positive note, where larger blocks of pine plantations planted during the late 1980s and 1990s have been actively managed, by timber thinnings and prescribed fire, turkeys are once again repopulating these areas.

This area's greatest limiting factor is the ever increasing fragmentation of turkey habitat caused by urbanization-fragmentation and the associated non-compatible uses of these small tracts by private landowners. Southeast Louisiana is where much of the state's human population lives, but it is woefully lacking in upland public lands managed for wild turkeys as well as related turkey hunting opportunities. Where turkeys still exist along the Pearl River basin flooding is an increasing problem. Annual river flooding is occurring more often than in the past and is impacting vegetation important to turkeys and other wildlife. American beech trees were once common on the Pearl River WMA but began to die off during the mid-1980s. It was determined that increased flood duration was killing the beech trees. Turkeys inhabiting the WMA were historically able to escape floods by flying across the West and East Pearl Rivers to adjacent high ground. These areas, which once served as secluded refuge from the floods, are now highly urbanized and are unsuitable for turkeys. The eastern most EGCP habitat is still recovering from damage caused by Hurricane Katrina. More upland EGCP turkey habitats have also suffered greatly from the loss of the once common flowering dogwood due to the spread of *dogwood anthracnose* disease. When first observed, dogwood trees infected with *dogwood anthracnose* lose vigor often resulting in parts of the tree dying. Within a few short years this historically dependable fall/winter food source became all but absent in the EGCP. In a study conducted in similar habitat in Alabama, dogwood berries were the primary fall food source (Exum et al. 1987). Dogwood flowers that once signaled the peak of turkey breeding season no longer show their beauty or provide much needed food for turkeys in the Florida Parishes. Only a sprinkling of this species remains. It is feared that this disease will soon spread to other areas of the state. Exacerbating the loss of this valuable turkey food source, is the continued growth of feral hogs which compete heavily for limited hardwood mast in the EGCP.

Upper East Gulf Coastal Plain Ecoregion

The upper east gulf coastal plain (UEGCP), which encompasses most of West Feliciana parish and Thompson Creek uplands of East Feliciana parish, contains a relatively stable wild turkey habitat that most consider the best habitat for turkeys in the Florida parishes (Figure 39). This area is dominated by loess soil which is highly erodible. This erodible soil and steep terrain features has limited farming potential which has resulted in less residential encroachment into turkey habitats. Much of this ecoregion is composed of upland hardwoods such as cherrybark oak, white oak, water oak, cow oak, nuttall oak, American beech, American elm, magnolia, hackberry, and hickory that supply excellent food sources for turkeys. Interspersed small pastures and steep hardwood covered slopes create some of the best turkey habitat in the state. Yet despite the habitat quality, turkeys here like many areas across the state have declined in recent years.

The greatest assets of the UEGCP revolve around the unique qualities of loess-hill type habitat. These hills and ravines packed with high quality hardwoods and other foods meet turkey habitat needs within smaller acreages than most flatland terrain hardwood areas. This was demonstrated in the smaller turkey home ranges found by LSU researcher John Gross (2015). The rugged terrain and high quality hardwood diversity also increases the carrying capacity for turkeys over other habitat types. The hills and slopes offer turkeys seclusion, escape cover, a wide variety of foods, open forests for predator avoidance, roosting sites, nesting habitat, loafing habitat, and brood habitat all in forest blocks of relatively few acres. It is not uncommon for loess-hill habitats to hold twice as many turkeys as compared to other ecoregion habitats. This ecoregion maintains several relatively large privately owned landholdings where wildlife is intensively managed. In addition, the UEGCP is actively managed for hardwoods and pine timber which creates a mosaic of habitat structure. This diversity provides both open and denser areas to meet various seasonal turkey habitat needs.

Mississippi River Alluvial Plain Ecoregion

The Mississippi River alluvial plain, often called the "*Mississippi alluvial valley*" (MAV), spans Louisiana from the Arkansas state line in Morehouse and the Carroll parishes, southward to the southeast coastal marshes of the Gulf of Mexico and includes the Atchafalaya alluvial flood plain (Figure 40). Today, were its original forests intact, the MAV would likely hold more turkeys than any other ecoregion. However, due to intensive agricultural activity within the MAV, only a few islands of suitable forests remain, mostly in Tensas, Madison, Concordia, St. Martin, and Iberville parishes. Much of this loss of forestland occurred during the 1960s as the price of soybeans and other row crops increased. So rapid was the clearing of bottomland hardwoods during this period, that many feared all of the larger forested tracts might disappear completely. Former LDWF biologist and Assistant Secretary Richard K. Yancey addressed the concern for this rapid loss of wildlife habitat in a report entitled *"The Vanishing Delta Hardwoods"* at the 1969 Governor's seminar on Mississippi delta hardwoods in Little Rock, Arkansas (Yancey 1969). Eerily close to his gloomy prediction of near total loss of MAV bottomland hardwoods in Louisiana, less than 15% of the MAV is suitable habitat today. His efforts and those of countless others resulted in the preservation of several thousand acres of remnant MAV forests. These critically important remaining forests are characterized by tree species such as sweet pecan, green ash, hackberry, box elder, water oak, nuttall oak, willow oak, overcup oak, American elm, sweetgum, cottonwood, and sycamore. Sweet pecan, native to alluvial plains of Louisiana's larger rivers, has been found to be very important to wild turkeys as a fall and winter food source (Bittner 1973). Areas of cypress and tupelo, also common in the MAV, are often preferred roosting sites. While larger expanses of cypress-tupelo forest in the southern MAV act as an expansion constraint to turkey range.

Figure 40: The below map shows the Mississippi River alluvial plain outlined in yellow. (Esri, DigitalGlobe, GeoEye, Earthstar, Geographics, CNES/Airous, DS, USDA, USGS, AEX, Geimapping, Aerogrid, IGN, swisstopo, and the GIS User Community)

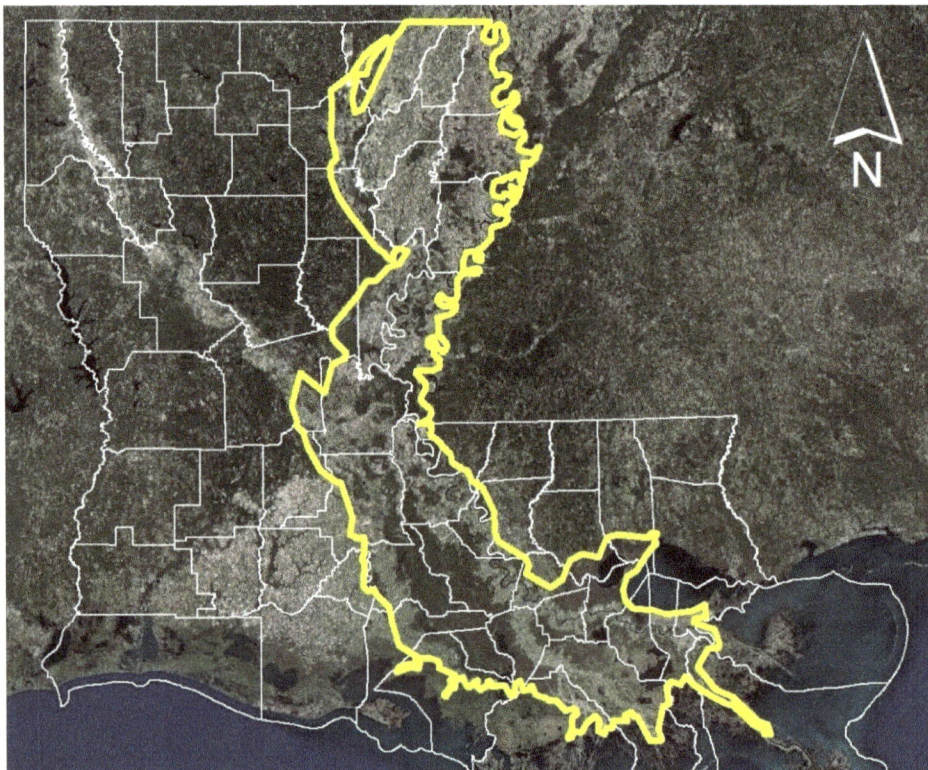

The most obvious asset of the MAV is the high fertility of its soils. Such soils quickly grow a diverse array of hardwood trees, vines, and herbaceous plants that produce turkey foods in mass. The fertile soils produce considerable insect concentrations in small forest gaps available to young turkeys deep within interior forests. Insects can be so plentiful within the forests of the MAV, especially in the southern MAV, that turkeys have been documented to avoid larger openings such as fields and rights of ways normally used in other ecoregions for brood rearing.

The remaining larger forested habitats throughout the MAV have been described as *"islands"* surrounded by agriculture and are primarily public owned lands that include Bayou Macon WMA, Big Lake WMA, Tensas River NWR, Richard K. Yancey WMA, Bouef WMA, Lake Ophelia NWR, Bayou Cocodrie NWR, and Sherburne WMA. The importance of these large contiguous forest blocks to wild turkeys cannot be overstated. A few other smaller privately owned islands of habitat also occur within the MAV but as aforementioned, sometimes lack connective mature forest corridors. These corridors must be contiguous and of adequate width and ground cover structure to facilitate use by turkeys. One of the most important recent improvements to this area for turkeys is the increase in acres now enrolled in the Conservation Reserve Program (CRP) and Wetland Reserve Program (WRP) offered by the Natural Resource Conservation Service (NRCS). These programs, encouraged by LDWF and the United States Fish and Wildlife Service (USFWS), have enhanced Louisiana black bear recovery efforts and helped a plethora of other wildlife species including the wild turkey. If properly maintained, the more than 500,000 acres of CRP and WRP should one-day result in expansion of wild turkey numbers within this ecoregion.

Many issues limit wild turkeys within the MAV. A glaring problem is that many areas where turkeys exist lack mature forested travel corridors to facilitate range expansion. This area also remains prized farmland that will always be under threat of the plow as farm commodity prices increase. Many of the remaining larger forested areas where turkeys might otherwise exist are choked with palmetto rendering them unsuited for turkey habitation.

Similar to other areas of the state, flooding is an ever increasing problem especially within leveed lands. Levees constructed to reduce flooding for man, have resulted in increased flooding of wildlife habitat within the levees. As rivers continually silt-in and man-engineered drainage rapidly directs greater amounts of water into the system, water restricted by levees can no longer spread naturally over the landscape. The result is higher water levels and more frequent batture flooding. It is believed by many land managers and wildlife biologists that increased flooding has greatly influenced the decline of turkey numbers within the MAV. Long time area LDWF biologist Cliff Williams reported that Lookout Point in East Carroll parish had one turkey per 40 – 50 acres in 1982 (Kimmel 1984), while today due to some 3 decades of increased flooding, turkeys are near absent from these same forests. LDWF MAV wildlife biologist John Hanks recently stated *"I fear that CRP/WRP lands will be slow to repopulate with turkeys as they come of age due to low turkey numbers within adjacent batture lands."*

CRP and WRP lands within the MAV, although planted in hardwoods, often lack the natural plant diversity of the original forests. Many of the native hard and soft mast species are lacking. Attention should be given during future management operations to broaden the array of native woody and herbaceous plant species that occur on these sites. Ensuring suitable openings within CRP/WRP lands will also benefit turkeys in the MAV.

Changes initiated by interfering with natural drainage have altered historic hydrology, tree health, and species composition. Many areas within the MAV have suffered *"oak decline"* as a result of these changes. When oaks begin to decline in health due to increases or decreases in normal flooding such areas slowly change to lower value tree species that can diminish a large area's value to wild turkeys.

Human initiated flooding is a growing threat within the protection levees of the Atchafalaya Basin. In recent years, this area has been relatively dry and wild turkeys have prospered. Yet in 2011, the Morganza Spillway was intentionally flooded when the water control structure was opened by the US Army Corps of Engineers (USACE) to reduce flooding potential in more populated areas southward along the Mississippi River. Prior to opening the public was informed that the water would be *"gradually"* released into the spillway. Although just a few of the many flood gates were opened, the result was anything but gradual. Water levels rose on Sherburne WMA by approximately 8 feet in less than a 24-hour period. Such a rapid rise is far outside of a normal Louisiana large river flooding event, and is suspected of causing significant wild turkey deaths in the basin. During the 2011 flood LDWF staff, working with the University of Georgia, captured and GPS/VHF radio monitored wild turkeys on Sherburne WMA. Due to the limited time allowed to capture turkeys before the flood, only a few were captured but each provided a wealth of information. The mortality rate for radioed turkeys during the flood was 60%. One hen was tracked daily via GPS for 21 days as she flew a large circular pattern from tree to tree searching for dry ground (Chamberlain et al. 2013). She died on day 21 (Figure 41). A radioed male survived 31 days before dropping into the floodwaters. It is believed that during a natural flood turkeys have time to move to natural elevated ridges that lead to even higher ridges which eventually lead turkeys to safety. The rapid man-directed flood did not allow this critical process of evacuation to occur for wildlife and losses were estimated to be great. The Sherburne WMA wild turkey harvest dropped from 77 turkeys the season prior to the flood to 13 the season after, confirming the deadly effect of this flood. The harvest has declined every year since, demonstrating that the flood was a serious blow to Atchafalaya Basin turkeys. LDWF MAV Region Manager Tony Vidrine reported that the Morganza Spillway flood of 2011 resulted in the greatest harm of any event to Atchafalaya area turkeys in his over thirty-year career. Despite actions taken by LDWF after the flood to reduce the hunting season length and number of hunters, many biologists fear that turkey numbers have fallen to a critically low point, warranting more drastic protective action. Future releases of water into the Morganza Spillway must truly be gradual or the future of wild turkeys there is bleak at best. This author believes that any floodwaters that rise greater than about 1 foot per day within large expanse bottomland forests where dry land is not readily available is very detrimental to wild turkeys.

Figure 41: The above photograph is of an emaciated GPS tracked hen that died as a result of the 2011 Morganza spillway opening. (T. Vidrine)

West Gulf Coastal Plain Ecoregion

The west gulf coastal plain (WGCP) in western and central Louisiana is the state's current stronghold for wild turkeys (Figure 42). This area of Louisiana was once dominated by longleaf pine forests. Today it is known for large blocks of public land containing regularly burned mature longleaf pine forests interspersed with numerous small hardwood stream bottoms. The WGCP is currently the most stable habitat base for turkeys in the state. Important hardwood tree species found in the WGCP include southern red oak, black gum, water oak, flowering dogwood, willow oak, white oak, post oak, elm, American beech, sweetgum, various haws, and viburnums. In addition to tens of thousands of acres of public land, large areas of industrial forest lands are found in the WGCP. It is not surprising that the number one parish for turkey harvests within the state, Vernon parish, is found in this ecoregion. Most of Vernon parish is lightly populated by people and contains the greatest number of forested acres of any parish. For this reason Vernon parish has led the state in turkeys harvested since tagging and reporting became law in 2009. In addition to Vernon parish, Natchitoches, Sabine, Winn, Grant, Rapides, and Beauregard parishes have also been relatively strong turkey harvest areas.

The Red River alluvial valley bisects the WGCP and offers little value as turkey habitat due to large areas of hardwood forests cleared for agriculture. Some areas have been reforested via CRP and WRP but most such areas are years away from being suitable turkey habitat again.

Figure 42: The west gulf coastal plain is outlined in yellow. (Esri, DigitalGlobe, GeoEye, Earthstar, Geographics, CNES/Airous, DS, USDA, USGS, AEX, Geimapping, Aerogrid, IGN, swisstopo, and the GIS User Community)

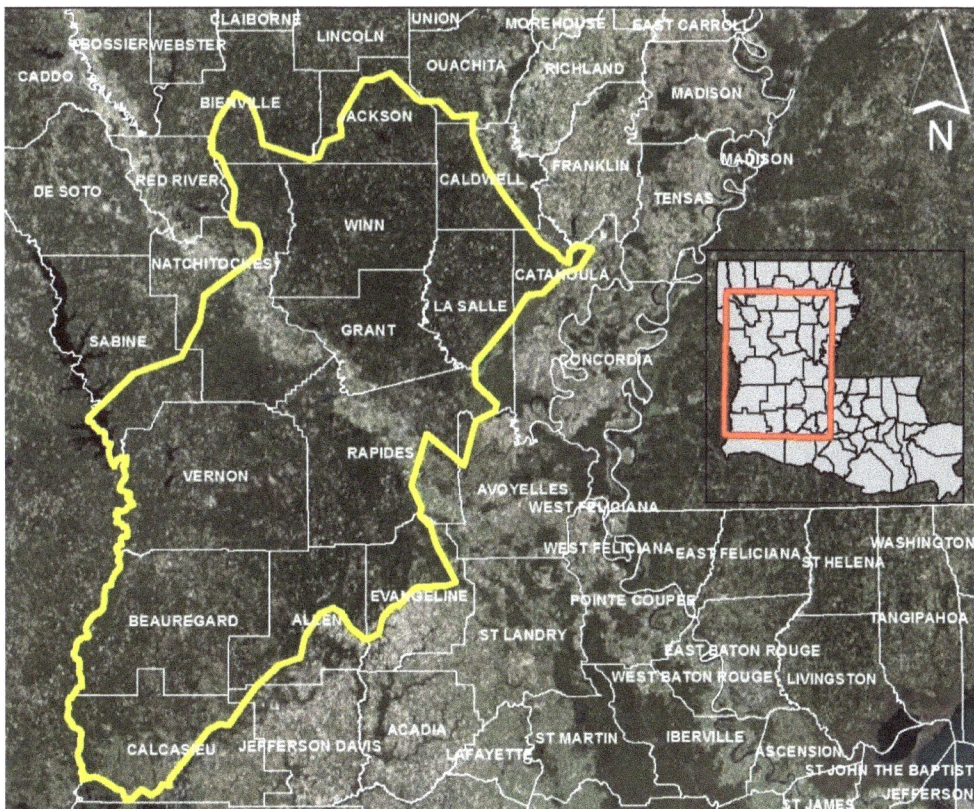

The large area of sparsely populated forests found in the WGCP is arguably the greatest factor influencing turkey numbers. Equally important is the area's large proportion of public land, most of which is managed by prescribed fire, which is tremendously beneficial to wild turkeys. More acres are burned in this ecoregion than any other in the state. Most of the more than 600,000 acres of Kisatchie National Forest (KNF), including Calcasieu, Winn, Kisatchie, and Catahoula Ranger Districts, are found in the WGCP. These KNF lands offer thousands of acres for turkeys and are open to turkey hunting for a 23-day period. State owned and/or leased WMAs such as West Bay, Ft. Polk-Vernon, Clear Creek, Peason Ridge, Little River, and J. C. "*Sonny*" Gilbert (formerly Sicily Island WMA) are also very important turkey areas and offer hunters generally fewer hunting days, but some of the best hunting in the state. These public lands should by nature of their ownership be resistant to encroachment from development well into the foreseeable future.

WGCP limitations include periodic restrictions on turkey hunting days and open areas on Ft. Polk-Vernon WMA and Peason Ridge WMA due to military training. However, most hunters understand the importance of these Department of Defense lands for military training. Like other areas, fragmentation and urbanization do affect the peripheries of WGCP public lands, but the impact has generally been less dramatic than in other ecoregions.

Upper West Gulf Coastal Plain Ecoregion

The upper west gulf coastal plain (UWGCP), located in northwest Louisiana, is characterized by mixed pine and hardwood rolling hills (Figure 43). Upland pines, including shortleaf and loblolly as well as a good mixture of hardwood species similar to those found in the WGCP, are abundant in this ecoregion. Away from its larger cities, much of this area is sparsely populated by people and has considerable industrial forestland acreage. Small farms are interspersed within large private and industrial forested areas providing turkeys a multitude of openings available for foraging broods. This ecoregion has in recent years experienced higher brood production compared to other ecoregions (see Appendix F). Many areas within UWGCP were some of the last restocked with turkeys. Hunting pressure on private lands within the UWGCP was documented to be relatively low in a recent gobbler mortality study (Byrne et al. 2014).

Figure 43: The upper west gulf coastal plain is outlined in yellow. (Esri, DigitalGlobe, GeoEye, Earthstar, Geographics, CNES/Airous, DS, USDA, USGS, AEX, Geimapping, Aerogrid, IGN, swisstopo, and the GIS User Community)

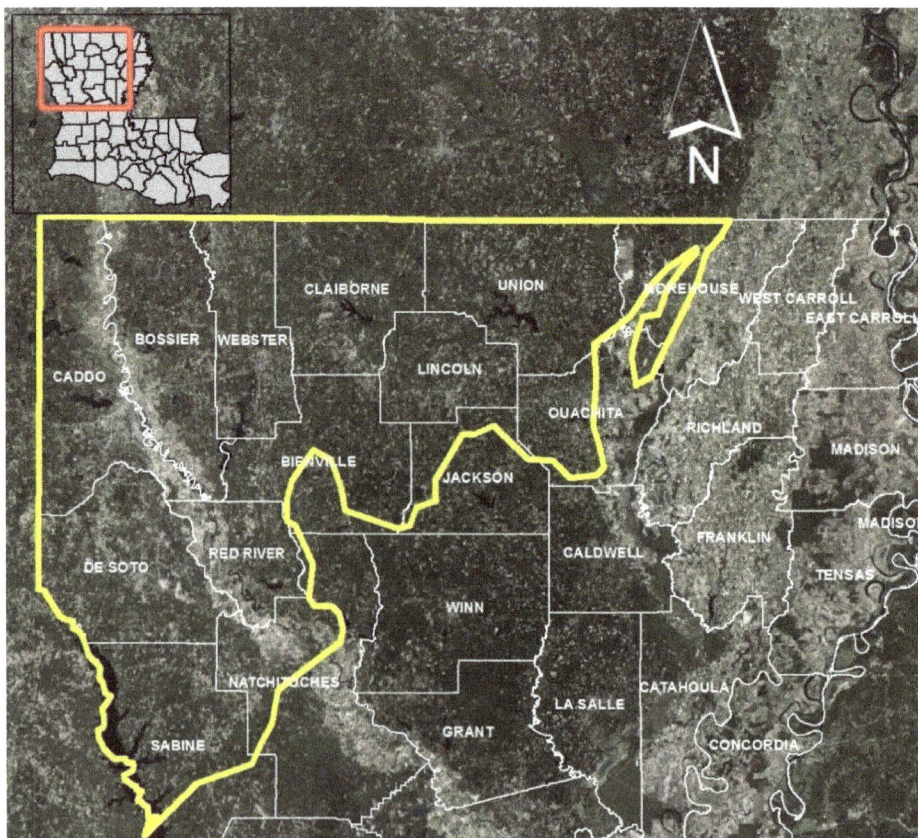

The leading parishes for turkey harvests within the UWGCP are Claiborne and Union which are comprised of large areas of forestland. Claiborne parish has the added benefit of the U. S. Forest Service KNF Caney Ranger District where turkeys are generally doing quite well. Bossier, Jackson, Bienville, upper Natchitoches, and Sabine parishes also offer quality turkey hunting opportunities both on private and public lands. This ecoregion has two important WMAs for wild turkeys: Sabine and Bodcau. With the loss of Jackson-Bienville, Georgia Pacific, and Union WMAs in recent years, as well as other ecoregion WMAs lost, maintaining current WMAs and increasing LDWF owned upland WMAs is a critical need. These WMA losses also increase the importance of wild turkey management and turkey hunting opportunities on federal lands within the UWGCP.

The Red River traverses from northwest to southeast within the UWGCP, but as in the WGCP, it offers little wild turkey habitat due to extensive clearing for farming. Increased development near Shreveport, along the I-20 corridor, and other larger cities has also limited suitable areas available to turkeys. Fragmentation and urbanization are an increasing factor in this ecoregion as much of the land base is in non-industrial private ownership. Prescribed fire has also greatly diminished as a forest management tool in this area from decades past. To add further to the degradation of the habitat, rapidly growing feral hog numbers continue to tax food resources diminishing habitat carrying capacities for wild turkeys and other wildlife within this ecoregion.

Habitat Requirements

There are 4 major habitat cover types needed by wild turkeys: nesting cover, openings/brood rearing cover, fall/winter cover, and roosting cover. Deficiencies of any one of these cover types will limit wild turkeys within a given area. The first requirement of each cover type is that it must afford ample escape from predation. In optimal habitats these cover types should also be present in the correct proportions and in proximity to one another. For a land manager, being able to accurately assess cover deficiencies is difficult, as no single text book can teach what turkeys instinctively know. Many try, but only a handful of more experienced biologists, wildlife managers, and turkey hunters have a sufficient understanding of year around wild turkey needs to accurately assess habitats for these cover type deficiencies.

A wild turkey's *"home range"* in Louisiana is about 1.5 square miles. Home range is defined as the area needed to support a turkey for the entire year. Louisiana studies found average home ranges encompassing 1,693 acres (Taylor 1969), 1,443 acres (Savage 1971), 1,049 acres (White 1986), 1,673 acres (Smith et. al. 1986), and 946 acres (Gross 2015). Gross found that GPS monitored males traveled an average of 2.3 miles in southeast Louisiana, Taylor documented 2.6 miles in northwest Louisiana, and Savage 3.5 miles in Tensas parish. Individual turkeys traveling further distances is not uncommon. Two jakes captured and released on site in East Feliciana parish by the author in 1985 were harvested in St. Helena parish the following year, one 9.5 miles and the other 12.5 miles from their capture site. Two hens captured and released on site at the Catahoula Ranger District (KNF) traveled more than 20 miles (Timmer 1998), while a 22-mile movement was made by a radioed hen in Union and Claiborne parishes (pers. comm. H. Cook).

If a needed cover type is present in the wrong proportions, the cover type itself may become a limiting factor to turkeys. If not proximal to other needed cover types, the habitat is also of lesser value. Optimal turkey habitats have all 4 cover types at the correct proportion and arranged throughout the forest expanse well beyond one turkey's home range. This larger expanse, often called *"landscape"*, transcends beyond a few hundred acres to several thousand acres in size. Habitat management actions with the greatest impact on wild turkeys will always come at the landscape level. State, Federal, and corporate entities can influence habitats at this grand landscape scale. Unfortunately, most turkey managers will never have the luxury to manage at the landscape scale, but instead must operate at a much smaller habitat scale. Yet even these small scale efforts, when combined with groupings of other similar efforts nearby, can net landscape results. Since more than 80% of Louisiana is privately owned, private landowners working together with neighboring landowners hold the greatest potential to affect the wild turkey's future.

Nesting Habitat

Nesting habitat, as defined by this book, consists of that specific spot where turkey hens establish their nest. Turkey nests have been found within any number of different vegetative covers, from briar patches, to broom sedge fields, to Virginia creeper covered forest floors, to wide open bottomland hardwood flats; turkeys will nest in a variety of vegetative substrates. Hens often select nest sites at the base of a tree, in brush tops, near a bush, or near a tall grass clump. Other hens may establish nests in vegetative structure with no discernable irregular vegetative features. The site selected will greatly influence the probability of the nest avoiding detection by predators or it being destroyed by flooding. Within the different habitats found in Louisiana hens select differing nest sites but these sites often contain similar plant structural characteristics. In bottomland hardwoods of the Atchafalaya, hens selected nest locations in areas that offered greater proportions of non-flooded bottomland forests and higher forest edge density than those generally available across the study site at all scales (Wilson 2005, Byrne et al. 2013). Byrne (2013) went on to report that most turkeys selected nest sites that were the result of small breaks in the forest canopy and that turkeys avoided larger managed forest openings such as clear cuts. In Tensas and Franklin parishes where bottomland hardwood forests are sometimes too open for nesting, longtime LDWF biologist Lowery Moak reported finding numerous nests underneath overhanging limbs in tall grass strips along roads. On the Kisatchie, Winn, and Calcasieu Ranger Districts of Kisatchie National Forest from 2014 - 2015, hens preferred nesting in mature forest stands burned 2 years previous (Yeldell 2016). An earlier study conducted on the Catahoula Ranger District during 1995 – 1997 reported hens using timber stands from age 5 to 111 (avg. 47.9) years old burned similarly an average of 2.2 years prior to the nest initiation (Timmer et al. 1998). In a recent study in southwest Georgia, hens nested more in shrub/scrub habitats of younger woody brush than in mature longleaf pine stands (Strelch et al. 2015). Regardless of the vegetation selected, most hens instinctively nest in the best cover structure afforded within their home range.

In Louisiana, flooding after nests are established, especially in flat terrain parishes can result in localized poult production deficiencies. Parishes prone to flooding by heavy rains include Livingston, Beauregard, Calcasieu, Ascension, Iberville, St. Martin, Pt. Coupee, Iberia, Assumption, St. Landry, East Baton Rouge, West Baton Rouge, Tangipahoa, St. Tammany, Concordia, Tensas, Madison, East Carroll, and Avoyelles. Many of these parishes were affected by the historic floods in 2016. Parishes within leveed Mississippi, Atchafalaya, and Red River batture lands are at even higher risks of regular flooding. In more upland areas traversed by countless streams and rivers, localized flooding can sometimes cause nest losses, but such losses in upland areas are usually buffered by production on nearby higher grounds.

Although hens will establish nests in a variety of vegetative structure, hens that select the best nest site are more likely to hatch young. Successful hens often select a larger expanse of nest cover rather than a small spot of nest cover (Figure 44), making it more difficult for predators to search out and find her nest. Think of it like a childhood Easter egg hunt. The odds of a child finding eggs within a yard with a few scattered clumps of cover are greater than finding eggs in a large yard completely covered in tall grass. Scattered clumps of cover are easily and thoroughly searched while expanses of cover are searched by random and incomplete sampling. Research conducted in the Atchafalaya basin suggests that managing habitats to create such expanses of nesting cover are preferred in order to improve nesting success (Wilson 2005 and Byrne 2016). Nests are often found within 25 yards of a road, trail, or other opening, allowing easy access for the hen and may also aid in leading poults to brood habitat when they leave the nests. Recent research done on Kisatchie National Forest confirmed hen preference for nesting along trails and roads but also found such nests some distance away from differing habitat transition zones (Yeldell 2016).

Figure 44: The nest in the center is hidden in a sea of Virginia creeper vines and leaves at Richard K. Yancey WMA. (D. Locascio)

Unfortunately, many nests located along roads, trails, and in fields are destroyed each year by mowing. Dennett (1997) recommended not mowing such potential turkey nesting areas from March 15 through July 15. After this date, mowing can be done with little risks of disturbing turkey nests.

Recent GPS telemetry studies indicate that hens may not pre-select nest sites, rather immediately before nesting hens may simply start walking in search of a nest site (Conley et al. 2016). A hen is instinctively pre-programed to look for certain vegetative structural qualities as she searches for a nest site. On rare occasions hens will simply run out of time to find her perfect nest site and lay a single egg in a road or other unsuitable spot. Needless to say, these eggs are quickly found by predators.

Openings and Brood Rearing Cover

The simple definition of an opening is any open area that turkeys might use. *Openings and brood rearing cover* may or may not be one in the same. Arguably the most important openings are those used by poults. These openings provide abundant protein-rich insect concentrations critical for rapid poult growth as well as cover and ease of access while poults are foraging. Such openings can be tree gaps within forests where sunlight reaches the ground or more open man-manipulated herbaceous areas. Good brood cover must provide plenty of insects and cover that is the correct height for the specific size of poults using it. Very small poults, 4 – 6 inches tall, will often be found in somewhat thin cover just under 4 to 6 inches tall. Older broods, 10 to 12 inches tall, might be found in cover just under that height. As a general rule, poults are often found foraging in cover that partially hides their body while feeding, but allows them visibility when they raise their head. Optimally, such cover is interspersed within clumps of taller vegetation to aid in predator avoidance. Road shoulders are a choice spot for foraging young as vegetation often exists along road edges at graduated heights to accommodate growing poults of various sizes throughout the summer (Figure 45). Roads and trails also allow for quick access to and from feeding and roosting areas.

Figure 45: Hens and poults foraging along a little used road in Livingston Parish (J. Stafford)

The more abundant insects are within brood habitats the less distance poults need to travel to meet daily food requirements, this reduces energy used and calories expended. The sooner poult crops are filled, the quicker they can resume more focused predator avoidance. Many studies agree that within a few weeks of hatching poults begin to consume higher volumes of grass seeds than insects. Therefore, it is also important that brood habitats have a significant grass seed component. In addition to grass seeds and insects, poult diets will often have a large proportion of blackberries when in season.

Broods heavily utilize openings from the day they leave the nest in May-June until early fall. Fields, food plots, road edges, rights of ways, trails, recently thinned forests, log loading sets, prescribed burned areas, clearcuts, and natural forest openings are commonly used by broods. The height and density of vegetation within an opening will determine its value to poults. In south Louisiana vegetative response to sunlight can be much more robust than north Louisiana, especially in the fertile soils of the MAV. This heavy annual growth renders some openings unusable to poults. A good turkey manager always monitors the condition of openings during the critical months of May – July.   Where openings are overgrown beyond use for turkeys, mowing is justifiable regardless of the month.

The LDWF annual *Wild Turkey Production Survey* which assesses statewide reproduction dynamics has been conducted by both conservation professionals and private volunteers since 1994. This survey, conducted from July 1 through August 31, determines a poult per hen (PPH) ratio that can be used from year to year to gauge production and predict future harvest success. It divides the state into 5 habitat regions where variations in rainfall and other factors may influence reproductive success quite differently in any given year. Habitat regions surveyed are: Southeast Loblolly Pine (Florida Parishes), Northwest Loblolly/Shortleaf/Hardwood, North Mississippi Delta, Atchafalaya and South Mississippi Delta, and Western Longleaf Pine. Traditionally biologists believed that a PPH ratio of 2.0 or greater was needed to maintain a population. New research indicates that a slightly lower PPH ratio may be capable of maintaining numbers (Byrne 2016). Figure 46 illustrates survey regions and recent poult production findings. Additional poult survey results from 1994 – 2015 are found in Appendix F while more current results may be obtained by contacting LDWF Wild Turkey Program Leader Cody Cedotal at *ccedotal@wlf.la.gov*.

Louisiana Wild Turkey Poult Production Index 2015

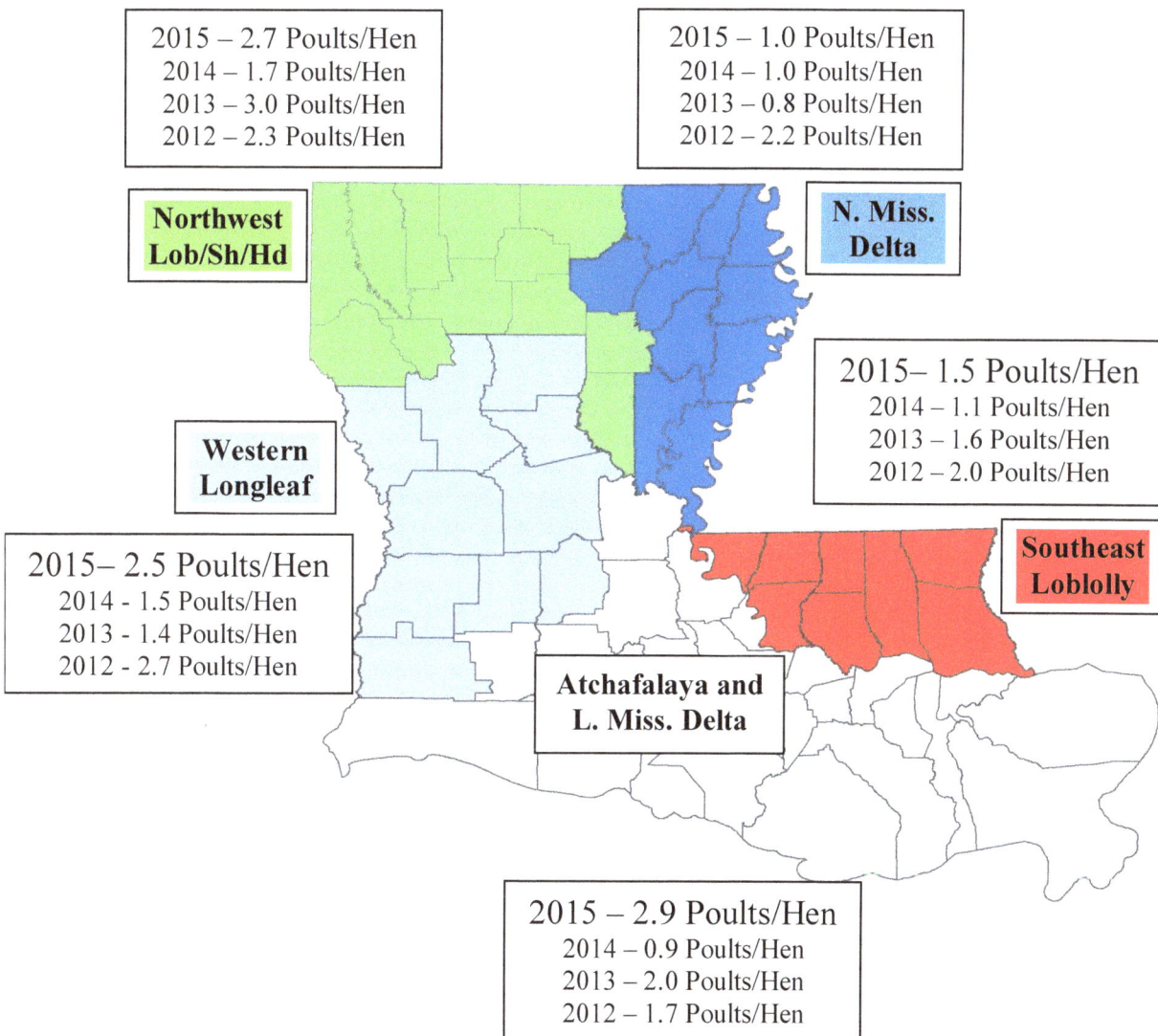

2015 – 2.7 Poults/Hen
2014 – 1.7 Poults/Hen
2013 – 3.0 Poults/Hen
2012 – 2.3 Poults/Hen

2015 – 1.0 Poults/Hen
2014 – 1.0 Poults/Hen
2013 – 0.8 Poults/Hen
2012 – 2.2 Poults/Hen

Northwest Lob/Sh/Hd

N. Miss. Delta

2015 – 1.5 Poults/Hen
2014 – 1.1 Poults/Hen
2013 – 1.6 Poults/Hen
2012 – 2.0 Poults/Hen

Western Longleaf

Southeast Loblolly

2015 – 2.5 Poults/Hen
2014 - 1.5 Poults/Hen
2013 - 1.4 Poults/Hen
2012 - 2.7 Poults/Hen

Atchafalaya and L. Miss. Delta

2015 – 2.9 Poults/Hen
2014 – 0.9 Poults/Hen
2013 – 2.0 Poults/Hen
2012 – 1.7 Poults/Hen

Figure 46 (LDWF)

In addition to their use for brood rearing, openings are important for hen pre-nesting nutrition and courtship. Prior to nesting, hens feed voraciously on insects, grass seeds, and green matter to prepare physiologically for egg laying and lack of nutrition during the 28-day incubation period. Pre-incubation openings sought out by hens include planted food plots, pastures, agricultural fields, utility right of ways, or openings created by fire or timber management within forests. Previously tilled or disturbed ground seems to be preferred as it may offer a greater variety of plants and insects than non-disturbed sites. Openings are important for social behavior prior to and during courtship. In addition, larger openings play an important role in predator avoidance during windy and rainy periods.

Fall/Winter Cover

Fall/winter cover may look very different than other cover types or very similar depending on the plant species composition and structure. Fall/winter cover must provide food and escape cover. As temperatures drop, turkey food requirements shift to high carbohydrate diets to aid in building fat reserves needed for maintaining body heat. Acorns, beechnuts, flowering dogwood seeds, beggar's lice seeds, sweet pecan, pine seeds, swamp dogwood, blackgum, and other fall/winter seeding plants are of major importance. Turkeys that might normally make a living in upland pine forests of southeast and west-central Louisiana during the summer and early fall will often travel considerable distances in the late fall and winter to find large hardwood dominant areas where food is more plentiful. The importance of diverse species composition within such hardwood forests cannot be overstated; this diversity ensures more dependable food availability. One food towers over the rest in importance; acorns. Forests with diverse species of oaks provide more reliable acorn crops and the best fall/winter habitat.

It is the fall and winter when hunters flock to the woods in search of deer. These hunter orange clad masses penetrate nearly every corner of the forest. During this time, turkeys seek more secluded areas that provide additional ground and mid-canopy concealment cover reducing visual hunter-turkey encounters. Such habitats often have a greater density of woody saplings and mid-story trees but are not so thick as to put birds at excessive risk of natural predation (Figure 47). Fall/winter cover may come in the form of 8 to 10-year-old regenerated forest areas that have a high stem count and above ground cover but afford turkeys good visibility at eye level. More mature timber stands periodically managed by timber thinning often have a well-developed mid-story of hardwoods that result in good fall/winter habitat. An example of a habitat that lacks fall/winter cover would be a mature closed canopy forest not actively managed for timber. Absentee landowner and neglected government owned forests are sometimes victims of fall/winter cover deficiencies due to inactivity in forest management. Industrial timber company forests seldom need worry as their regular timber management activities ensure plenty of fall/winter cover, except that mature hardwoods may sometimes be more limited within such upland pine areas. Fall/winter cover must have ample fall/winter foods interspersed throughout or be in very close proximity to mature hardwood areas that provide such foods.

Figure 47: This recently thinned fall/winter escape cover in Natchitoches parish offers increased concealment to elude people and predators. (J. Stafford)

Roosting Cover

Roosting cover is the forested site selected by turkeys to roost. Roosting in trees reduces predation risks. Depending on the ecoregion of the state where turkeys exist, differing site characteristics may be preferred such as roost tree species and forest stand structure. Mature turkeys often select trees containing at least one near horizontal limb about 1.5 to 3 inches in diameter. Young turkeys and hens tend to roost in smaller diameter trees. Turkeys prefer to roost on horizontal limbs because this aids in weight distribution and balance. Often limb diameter selection is based on the mechanics of how a turkey's foot operates. Without exertion, a turkey's three front toes and one back toe will automatically clasp a correctly sized tree limb as the bird crouches. This can be demonstrated on a freshly harvested gobbler if one bends the legs forward under the breast. The tight grip that is formed and a slight depression on the breast keel bone allows a turkey to securely spend the night sleeping without fear of falling. In the uplands of southeast and west-central Louisiana, adult turkeys often select mature pines for roost trees although beech, hickory, oak, and other trees with horizontal limbs are sometimes selected. During inclement weather on upland sites, turkeys may select pole-sized (11 to 14 inch D.B.H.) pine stands that are tightly stocked to decrease their exposure to wind and aerial predators.

Turkeys in the MAV bottomlands tend to prefer cypress/tupelo trees in standing water but also will roost in other species of trees away from water. Along river batture lands turkeys often roost along river front hardwood sites (Kimmel 1984). In northwest Louisiana and West Feliciana turkeys regularly use both pine and hardwood trees for roosting with seemingly less preference for one over the other. The habit of roosting over water and in pine trees is likely a survival adaptation. Many predators and other creatures of the night live in cavities of hardwood trees. When roosting in hardwood trees, turkeys avoid roosting in trees with hollow cavities. Pines seldom have cavities and offer the added protection of crackly bark alerting a turkey of any nighttime visitors. Median aged pole-sized (11 to 14 inches in diameter above the butt swell) cypress trees seldom have hollows and offer water as an added discouragement to predators. At times turkeys seem very selective of roosting sites, while other times not so selective. Gobblers following a hen during the spring may simply fly to the nearest tree at dusk or select a large one on a hill nearby to make sure he is easily heard far and wide when gobbling the next morning.

Turkeys fly to roost near official sunset each day and usually return to the ground slightly before official sunrise. On rainy days they may remain on their roost much longer in the morning. This author is not sure if this is a predator avoidance habit, or like me, they just don't care to get out of bed on rainy days. Gobblers will also linger on the roost during breeding season as they wait for the arrival of hens drawn to gobbling. In 2014, West Feliciana parish hunter Joel Smith reported a hen flying to and being bred in a tree by a slow-to-fly-down gobbler. Although I have witnessed many hens fly to gobblers early in the morning, this was the first time actual tree breeding has been reported to this author. However, there is no reason to believe that this does not occur on occasion, especially during spring floods where turkeys may be trapped in trees for a week or two during the peak of breeding season.

Important roost sites include timbered ox bow lakes, river front hardwoods, single or small groups of pines in large hardwood bottoms within upland ecoregions, pole-sized pine flats near hardwood transition zones, large pines/hardwoods near fields where turkeys traditionally congregate, stream or bayou bank cypress/tupelo trees, and head of hardwood drain pines. Availability of such roosting sites within a given tract will determine an individual timber stands overall importance as roosting cover. Where roosting sites are limited and heavily used by turkeys, all effort should be taken to avoid altering canopy and groundcover conditions near those sites. Relatively minor changes near roosting areas can significantly impact turkey use and sometimes cause turkeys to completely abandon the area.

The left shows pine roost trees at the back of a field and right shows a cypress/tupelo roost site. (J. Stafford)

In a study comparing the Texas Rio Grande subspecies to Louisiana's eastern wild turkey, little roost site fidelity was found in Louisiana turkeys compared to the Texas Rio Grande turkey (Byrne et al. 2016). Research conducted in West Baton Rouge, Washington, and West Feliciana parishes found that 28.2% of the time gobblers would return to previously used roost sites (Gross et al. 2015). The same study found that Louisiana gobblers use the same roost site on consecutive nights only 6.9% of the time. These findings may be relative to the quality and quantity of roost sites available but also indicate the important survival instinct of unpredictability. Greater roost site fidelity is most often associated with limited roost site availability.

Habitat Management

"Wildlife management is a science but the application of that science is an art." This often quoted statement is very true. For wild turkey management to be successful, a proper habitat evaluation must first be completed. Actor Clint Eastwood once said, *"A man has got to know his limitations."* So too must a wildlife manager know his habitat's limitations. Important limitations can be the size of the property, roost site availability, insufficient openings, habitat too open, habitat too thick, excessive palmetto, flooding, disease, predators, poaching, over hunting, and many others. Some limitations are well within man's ability to correct and some are not. An assessment is the first step to determine what necessary turkey habitat elements are insufficient. An experienced observer can start the process of assessment by using satellite images to determine missing or out of proportion elements. Many habitat features can be accurately quantified from above. Size of the forested area must always be the starting point. If a person has only 100 acres of forest to manage, he or she must understand that such minimal acreage does not supply a turkey's yearly needs. Even with 1,000 acres, turkeys using the property will spend considerable time on someone else's land. If a small tract of land, <500 acres, is not connected to a forested stream corridor or other large forested tracts, turkey management actions may result in little success. However, if small tracts are adjacent to much larger wooded areas where turkeys already exist, management efforts can make a considerable difference. On small acreages identifying the site's greatest current asset to turkeys is very important. Whether it is a roosting site, feeding area, opening, or combination thereof, such useful habitat features can be enhanced or protected for that purpose. A habitat evaluation form can be found in Appendix E to assist managers in assessing habitat limitations.

Habitat Management Practices

"The lazy do not roast any game, but the diligent feed on the riches of the hunt." Proverbs 12: 27. (NIV *Holy Bible*)

Well planned proactive habitat management efforts can net positive results for turkeys and hunters. Habitat management practices in Louisiana for turkeys most often include timber management, prescribed fire, opening management, and food plots. Of greatest importance to wild turkeys is proper timber management. Where timber management needs for turkeys have been met in upland pine forests, prescribed fire is equally important. In large well managed forests, most opening needs can be met with active timber harvesting activity, however, where timber harvests are sporadic over time, or fire is infrequent or absent, intentional opening maintenance is of greater importance. Although food is seldom a limiting factor in well managed forests with ample hardwoods, food plots, of lessor importance as a management tool, can be of value if created and maintained properly. The following sections will examine these habitat management practices.

Timber Management

Timber management sets the stage for vegetative conditions within the forest canopy, mid-story, and at ground level. It has the potential to rapidly improve or degrade large areas of habitat and can influence turkey numbers significantly. Occasionally, ground cover habitat conditions within larger closed canopy forests can become too open for turkeys. Timber management, if properly conducted, can very quickly remedy this habitat deficiency. It can also improve food and nesting cover availability. An often overlooked byproduct of timber management is that its application will also greatly influence the predator species present and their numbers. The manner in which a timber harvest is applied will determine the habitat's survival benefits or detriments to wild turkeys. One of the most respected minds in wild turkey research today, Michael Chamberlain, Ph.D. professor at the University of Georgia, stated to this author *"At the recent turkey symposium, Bill Porter, Ph.D. (also a great mind in wild turkey research) was presenting a paper attempting to convince the audience that habitats at some massive spatial scale are important to turkeys. As I listened to him, it struck me that it very likely isn't the turkeys that respond to diversity of habitats across these large areas, but rather, the predators that eat them. You put a huge chunk of mature pine forest out there with some hardwood stringers in it, and I can use fire to grow turkeys for decades. I don't really need lots of openings, as long as the forest structure (through timber management) mimics the successional state of an opening. However, we don't do that. We rip up that large chunk, run roads through it, sell pieces of it to all sorts of landowners with competing interest, create food plots, put power lines all over it, and dissect it in a way that makes it still ok for turkeys (they can make a living), but ideal for everything that eats them, they can do much better than just make a living."* (pers. comm. M. Chamberlain). Chamberlain's postulation might explain why nearly every vibrant population of turkeys in Louisiana is found in association with very large acreages of somewhat homogeneous habitats. Managers must remember that for every action conducted in the forest there is a reaction, sometimes with unexpected consequences. Even actions with good wildlife management intentions can sometimes have negative effects on turkeys. Some believe that if we as land managers would simply concentrate on managing lands to make habitats unappealing to predators, more success would be achieved at increasing turkey numbers.

There are two types of timber management; commercial timber management and wildlife timber management. Commercial timber management focuses on producing maximum timber yields for maximum economic return. Any benefits to wildlife are a secondary byproduct. Wildlife timber management, more specifically *"turkey timber management"*, has as its primary goal the increase of wild turkeys, with timber revenue being a byproduct of lesser importance. Few landowners are predisposed to select this maximum turkey benefit option. However, many interested in wild turkeys are willing to seek a reasonable compromise that helps turkeys but also keeps financial rewards at the forefront.

For any planned timber harvest to become a reality it must achieve or exceed an economic threshold for the timber buyer. A timber buyer will not stay in business long if he loses money on logging jobs in an attempt to make the perfect wildlife cut. The reality is that local timber markets will most often determine the degree of thinning and minimum size of an area that economically justifies logging for the timber buyer. Wildlife managers focused solely on *"doing good"* for turkeys sometimes forget this important fact. For example, in today's market a timber buyer may need to cut a minimum of 2,500 board feet per acre over a minimum timber stand size of 40 acres to make a profit beyond his investment of logging costs. Yet such small acreage timber harvests are of minimal value to turkeys. Harvests that occur on larger acreages distributed over even larger forest expanses are preferred. A removal of 2,500 board feet per acre by thinning may leave great turkey habitat in an initial timber stand that has 10,000 board feet to the acre, but if the original timber stand has only 5,000 board feet per acre, such a cut could quickly produce a post-harvest result too thick for turkeys. These are all important factors that must be considered when conducting timber harvests for the benefit of turkeys. As a rule, when harvesting fewer trees per acre to improve turkey habitat more acres must be cut to justify logging costs.

Unfortunately, the application of forest management for wild turkeys cannot simply be done by following a standard cookbook recipe. Like a dentist pointing out good practices such as brushing, flossing, and the use of fluoride, he is quick to point out that each set of teeth has its own individual problems that need correcting. A forest is no different, each has unique challenges that must be addressed to improve turkey habitat and thus turkey numbers. Both teeth and forests need experienced practitioners to determine problems and solutions. Such important considerations can be made by consulting an experienced wildlife forester.

Not all timber stands are in need of immediate timber management (harvest), but nearly all forests will at some point need corrective action to maintain value to turkeys. Again, habitat deficiencies must be identified before action is taken. If turkeys are plentiful and reproducing well, sometimes the best forest management action is no action at all. Many times important habitat features such as roosting sites and open loafing areas are altered by logging to the point that turkeys abandon the area for several years. These critical micro-habitat features are often best identified by avid turkey hunters and should be mapped as sensitive areas by forest managers while establishing timber harvest prescriptions. Simple adjustments to forest prescriptions pre-logging can reduce turkey range shifts post-logging. Landowners should be reminded that good turkey hunters tend to make the best foresters when it comes to managing for wild turkeys.

Habitats in north and west Louisiana respond differently to timber harvesting than do habitats in south and east Louisiana. Slight differences in temperatures, rainfall, and soils can result in very different vegetative response characteristics following a timber harvest. Vegetative response is often more robust in southern and eastern Louisiana which can result in logged areas becoming too thick for turkeys within a short period of time. While areas in the west and north may provide usable habitat with similar logging actions for much longer periods.

 In former LDWF Turkey Program Leader Dan Dennett's (1997) *A Guide to Managing the Wild Turkey in Louisiana"* publication several timber management recommendations are listed. Dennett, who had more than 40 years of wild turkey management experience, recommended timber management that favored the propagation and management of mast producing hardwoods. He saw firsthand the value of diversity in both the forest canopy and forest understory. Dennett recommended that managers maintain this diversity in plant species composition when managing for turkeys. He stated that when clearcuts are used they should be no greater than 40 acres and widely separated, recommending that no subsequent clearcuts be placed adjacent to another until the first opened sufficiently for turkey access. Dennett suggested that hardwoods be managed on an 80-year timber rotation (age of final harvest schedule) and pines 60 years. Depending on a particular area's soil characteristics, this author believes that these rotations may be considerably shorter and still benefit turkeys.

There are 3 general forest types that turkeys inhabit within Louisiana: pine, hardwood, and pine/hardwood mix. Each forest type should be managed appropriately. In general, pine management for turkeys is least complex, mixed pine/hardwoods slightly more complex, and hardwood management most complex. The importance of hardwoods and herbaceous wetlands to wild turkeys cannot be overstated (Cohen 2016). Within upland pine hardwood habitats of Caddo parish, Cohen found that turkeys spent most of their time in hardwood areas. Hardwoods provide food and habitat structural needs of turkeys. The complexity of hardwood management is in maintaining this preferred structure and plant species diversity within the micro habitats where each plant group grows. When using uneven aged management of hardwoods, insuring ample hardwood regeneration must also be a constant consideration.

At first glance, one might think that a forest composed only of oaks would be bests for turkeys. However, a more diverse mixture of hardwood species will provide a more sustaining year-round food source. Oaks are of great importance and should make up the greater percentage of the trees in a hardwood forest; however, other species such as American beech, elm, dogwoods, pecan, haws, holly, mulberry, maple, and black gum are important too. These and other plants found in well managed forests provide a time released food source at different points during the year. Figure 48 shows a hardwood timber stand with blue paint on trees scheduled for a wildlife timber harvest on Big Lake WMA.

Figure 48: Hardwood trees on Big Lake WMA paint marked for a wildlife timber harvest (D. Locascio)

Basal Areas

Basal area (BA) per acre is a forestry term used to describe the space occupied by trees. BA is the average area measured in square feet occupied by all tree boles at 4 ½ feet high within one acre. Regardless of the diameter of trees, BA generally increases over time as trees grow. High tree density (high BA) forests allow little sunlight to reach the ground which results in an understory that is too sparse. Less sun hitting the ground means less vegetation growing in the zone were turkeys live. Tree densities too low (low BA) can allow too much sunlight to reach the ground, creating excessively thick ground level habitats. Quality habitats will have areas with varying basal areas to meet year-round turkey needs. Again, proportions are very important. Reducing a site's BA is most often achieved through timber harvesting. For example, if the majority of a pine forest has achieved a BA of 180, shading out most of the ground cover, a timber thinning that reduces the BA to 70 – 80 would quickly improve foraging and nesting cover conditions for turkeys.

Thinning

BA reductions for turkey are best achieved through timber thinning, but can also be achieved by chemical injection of undesirable trees or by intentional use of excessively hot prescribed burns in younger pine stands. Today most pine forests on private lands are managed by a first thinning at about age 12 – 20 years, a second thinning about 8 – 10 years later, followed by a final cut (clearcut) around age 35. On some timber industry forests pines are thinned once, then clearcut about 10 years later at around age 28. Such short final harvest rotations are generally not as turkey friendly as are longer rotations. The longer rotations allow any interspersed slower growing hardwood trees more time to mature enough to produce food. The older trees also make better roosting habitat. However, in the immediate years post-thinning, turkey habitat is improved, even within short rotation stands (Figure 49). With the reduction in prescribed burning across the state in recent decades, thinning alone has become an increasingly important turkey habitat improvement practice. Nesting and brood rearing hens seek thinned areas during the first year after cut and many turkeys are harvested by hunters in recently thinned areas during the spring.

When thinning for wild turkeys in bottomland hardwoods one must first be very familiar with post-harvest vegetation responses for each site's hydrology, soil characteristics, and geographic location. These three factors will determine how thick and how quickly the vegetative response will be as well as its subsequent value to turkeys. There are numerous types of thinning methods, however in most cases light thinnings (those that remove fewer trees) favor turkeys most.   The *"variable retention"* method can be used to thin a large area at one time, thinning heavy in some places and light in others throughout the forest. This method can be more financially rewarding and if applied correctly works great for improving timber stand species composition. While another method that this book will call *"parcel"* thinning treats areas of several acres in a more homogeneous thinning then leaves similar sized areas untreated throughout a larger timber stand. Years later subsequent thinnings can be done in areas not thinned the first time to create both heavier and lighter cover areas. When conducting parcel thinnings it is important to thin parcels large enough to justify logging and benefit turkeys.

Figure 49: Recently thinned pines (< 2 years since thinned) provide optimal ground cover density and structure for foraging broods. (J. Stafford)

Clearcutting

Clearcutting is a timber harvest method that removes all merchantable trees within a timber stand at one time for maximum economic gain and in some cases to better facilitate reforestation. This method of harvest is often the scourge of turkey hunters, as so many of us have seen one or more of our favorite turkey hunting spots fall to such a harvest method. However, when used at a relatively small scale (<100 acres) within large forested landscapes, clearcuts can provide good turkey habitat and should not necessarily be shunned by turkey hunters. Clearcuts keep new, healthy, even-aged forests perpetually coming of age for future years while providing much needed escape cover as they grow. The key is to have clearcuts scattered over the larger area, have them as small as economically possible in size, and maintain significant mature hardwood buffers along streams that traverse through them. When done as described above, clearcuts are just another good turkey management tool. Clearcuts also make great places to hunt the first season after created.

Streamside Management Zones (SMZ)

Streamside management zones, sometimes referred to as *"riparian buffers"*, are forested areas left standing after timber harvesting located adjacent to streams, rivers, bayous, or intermittent drains. Ideally, SMZs should include dryer hollows and flats where hardwoods naturally occur. Hardwood SMZs improve water quality, provide wildlife feeding areas, and allow safe wildlife access routes as adjacent cutover areas become too thick for turkeys post-timber harvest. In effect, SMZs are often the primary travel lanes used by wild turkeys, complete with plenty of fast food outlets along the way. Proper SMZs should be wide enough to function as desired. If too narrow, sunlight from the adjacent openings will cause them to become too thick for safe turkey use. The wider the SMZ, the more it will function as it did prior to harvest. The narrowest of SMZs should be at least twice the height of its trees on both sides of a stream in order to function to the benefit of turkeys. In upland habitats, leaving a few mature pines within a hardwood dominant SMZ further enhances its value to turkeys as such pines make good roosting trees. The larger the stream, the larger the SMZ should be.   Within pine dominated landscapes, SMZs should occupy all areas where hardwoods would naturally be found. This includes the width of major bottoms, drains, and slopes near drains. SMZs should not be considered off limits to logging, however cutting within SMZs should be light and infrequent when performed. Within bottomland forests of the MAV and Red River valleys, SMZs are still of great importance near oxbow lakes, bayous, rivers, and streams to maintain open travel areas post-timber harvest. Private landowner and timber company landholdings with good SMZ practices are usually where turkeys propagate best in Louisiana.

Prescribed Burning

Left, a prescribed fire and right the same area 4 weeks later (J. Stafford)

While riding through the St. Helena parish forests with my uncle Jules Lindsey in the early 1970s, he pointed out a small 3-acre wildfire burn spot that had been plowed out by the local forestry commission staff. The 3 to 4-week-old burn spot was located within a several thousand-acre area of unburned forest. Uncle Jules said to me, *"Five gobblers have been killed in that little burned spot this year."* This statement from my uncle, an experienced hunter since the 1920s, reinforced to this young turkey hunter that fire was not only of great importance to wild turkeys, but great for turkey hunters also.

Without a doubt, returning prescribed fire to upland pine areas across Louisiana would have the greatest beneficial impact on wild turkeys. Fire that was once the most common natural landscape habitat influence in the southeast United States is today absent from many areas. Smoke, a natural byproduct of burning that once filled the skies across many states, is now over regulated by agencies that do not understand fire's importance to the natural ecology of pine forests. Nonetheless, the practice of prescribed burning is being revitalized by enlightened agencies such as the NRCS, USFWS, LDAF, and LDWF who promote its wise use for conservation and forest management purposes. Each of these agencies offer landowners financial incentives to use prescribed fire. Prescribed fire is also being used again by a growing number of wildlife conservation-minded timber companies.

Today thousands of acres across Louisiana have become too thick for wild turkey habitation due to the lack of prescribed fire. This thick habitat will remain of little or no value to turkeys unless restored by fire. If all Louisiana acres of burnable upland pinelands were regularly burned in an alternating mosaic (every 1 – 3 years), the state's wild turkey numbers would increase dramatically. Bobwhite quail and other declining grassland species would also increase in number.

As pictured in the photograph above much of the state's upland habitat is too thick for turkeys. Without the restorative application of prescribed fire, such habitats are practically useless to turkeys. (J. Stafford)

Turkeys must make their living during the day in a small zone that extends from the ground upward to about 3 feet. This small zone must provide food, ease of access, and reasonable visibility to avoid predators. Lovett Williams reported that turkeys need to be able to see about 100 feet to avoid predators (Williams 1991). When habitats no longer provide this visual safety zone, fire can be used to restore and maintain vegetative structure to its optimal condition for turkeys. Fire burns away dense layers of pine needles and thatch, kills unwanted hardwood brush, encourages herbaceous plant growth, and recharges soils with nutrients. With regular fire grasses and legumes favored by turkeys thrive and this creates optimal nesting and brood habitat. Multiple studies conducted in Louisiana have indicated that turkeys prefer nesting in habitats regularly burned (Timmer et al. 1998 and Yeldell 2016). Without the introduction of landscape level fire across Louisiana, upland pine habitats will never reach their full wild turkey potential.

There are two primary burning seasons: dormant season and growing season. Dormant season burns are conducted in the winter when hardwoods are dormant, while growing season burns are conducted in the spring and summer after leaves have sprouted. Each has a management purpose within Louisiana's upland turkey range. For years, growing season burns were considered by some to be detrimental in turkey habitats. It was reasonably assumed that such burns were destroying turkey nests and young. However, new research indicates that when properly applied, growing season burns destroy few nests and result in better turkey habitats that can increase future production beyond any short-term losses. Researcher Nathan Yeldell (2016) monitored 69 nests on Kisatchie National Forests from 2014 – 15 where burning regularly occurred and found none destroyed by fire. Other researchers in Georgia observed only 3 nests destroyed by fire out of 78 studied at a frequently burned longleaf pine forest (Little et. al. 2014). In the same study, only one brood out of 34 was lost to fire. Turkeys prefer sites burned more frequently than previously thought. Recent research in pine savannas demonstrated that both hens and gobblers seek sites burned every 2 years or less, over sites burned less frequently (Martin et al 2012). Turkeys avoid nesting in areas that have not been burned for more than 3 - 4 years. Such areas are in dire need of the restorative results achieved best with growing season burns. However, when growing season fire is applied in sites burned annually or every other year, nest losses can be higher. Generally speaking, most fires for turkeys should be dormant to early growing season (January - April) but where habitats have become too rank with hardwood brush, mid to late growing season fires (May – August) are more effective at restoring such areas to productive habitat. Growing season burns result in increased forb-legume diversity which can increase not only seeds but insects. When hens did occasionally select nest sites in upland pine sites not burned in 3 or more years, the failure rate on KNF was found to be 3.4 times greater than nests in stands burned the current year (Yeldell 2016). Nesting season fires used on sites not burned for 3 or more years have been found to destroy very few nests (Yeldell 2016 and Little et. al 2014). Longtime National Wild Turkey Federation turkey biologist James Earl Kennamer, Ph.D. stated, *"The use of prescribed fire during growing season is a win-win for wild turkeys."* The key in determining the best season to burn is to properly assess each site's needs beforehand, rather than simply applying fire any time of year with no regard for the type (dormant or growing season) of fire needed to achieve the desired vegetative result.

Burns have far less post-burn value to turkeys if timber stands are dense with trees. For proper herbaceous response, more open timber stands that allow ample sunlight to reach the ground are needed.   Generally, timber stands with lower BAs, 80 or less, provide far better turkey habitat after burning than stands with greater than 80 BA.

Burn intensity is also important. The temperature and flame heights that develop as a result of burn fuels, humidity, wind, timing, and application method can greatly influence the post-burn vegetative response. Many hardwood species are very susceptible to damage from hot fires causing most managers to avoid burning hardwood dominant timber stands. In the past, one of the best burn methods used to benefit turkeys was nighttime fire. These low intensity burns injured few hardwoods and produced good results in areas regularly burned. Today within pine dominant forests that have not seen fire for some time, hotter fires are sometimes initially preferred. However, forest managers should avoid very hot fires that remove most of the duff layer, thus exposing mineral soil. This can cause erosion, encourage more undesirable plants, and reduce plant species diversity. Hot burns can also severely scorch pine tree needles which then fall, inhibiting ground cover response.

One of the primary reasons wildlife managers and ecologists today recommend restoring longleaf pine ecosystems is that longleafs and associated plant communities thrive with the regular application of fire. It has been said that *"Fire in longleaf pine forests is like rain in a rainforest"*. Longleaf pine forests now occupy only 3% of their original range, making this unique ecosystem rarer than Southeast U. S. wetlands that occupy 65% of their former range and worldwide rain forests that occupy 43% of their former range (America's Longleaf 2009). Unlike other pine species, longleaf pines can be burned the first year after planting then as frequently as annually thereafter. This regular burning provides some of the best turkey habitat possible. Landowners planting even a small proportion of their property in longleaf pine which is then regularly burned, can see a noticeable difference in turkey use. Reestablishing longleaf pine forests managed by fire in effect creates large natural food plots for turkeys. Where longleaf pines historically occurred, restoring such areas (combined with regular fire) is one of the most beneficial turkey management practices that can be implemented.

Once actively managed through prescribed burning, larger forested blocks still remaining in much of the state are practically devoid of fire today. Industrial timber company policies, the increasing cost of burning, and private landowner fears of liability have all but ended the practice of annual prescribed burning. In past decades, active burning ensured abundant brood habitat and increased fall turkey recruitment rates. Turkeys studied on industrial pine forests of Washington parish from 1989 – 1997 at a time when forests were regularly burned saw random juvenile male captures comprising 67% (n=199) of total captures. Random juvenile male captures on the same sites from 2000 – 2007 when fire was no longer being used across the landscape, saw juvenile male capture rates drop to 44% (n=287) of the total captures (Stafford 2007). Several factors influenced reduced jake capture rates including improved adult carryover during the later study due to harvest management changes. However, juveniles became less common during the later study period concurrent with brood/nesting habitat degradation. Although not conclusive, lower jake observations, captures, and harvests in the study area over time indicate reduced productivity, likely the result of the only major land management change that occurred, fire exclusion.

To combat the loss of fire, LDWF, LDAF, USFWS, and NRCS programs were developed for private landowners to encourage the application of prescribed fire and its resulting wildlife habitat benefits. Louisiana private landowners are relearning how to conduct burns on their lands with assistance from forestry consultants and wildlife managers. Federal and state longleaf pine planting programs have helped increased acres planted and managed by fire. From 2010 – 2015 the LDWF prescribed burn initiative has funded the burning of some 15,484 acres of private land. LDWF also provides assistance with equipment needed to conduct these burns (Figure 50). Prescribe burning trailers purchased by NWTF and LDWF can be rented for a nominal fee and are stocked with burn equipment such as drip torches, fire flaps, water tanks, rakes, smoke caution signs, and other needed equipment. For more information on prescribed burning trailers contact ***www.wlf.louisiana.gov*** and click *"wildlife/private landowner assistance."*

Figure 50: LDWF prescribed burning trailer (J. Stafford)

91

Wildlife Openings, Food Plots, and Plantings

Openings are very important to wild turkeys. Openings are used by turkeys for predator avoidance, feeding, nesting, brood rearing, dusting, and breeding behavior. Dennett (1997) reported that 10 – 25% of a turkey's habitat should be in openings. Exactly which rate (10 or 25%) is better remains unclear and may depend on the type of habitat present. This author has observed no discernable difference in turkey numbers inhabiting habitats with 10% or 25% openings, however, well below and above this range does appear to negatively influence numbers. In well managed hardwood forests with 60 - 80 BAs and similarly stocked pine forests which are regularly prescribe burned, openings may be sufficient at a rate below the 10% opening threshold. Forest gaps in the canopy in such well managed forests can achieve desired opening percentages when applied over a large area. Where forests are managed less frequently by timber harvests, permanent openings are of greater importance. In areas where fire is infrequent, openings are critically important. Openings should be well distributed over the landscape and placed where they benefit turkeys the most. Ideally, openings should have native grasses and forbs for summer, fall, and spring foraging as well as winter plantings that provide grains and/or green foods.

Current LDWF Turkey Program Leader Cody Cedotal stated recently, *"Openings should be mitigated at each site. Since an opening can concentrate turkeys and easily become a kill zone for predators, mitigating the surrounding forests near the opening is important."* Mitigation is best done by reducing the density of vegetation adjacent to openings. Mowing, burning, using herbicides, or dozer clearing adjacent brush can make turkey access to openings much less hazardous. Figure 51 illustrates prescribed burning and herbicide spraying immediately adjacent to wildlife openings to reduce a predator's ability to hide.

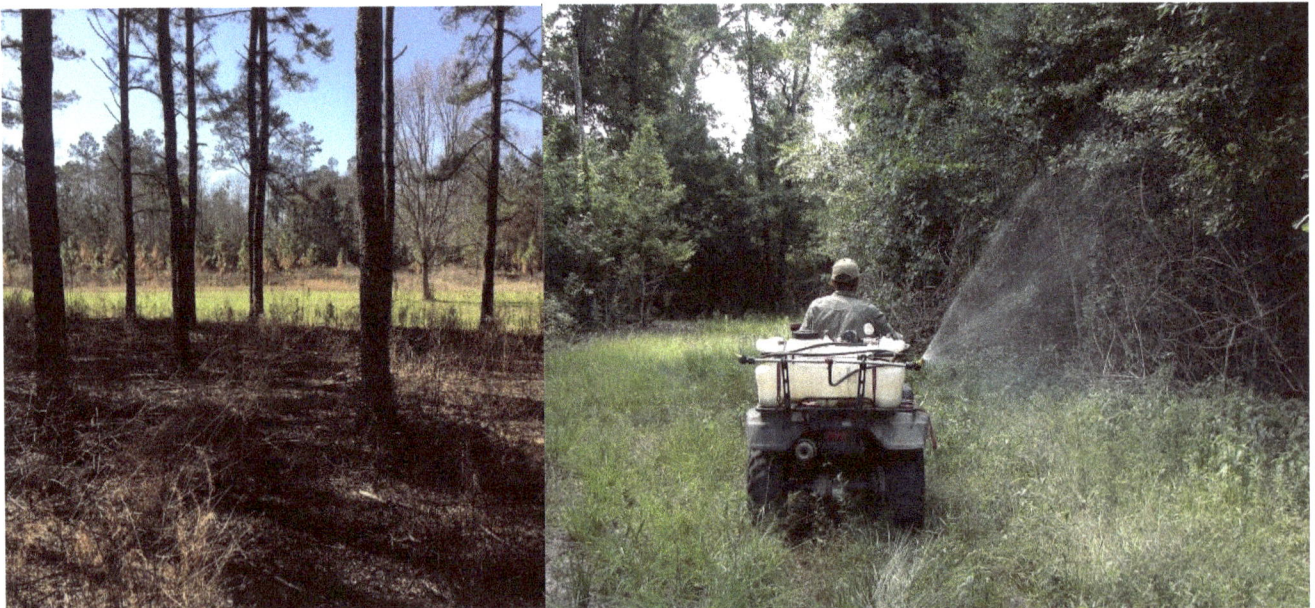

Figure 51: Burning adjacent to a food plot (left) and using herbicide along thick edges (right) reduces potential predation risks. (J. Stafford)

Some of Louisiana's highest turkey populations occur in habitats that contain wide areas maintained adjacent to road rights-of-ways (ROWs). One of the best ways to ensure quality openings in certain areas is to maintain one side of access roads to widths of 30 to 100 feet. Giving the appearance of pipelines adjacent to roads, these wide openings are heavily used by turkeys. Such linear openings that are allowed to grow in native grasses and forbs can be mowed or burned as needed while portions can be planted in clovers and wheat for fall/winter/spring foraging. Openings maintained on the opposite side of a road when the other side abuts the forest edge creates greater shade near the road, improving low risk access for turkeys. Creating wide road ROWs can greatly improve turkey habitats within young managed pine forests and hardwood forests that may have interspersed areas too thick for turkeys. These wide openings provide ease of movement from one forest stand to another and facilitates nearly unlimited options for turkeys to access or escape openings. Wide ROWs also ensure that in actively managed forests turkeys will still be able to feed and move through excessively thick areas somewhat secure from predators.

Food Plots

"Piney woods tend to be deficient of fall and winter turkey foods" (Williams 1991). Many of Louisiana's pine forests also lack adequate fall and winter foods due to hardwood shortages, lack of burning, lack of regular timber management, increasing feral swine occurrence, and other environmental factors. Among some biologists there is debate as to whether food plots help or hurt wild turkey populations. It is very evident that *"if you build it (food plots), they will come"*. No one argues that food plots are often heavily used by turkeys, but are these increased sightings the result of increasing populations over time or existing populations simply drawn to the easy food sources? Comprehensive research is lacking to answer these questions, but based on anecdotal observations this author believes that well distributed food plots can benefit turkeys and may even improve carrying capacities within lower quality habitats. Even within higher quality hardwood habitats, food plots with winter crops would be important in mast failure years (Wilson 2005).

Many erroneously believe that food plots are a panacea for turkey habitat woes. Holistically, addressing all habitat needs including timber management, native cover openings, prescribed burning, as well as cultivated food plots is the best approach.

There are many plantings that turkeys will readily use such as corn, sorghum, milo, wheat, clover, oats, rye, ryegrass, vetch, chufa, soybeans, millet, various fruiting trees, and shrubs. Combining two or more such plantings to provide food, lounging cover, and insect foraging habitat at the same site is optimal.

When planting food plots for turkeys, timing is of critical importance. Planting times listed on the seed bag may not be optimal for Louisiana turkeys. The following paragraphs list preferred plantings and best times for planting in Louisiana. The four most common mistakes made by novices planting food plots are: planting at the wrong time, using improper seeding rates, using too little fertilizer, and paying no attention to soil pH. Farmers know that soil pH is very important with all crops. Wildlife managers should understand that proper lime application is just as important as proper seeding rates and fertilization. Most plantings do well in a soil pH ranging from 6 to 7, unfortunately few areas in Louisiana have this condition naturally.

Timing is also important regarding when to manipulate or prepare sites. In most cases, mowing or disking food plots should be done before nesting in April. Some food plantings from the fall will mature then die in early summer. Managers can sometimes be overly eager to mow or disk such areas in preparation for subsequent plantings. This can sometimes remove valuable brood foraging habitat and destroy nests. Wise wildlife managers will postpone mowing and disking in areas frequented by adult turkeys and poults until mid-July.

Chufa is a nutsedge grass producing ¼ to ¾ inch long tubers underground that turkeys scratch up to consume (Figure 52). Chufa is likely the most preferred fall/winter food planting for turkeys, but is highly sought after by other non-target species such as feral hogs and raccoons. One major problem with planting chufa today is that, if hogs are in the area, they will find and leave little or no chufa for the turkeys. Some managers have found success by using hog proof fencing around chufa plantings. Unlike other plantings, chufa will often work best on sandy soil areas as long as ample moisture is present. In Louisiana, planting chufa in June and July works best. If planted earlier, chufa will grow well but will quickly be overtaken by weeds before the fall. Dense weeds can then cause turkeys to avoid such plots in the fall and winter. Planting in June and July has chufa maturing in September which is too late in the growing season for weeds to become a significant problem. A good broadcast planting rate for chufa is 40 – 50 lbs./acre. If using a row planter, that rate can be substantially reduced depending on row spacing. In areas where turkeys are not familiar with scratching up chufa tubers, light disking of a couple of strips can expose tubers. Once discovered, turkeys will then readily scratch the entire plot. Disking can be used to reestablish chufa each year without the need for replanting. Two diskings, one in early spring and the other in mid-summer, works bests. Due to the great attraction of turkeys to chufa, hunting over a chufa plot is thought by some to be unsporting except in the case of youths, senior citizens, or those limited with a serious disability.

Figure 52: Chufa tubers (J. Stafford)

Wheat is another highly-preferred turkey food during the fall, winter, and spring. During the fall and winter, wheat provides much needed green forage. In the spring as the plant matures turkeys will often fill their crops to capacity with green wheat seed heads (Figure 53). When mature, wheat also provides approximately 2 feet tall vertical cover that seems to give turkeys a sense of security while feeding. Turkeys have also been found to nest in standing wheat fields (Kimmel 1984). Wheat may be planted from late September to January. A broadcast planting rate of 1 - 2 bushels/acre works well. Row or drill planting rates are much lower depending on row spacing. Most wheat is planted in October – November for the added benefit of using such plots for deer hunting.

Figure 53: A West Feliciana turkey crop filled with green wheat seed heads (J. Stafford)

Clover is a highly utilized turkey food. In a recent study done by LDWF of spring turkey food habits, 32% (n=159) of crops examined contained clover (Stafford 2015). Clover was the most common plant found in spring turkey crops and represented the largest food volume. Clovers that persist throughout the year, such as Ladino clover varieties like Osceola, Patriot, and Dutch clover, provide the added benefit of massive quantities of insects sought after by poults. Such clover varieties that are heat tolerant and persist through the summer are more useful as a year-round food source for turkeys than varieties such as crimson clover that die in early summer. Clover should be at the top of any turkey food plot recommendation. Clover is most often planted in October – November to facilitate deer hunting which also allows this sometimes slower growing plant time to become established. Soil pH is especially important when planting clovers. Total clover crop failure is possible with improper pH. A good broadcast planting rate for Osceola clover is 5 – 8 lbs./acre. While crimson clover can be planted at 10 – 15 lbs./acre. Planting clovers at a lower seeding rate when mixed with other cereal grains or within native plant areas can produce a mosaic of high and low growing plants, offering added protection from predators while turkeys forage. Planting clover at reduced seeding rates after light disking within native openings puts clover, native grass seeds, and much sought after forbs at the same location.

An Osceola clover field where this gobbler was harvested (J. Stafford)

Brown-top millet is another highly utilized turkey food in the summer and early fall. Hens with young will travel long distances to forage on brown-top seed heads. Taller growing sorghum or milo can be mixed in small quantities (>10 lbs./ac.) within brown-top millet plantings to provide young turkeys added vertical predator cover. The key to achieving brown-top millet's greatest value is for it to be available as poults grow. Most poults begin to feed on seeds in June then continue feeding heavily on seeds throughout the summer and early fall. Brown-top seed heads mature in 45 to 60 days. Planting in April will produce mature seed heads in June. Planting other nearby areas in May will result in millet available for July. Planting still more millet in June will have seeds ready for August and maybe a September dove hunt as lagniappe. Staggering multiple crops throughout the spring and summer is optimal. A brown-top millet broadcast planting rate of 15 – 20 lbs./acre works well for turkeys. Adequate fertilization is also required for optimal seed growth.

Corn can be a good cool season food providing carbohydrates needed for fall/winter fat production. Standing corn also provides good avian predator protection. Deer and other animals will knock down corn once mature, producing a time released food source throughout the fall and winter. Corn can be an excellent food source during acorn mast failures and rare snow events. In Louisiana, corn is planted after the last frost in early spring (March – April). Corn can be planted as late as May if the soil is fertile and rains come regularly. Row planting is best, but broadcast planting of corn at a rate of about 30 lbs./acre can be done. Using herbicide resistant corn varieties (with herbicide) will improve corn production results. Small corn food plots under 1 acre are quickly consumed in the fall by deer and other species. If this food source is desired to last throughout the winter, larger corn plantings of $\geq$ 2 acres are most often required. Proper fertilization is critical when planting corn.

Shrubs and small trees can enhance an opening. Native or non-native food producing trees and shrubs provide proximal escape cover, shade, lounging cover, and food. Native berry or nut producing species that naturally create clean areas underneath are preferred. Black cherry, gallberry, chinquapin, fast producing oaks, persimmon, sumac, pawpaw, mulberry, wax myrtle, yaupon, cherry laurel, plums, huckleberries, blueberries, crabapple, mayhaw, dogwoods, pecans, and other turkey food plants are preferred. Most such trees are planted during the winter months. Encouraging dewberry and blackberry patches are also a great addition since such plants produce large quantities of berries and are highly sought after by turkeys during the summer. Be aware though that blackberries, dewberries, and other plants may require multiple years to reach fruit producing age. Any maintenance activities must carefully consider whether or not to set back such plants by mowing, fire, or disking. Native Polkberry, wild grapes, and other soft fruited plants should also be encouraged to further enhance food diversity.

Most food plots usually become established in whatever opening is easiest for those planting, with little regard for the consequences of its location for turkeys. Location and frequency of food plots is more important to wild turkeys than many other game species. Food plots, if done incorrectly, can actually harm turkeys by creating an ecological trap where predators have the advantage. For example, a single small food plot placed in the middle of a 3-year-old cutover with a single narrow trail leading from more open woods to the food plot, creates an easy kill zone for predators such as bobcats, foxes, and coyotes that frequent such thick areas. Larger food plots placed close to more open habitats and away from predator haunts, can be much better. Locating food plots where two or more habitat features converge can also be best, as long as the converging habitats are open enough not to work to a predator's advantage. Establishing food plots where differing timber stands converge in actively managed forests helps maintain the site's usefulness should one of the stands be temporarily rendered out of favor to turkeys as a result of timber harvests. The interface of 3 or more habitat types is called a *"covert"*. Locating food plots at coverts further enhances their longevity of use by wildlife. Having food plots more often across the landscape works more to the turkey's advantage than having just a few isolated plots. A food plot management program that is beneficial should consider the adage *"Go big or go home"*. Turkeys do better when they have plenty of options; having too few options can prove fatal. Having a multitude of options such as where to roost, feed, nest, and raise young are critical to increasing survival rates. A well planned food plot program with scattered plots over a wide area, combined with a good forest management program can make a noticeable difference for turkeys. Irregularly shaped food plots that incorporate existing habitat features, such as hardwood fingers and drains, are preferred by turkeys. Plot openings should have areas of planted foods and native grass/forb areas. An optimal opening has as many or more native grass/forb areas as planted food plot areas. Native areas can be maintained by fire, mowing, herbicide, or fallow disking. If large acreage native areas are allowed to grow to mature broom sedge and other modest height grasses/forb combinations and then left undisturbed from March - June, these openings can become valuable nesting areas.

Grazing

In years past, cattle were commonly allowed to graze freely across many parishes. Wildlife managers eventually saw cattle as a competing factor for newly established deer herds during the 1950s and 1960s, prompting efforts to keep free ranging cattle out of the woods. Some turkey biologists are rethinking the issue of managed grazing in today's brush laden forests. Moderate cattle grazing is beneficial to turkey habitat by suppressing brush, pruning vegetation, and creating trails (Williams 1991). In Louisiana where thousands of acres are overgrown and prescribed fire may not be a viable option, cattle grazing is looking more attractive as another tool for turkey managers. Some believe that managed cattle grazing would reduce dense woody brush and encourage grasses used by turkeys. The fact is the wild turkey is much more similar to a grassland bird like the bobwhite quail than to a brush-land bird such as the American woodcock. Like the quail the wild turkey thrives in grasslands that are of a proper structure, allowing ease of access and good visibility. Although grazing is seldom used as a wildlife management tool today, some areas could benefit from its use. Currently described as a useful management tool, cattle and other free ranging livestock can still become detrimental to turkeys if allowed to significantly over utilize the habitat of a given area. Land managers and ranchers using cattle to improve wildlife habitat must be vigilant in monitoring for such overgrazing.

Invasive Species

Invasive species and exotic species as defined for this writing are plants and animals introduced by man's activity that work to the detriment of native habitats and wild turkeys. Feral hogs are at the top of the mammalian list of problematic invasive species. Because of direct depredation, habitat degradation, and resource competition, wild pigs most likely negatively affect turkey populations (Jones et al. 2015). Although wild turkeys and feral hogs will coexist, hogs are a major competitor for food resources and can degrade habitats quicker than any other animal species. Hogs have also been documented to destroy turkey nests in Louisiana (Yeldell 2016). Unfortunately, many see feral hogs as just another game species to hunt; I too once saw reason in this belief. During the 1980s my opinion changed drastically while hunting on the Pearl River WMA as its hog population increased. One late October I bow hunted a favorite flat covered with hundreds of cow oak trees and littered with huge acorns, enough to feed turkeys and deer all winter long. Hogs were using the site and I managed to easily take 2 with the bow. When I returned to the same site in late November to deer hunt, virtually all of the thousands of pounds of acorns present earlier had been consumed by hogs. Never before had I seen a food resource meant to sustain wildlife all season depleted so quickly nor would I ever again underestimate the negative impact of feral hogs.

There are many plant species that occur in the Louisiana wilds that are non-native. Of these, *Chinese privet*, *Chinese tallow tree*, and *cogongrass* may be the most damaging to foraging, brood-rearing, and nesting habitat of turkeys (Jones et al. 2015). Chinese privet, sometimes used as a food source by wild turkeys, is a very prolific invasive plant. It grows in a wide variety of soil characteristics that allow it to outcompete native oaks and other more important food plants that turkeys need. Chinese tallow, sometimes call *"popcorn tree"* or *"chicken tree"*, can completely overtake areas previously covered in a plethora of hardwood species, pines, and other native foods. Once established, Chinese tallows like Chinese privet are nearly impossible to completely eradicate. Cogongrass has no known value to turkeys and is similar in its negative effects in that it replaces other beneficial plants, spreads rapidly, and is nearly impossible to control once established over a large area. Chinese tallow and privet are found over the entire state while cogongrass is currently found only in southeast Louisiana, but may soon spread to other parts of the state. The key to stopping these invaders before they become well-established is to learn how to identify each, watch for their appearance, and aggressively treat with appropriate herbicides (Figure 54). Herbicide information can be obtained from your local LDWF private lands biologist, NRCS, USFWS, LDAF, or the LSU extension service.

Figure 54: The top left is invasive cogongrass in fall and right flowering cogongrass in the spring. (J. Stafford)

Left is invasive Chinese tallow and right Chinese privet (J. Stafford)

Protection

Protection is another important consideration in wild turkey management. Protection from excessive predation, harassment, and poaching is important. Poaching, and in some cases excessive legal harvests, can greatly impact localized turkey populations. Regarding the illegal take of wild turkeys, it was best stated by E. B. Cope, *"A citizenry educated to the necessity of practicing conservation would not look with indifference upon violations ..."* (Cope 1932). In virtually every writing about wild turkeys during Louisiana's lowest population period (1930 – 1955), excessive poaching was noted as the primary culprit of turkey scarcities. An effective law enforcement effort was needed then and is still important today. Illegal turkey hunting should not be tolerated nor glorified in any way by those who care about the future of turkey hunting. Working closely with LDWF enforcement agents both before and during the season will let others know that one is serious about stopping poaching. Illegal baiting continues to be a serious issue facing wild turkeys. Legal *"feeding"* is also a problem. Several years ago politics again raised its ugly head when feeding was allowed in Louisiana as long as hunters stayed 200 yards away from such feeding sites. This rule change has greatly complicated law enforcement of baiting violations and allowed many turkeys lured to feeders to be *"legally"* killed. In this author's opinion, no *"feeding-baiting"* should be allowed from March 1st through April 30 where turkeys are hunted with the exception that hog baits and other feeds typically not consumed by turkeys may be used. Additional regulation change placing the onus on deer hunters to remove all bait from feeders prior to March would aid in reducing the liability of those turkey hunters that might unknowingly stumble upon another person's deer feeder with grain inside.

Other illegal activities include harvesting over the limit and taking turkeys outside of the spring season. Contrary to reason, some people consider the illegal take of turkeys more attractive as they become rarer in an area. Such illegal kills in low population areas have an even greater detrimental effect.

Many who worked with the LDWF during the 1970s are convinced that unrestricted legal hunting on open lands where turkeys were first stocked greatly reduced the success of these early restoration efforts. Charles Jordan, who hunted during a much earlier time of few turkeys said, *"every old gobbler...is a marked bird. It is given no rest until it is killed"* (McIlhenny 1914). His statement still holds true in many Louisiana locations today. *"The take of turkeys out of season has remained more culturally acceptable in Louisiana than more northern states,"* reported long time LDWF biologist and LSU wildlife management professor John Haygood. He further stated to this author, *"You just don't see turkeys in people's yards as much here as in other states to the north. If people would just give them a break during the off season, we could have turkeys all over."*

Turkeys must be afforded protection by giving them areas and periods of the year without human disturbance. In recent years, some public land wildlife officials have fallen victim of special interest groups that seek access to critical turkey habitats during periods of the year that were once restricted from public access. Other interest groups have successfully lobbied for more vehicle, horse, boat, ATV, dog, and UTV access into interior forest areas where once such activities were prohibited. No one wants to say *"No"* to these fellow outdoor groups simply desirous of more use opportunities, but for turkeys to prosper, wildlife agency leaders need to ensure that such activities are done at times when the least potential harm occurs to wild turkeys. Encouraging *"walk in only"* areas has proven to reduce illegal *"drive by"* harvests and given turkeys much needed privacy during off-season periods. Turkey hunters generally support establishing such areas where less pressured turkeys can be found. Private lands are not immune to the issue of excessive access either. Private wildlife managers should determine what access routes are essential and during what times of the year they can be used. Consideration should be given to nesting, brood rearing, roosting, and breeding to determine what areas need restricted access the most.

Industrial Forest Lands

This book would be lacking if it did not specifically address industrial forest (*"timber company"*) lands. Industrial forestlands that represent about 28% of all private lands in the state have been much maligned by turkey hunters for practices performed (or not) within their landholdings. Nonetheless, such companies represent some of the state's most reliable turkey habitats. These large contiguous blocks of forested habitat have been much slower than individually owned private lands to fragment or urbanize beyond turkey use. For this reason, timber company lands act as important habitat reservoirs for turkeys. Some of these lands have been sources for restocking, some have provided public hunting opportunities through free or low cost leases for WMAs, while most others provide private hunting lease opportunities. For turkey hunters to automatically disparage these companies for prioritizing maximum timber production is somewhat short sided. Are there sometimes practices performed that work to the detriment of turkeys on timber company lands? Yes. Practices most detrimental include conversion of natural hardwood areas to pine, short pine timber rotations (< 28 years), prescribed burning bans, excessively large clearcuts, and harsh herbicide treatments. Are there companies that work to mitigate timber management practices to make them more beneficial to wildlife, including wild turkeys? Yes. These beneficial practices include managing natural hardwood sites for hardwoods, establishing substantial streamside forested buffers (SMZs), prescribed burning, longer pine timber rotations (> 30 years), smaller clearcuts, and the use of more selective herbicide applications that maintain a greater variety of preferred herbaceous turkey foods. It simply makes good business sense for timber companies to conduct timber management practices that are good for wildlife. Doing such increases the land's value and acts as a positive advertisement for the company that does so. Managing for both timber and turkeys, depending on markets, can actually be more economically rewarding than timber management alone (Dutrow and Devine 1981). It makes for happy hunters and encourages other private landowners interested in conducting timber work to seek out those companies with good wildlife practices. Companies that operate with little or no regard for wildlife quickly get a reputation for such, regardless of how they might try to whitewash their activities with slick advertising. This writing will not attempt to call any specific company out for misdeeds, but has simply pointed out the practices that help turkeys most. It is up to the reader to decide where his or her local timber company stands. I will, however, take this opportunity to thank wildlife conservation minded companies that actively manage for wildlife and those that allow public hunting through free or low cost leases to the LDWF. Turkey hunters of Louisiana owe these companies a great debt of gratitude. The names of some such companies can be found each year in the WMA section of the *Louisiana Hunting Regulations* brochure.

Turkey friendly timber companies provide turkey hunting opportunities, use clearcut harvest methods in small blocks (<100 acres), and do not regularly place clearcuts adjacent to other stands too thick for turkeys. These companies thin timber stands often, burn significant acreages in pine habitats, have good streamside management zone (SMZ) policies, and encourage retention of hardwood mast producing trees. Companies that manage pine plantations with longer timber rotations provide better habitats for turkeys. Setting aside areas for permanent openings where needed and allowing/encouraging log sets to be maintained as food plots/native openings are additional turkey friendly practices. MAV companies that have hardwood dominated forests should take special care to protect historic roosting sites if such areas are a limiting factor for turkeys and maintain well managed road/trail rights of ways to provide useful openings. Private land managers as well as state and federal wildlife biologists would be well advised to work closely with industrial timber companies then give such companies well deserved praise when they operate to the benefit of wild turkeys. It is this public praise that can have the greatest value to the company and perpetuate good wildlife management practices.

Ecoregion Specific Habitat Needs

The ***east gulf coastal plain*** *(EGCP)* ecoregion of southeast Louisiana has seen turkey numbers decline in recent years. The primary reasons are habitat loss through the fragmenting of former turkey range and lack of turkey friendly habitat management practices. Fragmentation is a problem that is not readily overcome. Over time, large single ownership forest blocks tend to become smaller as they are passed down to heirs or sold in parcels. When once contiguous large blocks of similarly managed forests become too heavily fragmented by open areas and residential or commercial development, turkeys are no longer able to sustain their populations. Where larger forested parcels remain in the EGCP, turkey friendly management practices are badly needed to improve such lands. Prescribed burning within southeast Louisiana pinelands is the greatest current need and if increased significantly, would greatly improve turkey numbers. In a study of intensively managed loblolly pine plantations in Alabama, it was determined that poult mortalities exceeded 87% in the very dense groundcover of pine plantations. Burning within pine plantations as early as possible can decrease poult mortalities by increasing the ability to detect predators and improve foraging habitat (Exum et al. 1987). Increased use of SMZs, prescribed burning, and permanent openings would greatly improve turkey habitat on the EGCP's intensively managed private and industrial pine lands. Hardwoods have also greatly diminished within this ecoregion. Hurricane Katrina did considerable damage in 2005 to hardwoods on the eastern side of the EGCP where turkeys were once abundant. Turkey numbers in this area have been slow to recover. Hardwood timber prices have also increased considerably in recent years, prompting many landowners that once may have retained standing hardwoods to now heavily cut such areas. When possible, harvesting hardwoods by single tree selection logging is often the preferred method to manage for wild turkeys. Leaving a mixture of oak species, American beech, American elm, and other food tree species at residual basal areas of not less than 70 square feet per acre will benefit turkeys. Where low wildlife value hardwood forest stands exist, such areas should be considered for clear cutting and reestablished in more turkey friendly hardwood species. Quality hardwood management on private lands has been the rule within much of the northwest EGCP for decades. In such well managed areas, turkeys have maintained good numbers.

The ***upper east gulf coastal plain*** (UEGCP), comprising West Feliciana and the Thompson Creek uplands of East Feliciana, remains a remnant jewel of great turkey habitat for the state. However, this ecoregion's rugged terrain is not immune to threats of fragmentation. Fortunately, the fertile soils of this area allow the quick recovery of man's detrimental actions. Where man has converted hardwood areas to pine or excessive openings, nature fights back with fast growing hardwoods. A need within this area is for more lands to be restored to high quality historic upland hardwoods. Other areas that have been overtaken with low quality hardwoods and exotic species should be restored. In most cases, openings are ample in the UEGCP and the greater need is to increase contiguous forested acreage. Where pines exist in this ecoregion, active timber management and more prescribed burning is the immediate need.

The higher quality of the habitat in the UEGCP produces an abundance of foods supporting a large number of small mammals including squirrels, mice, and chipmunks sometimes resulting in higher predator populations. It is important that openings and food plots in this ecoregion be managed with this in mind. Special attention should be given to vegetation height and opening access routes for turkeys to reduce predator ambush success. Managers of this area, like many others in the state, should intensify their efforts to remove feral hogs. Like the rest of southeast Louisiana, the UEGCP lacks adequate public lands for wild turkey habitat and hunting. Greater emphasis to acquire such public lands is needed.

The **Mississippi River alluvial plain** *(MAV)* has long suffered a lack of habitat due to clearing for agriculture. Yet turkeys have remained in a few isolated pockets of residual high quality habitat. In the management of these habitat pockets, many of which are publicly owned, turkey management efforts should be intensified. Turkey management is somewhat different than deer management in that timber harvests must be relatively light when done to prevent areas from becoming too thick. Where timber management is active and well distributed openings are generally ample, however, there exist areas within some MAV public lands where more maintained openings are needed. State and Federal agencies are sometimes resistant to new permanent openings for a variety of reasons. Where needed, this resistance to openings should be moderated for the benefit of wild turkeys. Additional effort should be made to see that openings are better juxtaposed, either by timber management or addition of more permanent openings, throughout larger MAV forest blocks. If established, permanent openings must be properly maintained to have long-term value to turkeys.

Closed canopy bottomland hardwood forests of the MAV can sometimes become too open at ground level. Although *"parklike"* habitats are very important to turkeys, too much of this habitat can be a bad thing. Parklike habitats are often characterized by mature forests with little or no mid-story or groundcover vegetation. In such open areas turkeys can see for long distances. Definitive research is lacking in determining just how open is too open for optimal turkey habitat, but anecdotal observations point to turkeys spending little time in very large expanses of open habitat. Dozens of factors may influence whether or not a habitat is too open. Terrain relief, waterways present, height of trees, age of forest, hunting pressure, distance from residential areas, habitat fragmentation, and many more influences can determine turkey use of open forests. Some more remote open forests that experience little human encroachment can see considerable wild turkey use while other open forests where man's activity is more prevalent may be uninhabited by turkeys. In such sites a wildlife timber harvest directed to favor turkeys can be the best corrective action. This can be done by various timber harvest strategies such as light thinning of large areas, variable retention harvests, and/or parcel thinnings.

Other areas of the MAV have the opposite problem and are choked with palmetto, preventing turkeys from using these areas (Figure 55). Palmetto densities are often determined by elevation of the land and are a natural vegetative response that may render large areas unusable to turkeys. Lovett Williams (1991) reported, *"Saw palmetto growing inside of hammocks sometimes is so dense that it causes wild turkeys to stay out. Mowing with an extra-heavy rotary mower will usually kill palmetto in heavily shaded hammocks."* Recently thinned timber areas in Louisiana where dense palmettos occur will often have nearby turkeys relocate to these areas due to reductions in palmetto caused by logging. Where logging is not possible or too infrequent, Williams suggested mowing 40 to 50 feet wide travel corridors in areas where palmetto are excessive. Mowing may be one's only option, but is an expensive management practice and can treat only a few acres each year. Where feasible, intentional flooding of palmetto areas can sometimes reduce palmetto loads enough that when drained nearby turkeys inhabit the area. Active timber management is by far the best method to treat large areas of palmetto but this too can sometimes result in increased palmetto densities if too many trees are removed. Where timber management is not an option, mowing palmetto along the edges of openings, roads, and trails can improve turkey usage of certain areas. Figure 55 shows a palmetto choked habitat on Buckhorn WMA.

Figure 55: Dense palmetto habitat limiting wild turkey access (J. Stafford)

Turkey friendly timber management practices should be implemented on WRP and CRP lands as they come of merchantable age within the MAV. CRP and WRP lands should be improved for turkeys through light thinnings and permanent openings where needed. It is not expected that urbanization will be an immediate problem on such lands and turkeys should increase in the MAV for decades to come as long as CRP/WRP lands stay forested and perimeter turkey populations remain available for expansion. Although CRP/WRP acreages have increased in recent years, acres currently forested are still only a fraction of what they were several decades ago. The MAV's greatest turkey need continues to be more acres returned to forestland.

The **west gulf coastal plain** *(WGCP),* located in central and western Louisiana remains in a more stable habitat condition for turkeys than other ecoregions of the state due to the large publicly owned land base. Prescribed fire is a common practice on public lands and is used more on private lands within the WGCP than other areas of the state. However, fire use on private and industrial timber lands is still insufficient. Increasing the acres burned each year on private and industrial lands would greatly improve turkey habitat and turkey numbers. Public land managers have generally done a superb job of maintaining historic hardwood areas within the WGCP. Improving SMZs on private industrial timber lands, especially in the pine *"flatlands"* of Beauregard, Calcasieu, Allen, and Evangeline parishes, would improve hardwood availability and increase turkey carrying capacities. In pine dominant areas of the WCGP where hardwoods are scarce, a well distributed food plot program can enhance such areas for turkeys.

For years there has been concern among some that excessively large burn patch sizes on public lands within the WGCP may negatively affect turkeys. A recent study on Kisatchie National Forest found the average burn patch size during the two years examined was 1,198 acres (Yeldell 2016). These burns ranged from 18 acres to 3,873 acres in size. The study determined that such larger burns may not present optimal juxtaposition of resources since turkeys tend to primarily use large burned area perimeters while avoiding interior spaces. However, as the number of days increased from the date burned, turkeys increased use of large burned area interiors. The study suggested that smaller burn patches adjacent to stands that had not been burned for 1 to 2 years prior were optimal for turkey use. Regardless, these same KNF forests continue to hold some of the largest turkey numbers in the state. Although smaller burn patches are optimal, if efforts to achieve smaller burns result in fewer total acres being restored by fire each year on KNF, this too would not be optimal for turkeys. Currently, studies are being conducted by LSU on Peason Ridge WMA to examine turkey use of smaller scale habitat manipulation areas compare to larger manipulated areas in the KNF.

Within the WGCP's short rotation industrial pine forests, increasing the use of prescribed burning and improving SMZs would have the greatest impact on creating usable space for turkeys.

Much of the ***upper west gulf coastal plain*** *(UWGCP)* in northwest Louisiana is in private ownership, but like the EGCP in southeast Louisiana it has only a small amount of area that is publicly owned or managed. Turkey numbers are relatively good in Claiborne, Union, Bossier, Jackson, Bienville, Winn, Natchitoches, and Sabine parishes. Parishes such as DeSoto and Caddo have failed to respond to earlier restocking efforts compared to other parishes within the UWGCP. Regardless, much of this ecoregion is in a habitat state that is very similar to the EGCP during the 1990s when its turkey numbers were good. The UWGCP is likewise subject to some of the same influences that gradually diminished turkeys in southeast Louisiana, such as lack of burning and habitat fragmentation. Fortunately for turkeys, the UWGCP will not likely soon experience the same accelerated urbanization as experienced in southeast Louisiana. The UWGCP area is generally blessed with a greater abundance of mature hardwoods intermixed within pine areas. Hardwoods, although a tremendous asset within the UWGCP, can sometimes experience years when hard mast availability is low. Extended droughts and late season frosts can diminish these valuable food sources. In such years, a well distributed food plot program can ease life for turkeys. As with other upland ecoregions, increasing private land prescribed burning would expand areas of good turkey habitat.

The recent increase in oil and gas activity within the UWGCP has affected turkey habitat by further fragmenting larger forested blocks. Finding new ways to manage the multitude of associated openings, roads, and pipelines as turkey friendly habitat would be a wise conservation move for the petroleum industry as well as private landowners. Rather than completely covering large oil/gas openings with gravel and planting low wildlife value grasses like Bermudagrass and Bahia grass, using a native grass-forb mix would provide usable nesting cover and food. Adding patches of properly maintained clover or brown-top millet would further increase their use by turkeys. Encircling oil/gas production sites with green winter planting sought after by wild turkeys would also aid in wildfire hazard reduction.

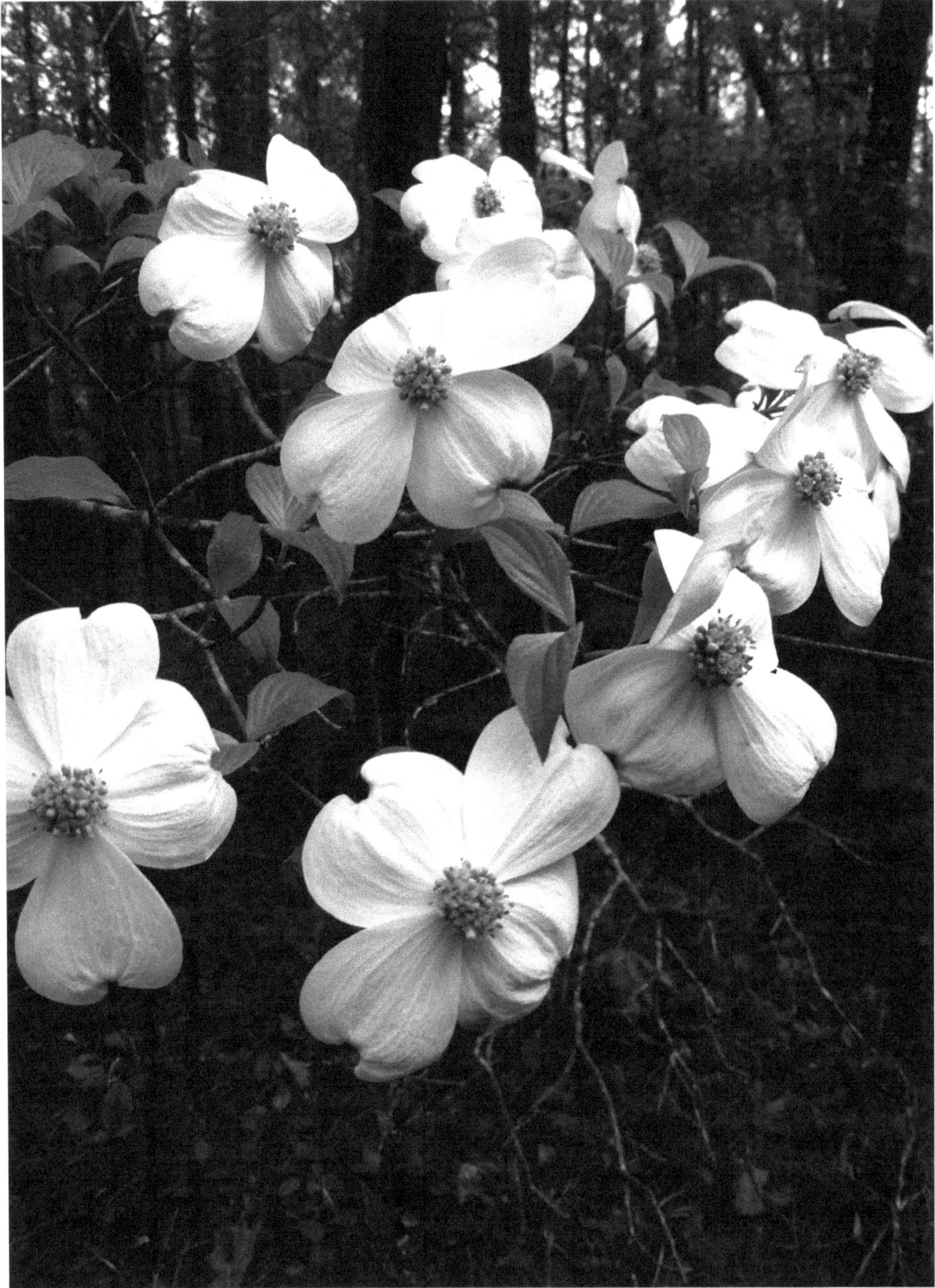

Sabine parish dogwoods produce berries that are an important fall food source for turkeys. (J. Stafford)

Wild Turkey Hunting in Louisiana

Length, Timing, Bag/Season Limits, and Politics of Turkey Hunting Seasons

"The hunter is a very important, probably the most important, single limiting factor on the wild turkey population."
(Henry Mosby 1943)

Length & Timing of Seasons

Wild turkey numbers are a product of their habitat and survival rate. Habitat, predation, and hunting most affect turkey survival. Of those, hunting is often the easiest for managers to manipulate. The first wild turkey hunting season in Louisiana was established in 1902. Prior to that time, the harvest of turkeys was unregulated. This first wild turkey season started November 1st and ended March 31st (Hollis 1950). Both hens and gobblers could be harvested throughout the season with no bag limits. By 1905 the first bag limit, set at a mere 25 gobblers per day, was imposed as well as a reduced December thru March season. In 1911 the season dates were shifted to November 15 thru April 15. The bag limit that year was reduced to one gobbler per day. By 1925 much of Louisiana's upland virgin forests had been cleared resulting in significant habitat losses. That year the turkey season was reduced to 2 months (December – January) and the first season limit of 12 turkeys was established. As turkeys became increasingly scarce winter hunting was abandoned in 1926 - 27 and the first spring only season was set during the month of March. The season bag limit was further reduced to 5. By 1933 turkey numbers had dropped so dramatically due to habitat loss and overexploitation that all turkey hunting was suspended until 1945 when a limited 15-day season opened April 1st and was held for four consecutive years thereafter. This season was put in place by politicians despite vigorous objections from wildlife biologists. Turkey numbers continued to flounder and in 1949 the turkey hunting season closed again for a period of six years. From 1955 thru 1958 a very limited season reopened. During this time the season opened as early as March 29th and as late as April 5th, but only in selected areas for 7 days or less. The season limit was one gobbler. In 1959 thru 1967 (about the time that this author began to hunt turkeys) the turkey season opened between April 1 – 8 and closed between April 8 – 23, lasting some 7 to 23 days. A list of turkey season dates (1902 – 2017), limits, and other information is found in Appendix B.

During the 1940s and 1950s many states, including Louisiana, attempted restocking with pen-raised wild turkeys. These efforts failed to establish viable populations. But with improving habitat conditions and advancements in native wild turkey trapping techniques, numbers began to grow. As turkey numbers increased, the Louisiana season limit was raised to 2 gobblers in 1968. That year the season opened March 30th, never to return again to a statewide April opening day. From 1969 thru 1975, season openings varied from March 15 to March 29 and season lengths ranged from 23 to 44 days long. In 1976 the occupied range where turkeys were hunted was parceled into turkey hunting *Areas* denoted by letters of the alphabet. These areas often had differing start dates and season lengths depending on turkey densities or the number of years since they were restocked. Certain south Louisiana areas started as early as March 11th while others in north Louisiana started as late as April 23rd. In 2002 it was decided to continue varied season lengths for different turkey hunting areas, but to move all area opening days to the same date to reduce hunter migration from one area to the next as each area opened. Today wild turkey season opens on the 4th Saturday in March for all designated turkey areas. Based on turkey hunter surveys conducted by the LDWF, the decisions to open all areas on the same date and on the 4th Saturday in March were supported by the majority of turkey hunters statewide. However, are such decisions designed to satisfy most of the hunters always best for sustaining wild turkey numbers and hunting success over time?

Ask any 10 turkey hunters when they believe turkey season should open and you will likely get 10 different answers. Yet ask turkey biologists at the state, federal, or university level who study wild turkeys as a profession and you will find answers not so diverse. Almost without exception these experts have little issue with the popular uniform opening date, but disagree with many hunters that support *"early"* opening seasons. Most biologists in Louisiana and across the nation are united in a desire to see later season start dates. In fact at a recent gathering of wild turkey experts (state wild turkey program leaders) from across the southeast United States a single resolution was drafted encouraging all state agencies to resist public and political desires for earlier turkey season start dates. The resolution strongly supported the establishment of season openings that occur after peak nesting periods. This resolution was penned despite the fact that many of the states represented had *"early"* seasons. The primary reasons cited for this unified stance were long-term reproductive and survival benefits to wild turkeys with later season start dates.

As an avid wild turkey hunter since the 1960s, I have a personal preference of when "I" like to spring turkey hunt. That preference is based on hundreds of encounters with wild turkeys, but so does every other turkey hunter based on similar personal experiences. In 2011 the LDWF surveyed turkey hunters in an attempt to learn more about these preferences and found a greater preference for later season start dates from north Louisiana turkey hunters than south Louisiana hunters, who preferred earlier openings. But should hunter preference be the primary driver in the setting of turkey season dates or should science based recommendations best for sustaining long-term turkey numbers and high quality hunting be paramount?

With each species that sportsmen *"take"* (remove from the environment), regulations are imposed to protect, conserve, and proliferate the species which is taken. Unlike some species, numerous studies have indicated that wild turkeys have a relatively brief period of time when most of the breeding and nesting occurs. This brief period is of critical importance to wild turkeys. Based on telemetry studies and decades of production surveys, Louisiana findings have shown that peak nest initiation, incubation, and hatching date averages are similar from one end of the state to the other. So if we know when most turkeys are nesting, and harvest records tell us that most turkeys are harvested during the first week of the hunting season, is it wise to hunt them before this peak nesting-breeding period occurs?

Each state is responsible for setting its turkey seasons and bag limits. Biologists are tasked with establishing season and bag limits that are biologically responsible and sustain wildlife populations over time. Of primary concern to biologists during this decision making process is that turkey population maintenance and growth never become hindered by over taxing of the resource. Biologists understand that seasons can never be set solely for those areas in the state with the highest turkey densities, but must consider both low and high density populations. With that said, the act of hunting gives the wild turkey its greatest public value. Without its hunting, a wild turkey would have no greater societal value than a house wren or a mockingbird. Regulatory decisions must be rooted in turkey biology, but also consider the importance of the hunting tradition. So, what happens when *"politics"* enters the decision making arena? During the early years of the LDWF, strong political influences from local parish governing authorities sometimes hindered wildlife management efforts (Herring 1959). During that time some biologists, who were simply doing their jobs, were threatened with arrest by local sheriffs that did not agree with their activities (pers. comm. J. Herring). These early conservation pioneers somehow managed to move wildlife restoration forward while navigating a minefield of political influences. Even today, decisions regarding the Louisiana wild turkey season are not free from occasional political influence. For the record, *"politics"* is not always a bad thing, for it is often the most expeditious way that opinions of the majority and minority can be considered in the regulatory process. Today, checks and balances have been established within the regulatory process ensuring that science alone does not automatically trump the will of the people. Each year hunting regulation proposals are presented by biological staff in advance of hunting season to the Louisiana Wildlife and Fisheries Commission (a board of private citizens appointed by various Governors to oversee the decisions of the Department of Wildlife and Fisheries). The science-based proposals presented to the Commission are then followed by a public comment period. But what happens when the will of the people runs contrary to sound biological recommendations? Can certain overriding public preference motivated regulations, which have been maintained over time, work to the detriment of a valuable resource like wild turkeys?

Often when public opinion runs contrary to biologically based regulation proposals, scientists have failed to adequately make their case. Fortunately, today's turkey hunter has much more access to science-based information than those 30 or 40 years ago and today's hunter rightfully demands facts before supporting change. If turkey hunters are aligned against turkey biologists (many of which themselves are avid turkey hunters), a failure has occurred in getting the necessary information (facts) out to their greatest partner in conservation.

The *"later season"* argument may be the most controversial subject that can be broached between turkey hunters themselves, or between biologists and turkey hunters. Short of kicking a turkey hunter's dog or denigrating his religion, this subject runs a close second in its likelihood of starting a fight. It divides lifelong friends and even family members, but for a moment I ask that each turkey hunter try to consider the subject devoid of personal bias. I must confess that 30 years ago as a young biologist I argued in support of early (mid-March) opening days. My case was built on many of the same arguments heard today: cooler weather, fewer mosquitos and snakes, gobblers in groups (easier to pick the one with the bigger beard), fewer leaves on the trees means you can hear them gobble farther, you are in the woods when birds first start gobbling good, and most importantly, you *"get at um"* before they are *"all henned-up"*. Yet, none of my somewhat selfish reasons considered what was best for turkeys and maintaining high quality hunting for years to come. Like most who support these same arguments, I was focused on the short term. The fact was, I was simply short on patience and just wanted to get out there in the woods as soon as the first green leaves appeared to get my turkey. However, with the graying of my hair and the study of thousands of turkeys over several decades has come the realization that my youthful preferences were not what was best for sustaining wild turkeys or quality wild turkey hunting into the future. And most turkey experts across the nation agree.

A common misconception of some hunters is that turkeys will *"gobble out"* if you don't start hunting them in March. This perception likely rooted in the fact that significant gobbling can occur during two seasonal peaks; one peak occurring in mid- to late-March and the other in mid- to late-April. The lull between peaks can vary in length and intensity or be virtually unnoticeable during certain years. These gobbling oscillations could easily lead an early season proponent to think that it is all over by the end of March. Another contributing factor to reduced gobbling following the opening week of the turkey season, is hunter caused disturbance and the fact that many gobblers will quickly be harvested. Science has proven beyond a shadow of doubt that dead turkeys don't gobble! If a hunter hears 5 gobblers the week prior to turkey season, then two weeks later hears only two, the other 3 may very well be dead. From 1999 through 2008 the LDWF conducted gobbling surveys across the state. These surveys started 3 weeks prior to the start of the season and ended the day before opening day of turkey season. The survey documented increasing gobbling until the start of hunting over several years with differing opening dates, proving that turkeys did not gobble out prior to the season. In 2005, the LDWF conducted a post-season gobbling survey using similar protocols on Union WMA, Ben's Creek WMA, and Mosher Hill hunting club in Washington parish. These surveys, conducted from May 2 to June 3, documented fewer individual gobblers gobbling post-season as expected due to season harvests, but also documented an increased number of gobbles per bird post-season which was not expected by some. Union WMA saw only a modest post-season increase in gobbling of 5%, while Ben's Creek WMA had an 83% post-season increase, and Mosher Hill hunting club a 75% increase in post-season gobbling. Gobbling did finally diminish greatly by the first week of June but this result demonstrated that gobbling intensity does not necessarily decrease with the close of hunting season in April. More recent gobbling studies, yet to be published from South Carolina, also found pronounced gobbling post-hunting season (pers. comm. B. Collier). This might explain why more *"avid"* turkey hunters, those hunting 10 or more days during the season or having harvested two turkeys, surveyed in the LDWF *2011 Turkey Hunter Survey* were more likely to support a later opening date than less avid hunters taking fewer turkeys and hunting less often.

So what about those *"henned-up"* gobblers? Any experienced turkey hunter has had to deal with this unfortunate but common circumstance. Henned-up gobblers are usually not receptive to calling due to the presence of hens. I have personally found this to be a greater problem during mid-March when winter flocks are breaking into smaller groups prior to peak nesting. Since most early season turkeys have not been *"monkeyed with"*, many hunters are able to harvest turkeys quite readily during this period. The simple fact of being in the woods during this time of flock dispersal will often result in success. Regardless, gobblers are generally most vocal and most receptive to the call when those hen groups dwindle or when hens leave gobblers completely to nest. This scarcity of hens grows rapidly in April and can cause a reluctant Tom, considered call proof in March, to charge in without reservation to a hunter's call in April. Hardly a better illustration is available to demonstrate how season opening dates affect harvest than the WMA youth lottery turkey hunting results from 2007 – 2014 (Figure 56). The numbers on the left indicate both the harvest and date of opening in March. The later the opening day of youth season indicated by the red line, the higher the youth harvest indicated by the blue line on various WMAs across the state. It is believed that this increasing harvest rate would continue if regular seasons were shifted even later.

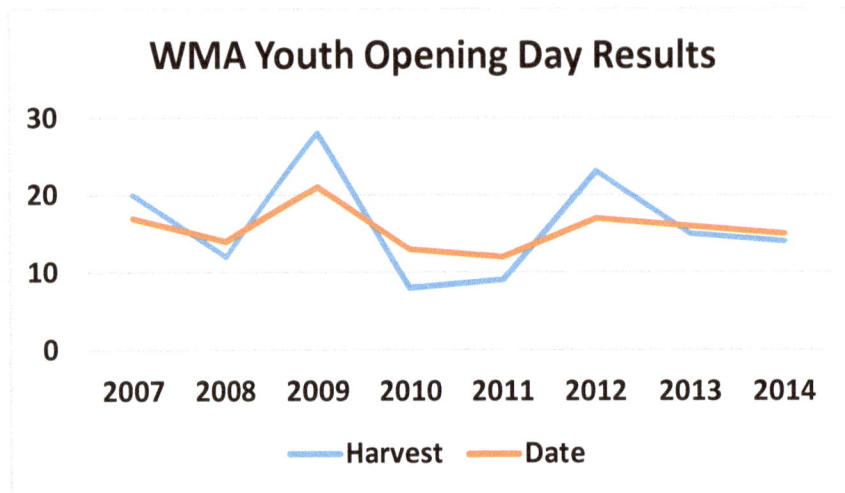

WMA Youth Opening Day Results

Figure 56

As with any species, there is a genetic consideration to healthy wild turkeys that originates at breeding. Dominant gobblers tend to be the better specimens within groups and should be allowed to do most of the breeding to ensure that the best physical traits are passed on to the next generation. Very little research has been done to determine the exact timeframe when a wild turkey hen is bred by a gobbler in relation to when she lays her first egg. Based on the best information available, that period of breeding likely occurs 25 – 30 hours before the first egg is laid since it must occur before egg shell calcification when the first egg is still in the oviduct or the egg will be infertile. Once bred, it is believed that hens can store sperm for many weeks (56 days) allowing for subsequent nesting efforts without additional breeding if the first nest is lost (Marsden and Martin 1955). Hens that have had nests predated over an extended period of time since initial breeding likely revisit gobblers for subsequent breeding during the late spring and summer, further demonstrating the need for an ample percentage of gobblers to survive the hunting season. The peak nest initiation date (date of first egg being laid) for Louisiana wild turkey hens is April 8th. This median date was determined using radio telemetry studies, back dating of poults, and egg embryo aging across Louisiana over several years and averaged for the state. There may be slight differences in breeding dates from one part of Louisiana to another during certain years, but generally most turkey hens are likely bred between the last week of March and the first 2 weeks of April.

Contrary to popular belief, most hens do not breed when gobblers first begin to strut and gobble any more than white-tailed does breed when the first buck rubs appear in the forest. With both turkeys and deer, it is up to the female when breeding occurs. The strutting and gobbling activity typically associated with breeding may go on for several weeks before the first hen is actually bred. Exceptions to this do occasionally occur, as this author has documented at least one successful nest being initiated the first week of February. (Additional specific nest initiation dates for backdated poults observed in southeast Louisiana are found in Appendix C.) Turkey hens are naturally programed to use visual stimuli to become receptive. That stimulus is likely base as much on day length as any other factor. So, if most Louisiana hens lay their first egg near April 8th, peak breeding likely takes place somewhere within one to two days prior to that date. If we want the best genetics from the dominant (largest, strongest, and healthiest) gobbler, he must be allowed to live until he breeds most of the hens. Unfortunately, many dominant (generally the single strutter within groups of Toms) gobblers are the first selected for harvest by hunters during March hunting. With mid- to late-March season openings, it is theoretically possible to harvest most of an area's dominant gobblers within low population sites prior to the natural breeding period.

As early as 1920 William Holmes (La. Dept. of Conservation) reported *"the present season…is in need of revision…the month of March at least should be excluded from the turkey season"* (Holmes 1920). In 2016 only 17 out of 52 parishes having a turkey season reported harvesting more than 50 gobblers, just three of which reported more than 100 harvested. Obviously these are reported harvests and actual harvest numbers are higher. Nonetheless, most of Louisiana can reasonably be considered as having a low population. In those few areas with high turkey numbers, harvesting a considerable number of gobblers early in March is likely not a serious biological concern. It is often hunters from these higher population areas that are the most vocal supporters of early seasons and increased bag limits. However, due to increasing habitat fragmentation and the ever diminishing use of prescribed fire, much of Louisiana is now considered marginal habitat maintaining only modest to low turkey numbers. Hens may go un-bred in such very low population sites and will lay unfertilized eggs that will not produce young. Some biologists fear that hunting low turkey population areas over multiple years during early seasons is not sustainable and will result in long-term declines in turkey numbers and harvests. Some believe that this decline has already begun in many areas.

Louisiana is a leader among Gulf coastal states in conducting some of the largest eastern wild turkey gobbler harvest studies. Harvest rate information collected from hunters reporting harvests of banded gobblers is believed to accurately reflect harvest rates, based on a compliance study using monetary reward bands that indicated reporting rates of non-reward banded gobblers as high as $100 reward banded gobblers. These harvest studies have shown researchers that certain areas can be over-hunted under certain circumstances. Also, a large proportion of the harvest has been found to occur during the first week of hunting. Based on 4 separate studies conducted in Louisiana from 1989-2007, 46 – 59% of the total harvest of gobblers occurred during the first week of hunting season. The second week saw a much reduced harvest of 12.5 – 25% and the third week 12 – 29%. These same studies also indicated that when hunting seasons started later, harvest rates by week were more proportional throughout the season. Today's season which starts some years more than 2 weeks before peak breeding can see approximately 60 to 90% of the season's total harvest occurring prior to peak breeding.

Research in some states indicates that illegal spring hen harvests can have a significant impact on turkey numbers, especially in those states that harvest additional hens during fall either sex seasons. Turkey experts in these states prefer a season that does not open until the peak of incubation (a couple of weeks after peak laying starts, when hens stay on the nest both day and night). The belief is that incubating hens are far less likely to be shot than those walking around prior to incubation. In Louisiana this incubation peak is around April 21 - 28. Since Louisiana has no fall season and in-state telemetry studies have not indicated illegal hen harvests as being excessive, this much later opening strategy may not be justifiable in the Bayou State. Besides, few Louisiana hunters are desirous of a hunting season start the last week of April.

What about hunting success during later seasons? Turkey seasons have historically opened at any number of dates throughout the country and within this state. The greatest proportion of the annual turkey harvest at any location will likely occur during the first week of turkey season, whether it opens March 15th, April 15th, or May 15th. Therefore, managers and hunters must consider which opening date will most benefit turkey population growth, health, and last but surely not least, hunter success. To decide this date, we must first examine the turkey breeding cycle. Social breeding behavior of gobblers begins while birds are still in winter groups. These groups of 2 or more males have spent much of the year together and with the changing of seasons begin to gobble more often as March progresses. As temperatures warm, day length increases, and as hens are drawn to gobbling, tensions build and dominance, if not already established, is determined through sparring. Breeding increases in late March and peaks in early April. Early in this period gobblers may remain together since large groups of hens are present. It is during this time in the breeding cycle that hunting (calling) success can be at its worst, but in a week or two as hens begin to leave for nesting gobbler rivalries grow and hunter success odds begin to increase again. By mid-April many gobblers that have not fallen to the gun are alone or with small hen groups. As these few hens break away to nest, formerly impossible to call gobblers become more receptive to the lure of a hunter's call and thus harvest success can increase. Time has demonstrated that seasonal weather conditions are also a huge factor and can influence harvest success. In years when spring comes early hens break away to nest sooner and in years where winter holds on longer hens depart for nesting later. Therefore, if season lengths (number of days) are decided based on various designated *"area"* turkey densities and those days are limited in number, it only makes sense to place those limited hunting days when the odds of turkey hunting success are best. All too often, due to the *"all areas open on the same date provision"* public lands and private land areas with short seasons find themselves closing before the best hunting period of the breeding cycle occurs. This can be equated to deer season closing a week before the rut peaks. Such seasons put hunters at a big disadvantage and often has them sitting at home when gobblers are most receptive to calling.

What part should weather play in setting turkey season? During the opening weekend of the 2010 turkey season many Louisiana turkey hunters found themselves hunting in snow flurries. The March 20th opening coincided with a frigid weather event that became a major factor in the suppressed harvest that year. Again in 2013 Louisiana hunters experienced several frosty mornings and wintery afternoons throughout the season and reported the lowest harvest since tagging was reinstituted in 2009. Once more in 2014 Louisiana saw a cold winter and gobbling very suppressed across the state during the first weeks of the season. Thirty years of sitting in blinds watching turkey behavior while trapping turkeys teaches one a few things. I found that on cold days turkeys will prioritize finding food. They exhibit much less social behavior, generally gobble less, and focus more on finding food. Rainy days are similar, except turkeys tend to congregate in more open areas such as fields or other more substantial openings. Warm days stimulate male breeding behavior as well as discontentment with other male turkeys in the area. Gobblers strut more, fight more, feed less, and generally gobble more on warmer days. Let's face it, Louisiana has crazy weather, but any climatologist can verify that as the calendar rolls into April, on average, fewer cold weather extremes will occur than in March. With each day later into spring warmer average daily temperatures will occur, stimulating more consistent breeding behavior. As the calendar moves later, even unseasonably cool mornings will cause little if any reduction in gobbling. Later season starts tend to reduce the likelihood of weather negatively influencing annual harvest rates.

Figure 57 illustrates the daily reported harvest from 2009 thru 2011. This graph shows typical harvest proportions throughout the hunting season. During the first days of 2010 cold weather moderated the harvest. Weather and first week harvest rates in 2009 and 2011 were closer to normal despite the two season opening dates being about a week apart. Both years experienced typical high first week harvest rates compared to the suppressed first week harvest caused by cold weather in 2010. During 2009 when the regular hunting season opened March 28th, 64% of the reported season harvest occurred prior to the peak of nest starts and suspected peak breeding. While the earlier starting seasons of 2010 and 2011 that opened March 20th and March 19th, saw 82% and 93% respectively of the season harvest prior to estimated peak breeding and peak nest starts. Incidentally, the later starting 2009 season saw an 81% higher opening weekend reported harvest than 2010 and 42% higher than 2011 suggesting improved hunting success with the later season start.

2009 - 2011 Harvests & Reporting Dates

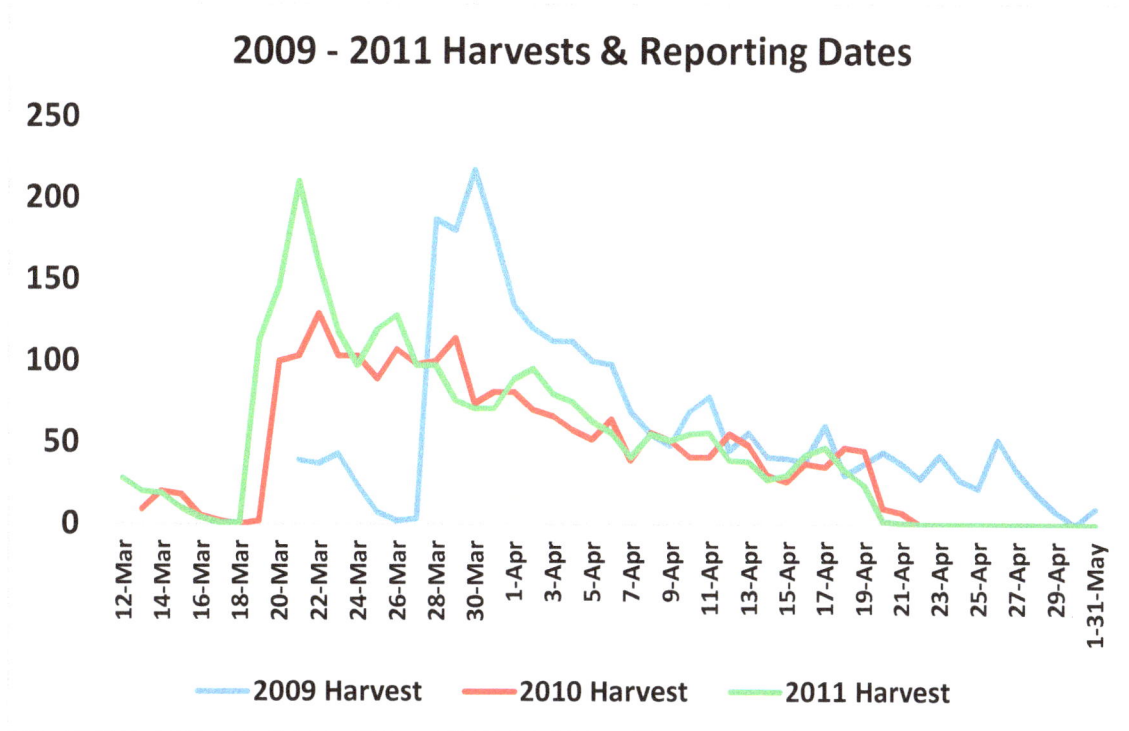

Figure 57

So, just what kind of an opening time period is best to ensure healthy turkey populations and successful turkey hunting in Louisiana? The current season that opens before peak nesting, the author has been told, was established that way many years ago by design. The idea was to set the season when harvest rates would be lower as peak numbers of hunters entered the woods during the first week of hunting. Then as the season progressed into peak nesting, hunting areas would be less populated with hunters. When Louisiana hunter numbers were relatively low and public hunting grounds abundant, this strategy had some merit. In more recent years hunters often find themselves more concentrated. Hunters today, being quite willing to travel and proficient at harvesting turkeys, combined with research demonstrating that a large percentage of gobblers are taken during the first week, prompts increased concern for marginal population areas. The resolution adopted by a consensus of top wild turkey experts throughout the southeastern states suggests that the actual best date to open is much later than nearly every Gulf coastal state's current turkey season opening. These opinions represent the purest biological recommendations available today. If Louisiana adopted the more conservative dates that protected turkeys throughout peak breeding, laying, and incubation, that opening would occur in late April. Such an opening date would be nearly a month later than the current opening date.

Research conducted in Louisiana has found little evidence that illegal hen harvests during the spring is widespread, therefore the primary focus in season setting here should simply be to ensure that gobblers live long enough to reach the period of peak breeding. This peak occurs on average sometime around the first week of April throughout Louisiana. Ideally starting turkey season just after this peak would be best, but most biologists believe that a more modest shift of opening day to the first Saturday in April or even a lesser shift to the Saturday closest to April 1st would be a huge step in the right direction for long-term sustainability of turkeys and hunter success across the state. Each later start date shift allows a larger percentage of hens to be bred prior to gobblers being removed by harvests. However, based on hunter surveys, the majority of turkey hunters in Louisiana currently do not support such a change. Biologists wonder if presented the biological arguments, will hunter opinions will change or stay the same. Only time will tell.

Bag & Season Limits

The daily bag limit of one turkey has remained unchanged in Louisiana since 1911, while season limits have been more variable. In 1925 a season limit of 12 either sex turkeys was established. By 1927 the season limit was dropped to 5 as turkey numbers declined. In 1945 the season limit was further reduced to 1 turkey during a very short season and from that year on would be gobbler only. Not until 1968 had turkeys rebounded enough to raise the season limit to 2 gobblers. As numbers grew, the season limit was raised again in 1977 to 3 gobblers. In 1983 a somewhat unusual change occurred when the season limit was removed completely, allowing the harvest of one gobbler per day for the entire season. The rational was that there were plenty of turkeys and the belief that the wildlife management principle called the *"law of diminishing returns"* would result in reduced hunting pressure as area populations decreased and that harvest numbers would self-regulate without detriment. This unrestricted season limit was short lived as most hunters and many biologists, including this author, strongly objected for a variety of societal and biological reasons and by the following year (1984), the 3 gobbler season limit was restored. Due to biological and management reasons, the season limit was reduced from 3 gobblers to 2 in 2002. This change has, from time to time, prompted some to request that the LDWF return this third bird in some manner to the season limit.

The following information regarding the bag limit change was first compiled from data collected by LDWF biologists Larry Savage and Fred Kimmel then later updated by the author.

Research conducted on both private and public land in Washington parish from 1989 - 1997 revealed that 70% of the adult gobblers were harvested each year and *"annual survival"* was only 16% (Stafford et al 1997). [Note that annual survival rate estimates are determined by statistical modeling that takes into account a variety of survival risk factors then estimates survival for one year.] This harvest rate was much higher than reported in other areas of the southeastern United States. Adult gobbler harvests in other southeastern states ranged from 17% - 32% and annual survival in hunted populations ranged from 36% - 63%. Additional in-state harvest mortality studies conducted during the 1990s and early 2000s on both public and private sites indicated lower annual harvest rates (0 to 37.5%) than the Washington parish study. Harvest rates above 30 – 35% lead to decreases in adult populations and hunting quality (Vangilder and Kurzejeski 1995). Since annual gobbler survival is generally very high (at least 80%) in the absence of hunting, a high harvest rate reduces the number of birds available in subsequent years and reduces the average age of adult gobblers harvested. The continued viability of isolated populations or low-density populations may be adversely impacted by high gobbler harvest rates.

LDWF WMA Supervisors Tommy Bruhl and Calvin Waskom banding an adult gobbler for mortality studies in southeast Louisiana. (J. Stafford)

A flock of West Baton Rouge parish turkeys just prior to capture then seconds later as the author and LSU researcher John Gross secure turkeys prior to fitting the birds with GPS telemetry units for movement and hunting mortality studies. (J. Gross)

Allowing fewer gobblers to reach 3 years or older creates a situation where the harvest each year is highly dependent on production 2 years prior. Such a situation is not a problem during consecutive years of good production. However, when consecutive years of poor production occur, adult gobbler populations and hunter harvests will drop to low levels. Once the gobbler population reaches low levels it will take several years to recover even if production is good. During 2009 – 2014, poult production in 4 of the 5 Louisiana habitat regions was below 2.0 poults per hen (less than 2.0 is considered poor) most years except in the Northwest Loblolly/Shortleaf/Hardwood region which maintained better production. A preferable situation is to have a moderate harvest level that results in a diverse gobbler age structure so that harvests can remain relatively stable even following years of poor production. A moderate harvest rate will help avoid a *"boom or bust"* harvest cycle.

Over time, large forested areas of private lands within Louisiana have continued to become fragmented. Turkeys have become extirpated (geographically extinct) from many areas where suitable forest blocks have diminished in size. Urban sprawl is a growing factor that has negatively affected turkey habitat especially in southeast Louisiana. Expansion of suburban areas near Monroe, Shreveport, Lake Charles, Alexandria and other cities has also accelerated in recent years. Additionally, much of Louisiana has been converted to monoculture pine, which is less suited for turkeys than previous mixed pine/hardwood forests. Populations dependent on marginal habitats are less productive and less resilient than those in better habitats. High harvests and/or predation rates combined with poor production have a greater and longer lasting impact on populations in marginal habitats.

The two turkey season limit seems to have moderated the statewide harvest and anecdotal information indicates increased hunter satisfaction due to gobbling activity in many areas. Hearing gobbling turkeys is a key element in turkey hunter satisfaction. The more restrictive regulations were intended to increase the proportion and number of adult gobblers, thus increasing the amount of gobbling heard by hunters.

Research conducted during 1989-94 on the former Ben's Creek WMA and neighboring private lands revealed that 70% of adult gobblers and 23% of jakes were being killed each year. A follow-up study from 2000-07 at the same sites following reductions in hunting days and season limit found annual adult gobbler harvest rates dropped to 36% and the jake harvest rate dropped to 6%. This lower harvest rate was closer to harvest rates observed in other southeastern states, indicating that the regulatory adjustments made did impact harvest rates. Lovett Williams, Jr. (1991) ranked protecting turkeys from over-hunting as the most important action that managers can do.

Gobblers with spurs greater than ½ inch are usually adult birds (at least 2 years old). Spur length of gobblers captured by LDWF personnel during the Washington Parish research project during 1989-94 and 2000-07 were measured, documented, and compared. During 1989-94, 54% of adult gobblers had spurs greater than ¾ inch. This increased to 76% in 2000-2007 after the limit was dropped to 2 birds and season length was reduced. These results indicate an increase in the quality and average age of harvested gobblers with the more conservative harvest strategy.

Most licensed turkey hunters fail to harvest a turkey during most years. It is estimated that increasing the season limit to 3 gobblers would have the potential to affect 3 - 10% of the hunters that now harvest 2 birds. In 1995, 3% of turkey hunters surveyed reported harvesting 3 birds. However, the third bird in the bag accounted for 21% of the total harvest. This means that the birds harvested by a handful of very successful hunters represented a much greater portion of the total harvest than might be expected. The bag limit reduction was implemented to reduce the overall harvest by at least 10%.

The goal of the more restrictive season limit was to reduce the harvest in response to declining turkey populations and concerns about excessive harvest. Approximately 4% of the hunters might successfully harvest a third bird, but it is estimated the third bird would comprise about 10 - 20% of the total harvest today. Such an increased kill could negatively impact the proportion of adult gobblers in the population in some areas and ultimately result in reduced hunter satisfaction. The impact would be most apparent following years of poor production and in those areas with marginal habitat.

Each season hunters pursue a finite number of gobblers. Some believe that allowing a third turkey to be harvested diminishes opportunities for young, old, or more novice hunters. It may also encourage some to keep hunting longer for themselves rather than taking someone else hunting. For these and other reasons it is important at this point in time that Louisiana maintain the current 2 turkey season limit.

Jake Harvests

Louisiana puts no restrictions on the harvest of jakes. In days of old, harvesting a jake was considered by many hunters just as rewarding as harvesting an adult gobbler. However, hunter opinions have changed in recent years and many who once would have jumped at the chance to harvest a jake, now let jakes walk by unmolested as if they were hens. Many studies, both in-state and out, have demonstrated that jakes surviving the first hunting season are very likely to live until the next season. In a good production year, jakes can make up the majority of males in certain populations. The 1989-1997 Washington parish gobbler study indicated a relatively high jake harvest rate of 23% and an estimated survival rate for jakes of 46% (Stafford et al 1997). Following harvest restrictions at the study site, that included reducing the season limit to two and reducing season hunting days during 2000 – 2007, only 6% of jakes were harvested and the jake survival rate was estimated at 56% (Chamberlain et al. 2012). In a similar study conducted in the northcentral parishes of Union, Jackson, Bienville, and Lincoln just 7% of jakes were harvested from 2002 – 2009 and annual survival was estimated at 55% (Byrne et al. 2015). In a more recent study done on Kisatchie National Forest, 8% of banded jakes were harvested the first season after capture, further indicating that today both on private and public lands within Louisiana jakes are not excessively harvested. These three later studies represented a large sample of jakes (n = 312) where only 22 were harvested as jakes. These and other recent studies conducted in Concordia, Iberville, St. Martin, Tensas, Madison, Franklin, West Feliciana, West Baton Rouge, Vernon, Rapides, Natchitoches, Winn, and Claiborne parishes indicate similar low jake harvest rates. Since such a small percentage of jakes are harvested from the jake population, LDWF finds little evidence to support additional restrictions preventing hunters who may not otherwise take an adult bird from taking a jake. Having said that, passing up jakes is still a wise conservation practice for most Louisiana turkey hunters and this author highly recommends this voluntary practice. In 1998, Mississippi implemented a *"Jake Law"* restricting the harvest of jakes. Based on their aging techniques, 41.2% of turkeys harvested prior to restrictions were >3 years old. After restrictions, 47.6% were >3 years old (Austin 2012). Mississippi researchers also reported improved gobbling activity and greater hunter satisfaction after passage of jake harvest restrictions.

Fall Hunting

In 2010 Louisiana instituted its first fall turkey season in the state since 1924. This season was confined to the Peason Ridge WMA. The season proposal was not initiated by LDWF biologists. Ultimately, this lottery type gobbler-only hunt harvested less than 15 birds over the 3 years that it occurred. The lack of fall gobbling, difficulty of calling birds in, and hot weather caused interest to drop over time. In 2012 the fall season was ended with no plans to implement it again.

Louisiana Hunting Statistics

During early years of turkey hunting in Louisiana, acquiring accurate harvest information was difficult. However, from the reopening of turkey hunting in 1955 until the mid-1970s it is safe to say that the harvest was very low. From 1955 – 57 it was reported that only 250 turkeys were harvested statewide and that low harvests were the result of rampant illegal hunting (Newsom 1957). LDWF biologist John D. Newsom reported *"Dogs have been and are still being used to hunt young turkey in the fall of the year. The hunter in this case is not particular about the sex of the bird he is taking and, in most instances, will kill the entire flock if possible."* In 1971, biologist Cliff Williams reported only a slightly increased statewide harvest of 300 – 350 turkeys (Williams 1971). For a period of time during these early years hunters were issued tags to place on harvested gobblers and were then required to turn in any unused tags after the hunting season. Deer, turkey, and even a bear tag was issued to each *"big game"* hunter starting in 1961. Even though having never as much as seen a bear track in southeast Louisiana, I can still remember getting my one bear tag then looking at my trusty 20-gauge single shotgun and thinking "*A bear better not cross my path this season.*" By the early-1970s tagging was found to be of little biological value because too few hunters were reporting harvests or turning in unused tags. Since there was no effective way to track the paper tags or their use, tagging was abandoned. A close inspection of some of the older photographs in this book reveal such tags.

Wild turkey populations have always been vulnerable to both excessive legal and illegal harvests. This makes it ever more important for biologists to keep abreast of annual harvest rates and enforcement of turkey law violations be aggressively administered.

Since 1980 the LDWF has conducted mail out game harvest surveys to monitor harvest rates and hunter numbers. This important annual survey is mailed to 6% of randomly selected licensed resident hunters and asks specific questions about a variety of games species and the previous season's hunting success. Information about turkey hunting is obtained from those who respond to the survey and is extrapolated to create statewide estimates of hunters and harvests.

Since 2004 a special statewide youth turkey season on private lands has occurred the weekend prior to the regular opening of hunting season. About 20% of turkey hunters surveyed reported taking a youth turkey hunting. Youth hunts are a great way to introduce young hunters to the thrill of turkey hunting and gives them very good odds of having a close encounter with a gobbler. Youth hunter harvests add about 15 – 25% to regular season harvests. Figure 58 illustrates the *Louisiana Big and Small Game Harvest Survey* turkey hunting results from 1980 – 2015. Note that no survey results are available for years 1988, 1989, and 2004. Also note that due to a survey anomaly in 2014 that overestimated the youth harvest, the actual 2014 harvest is likely far less than illustrated below.

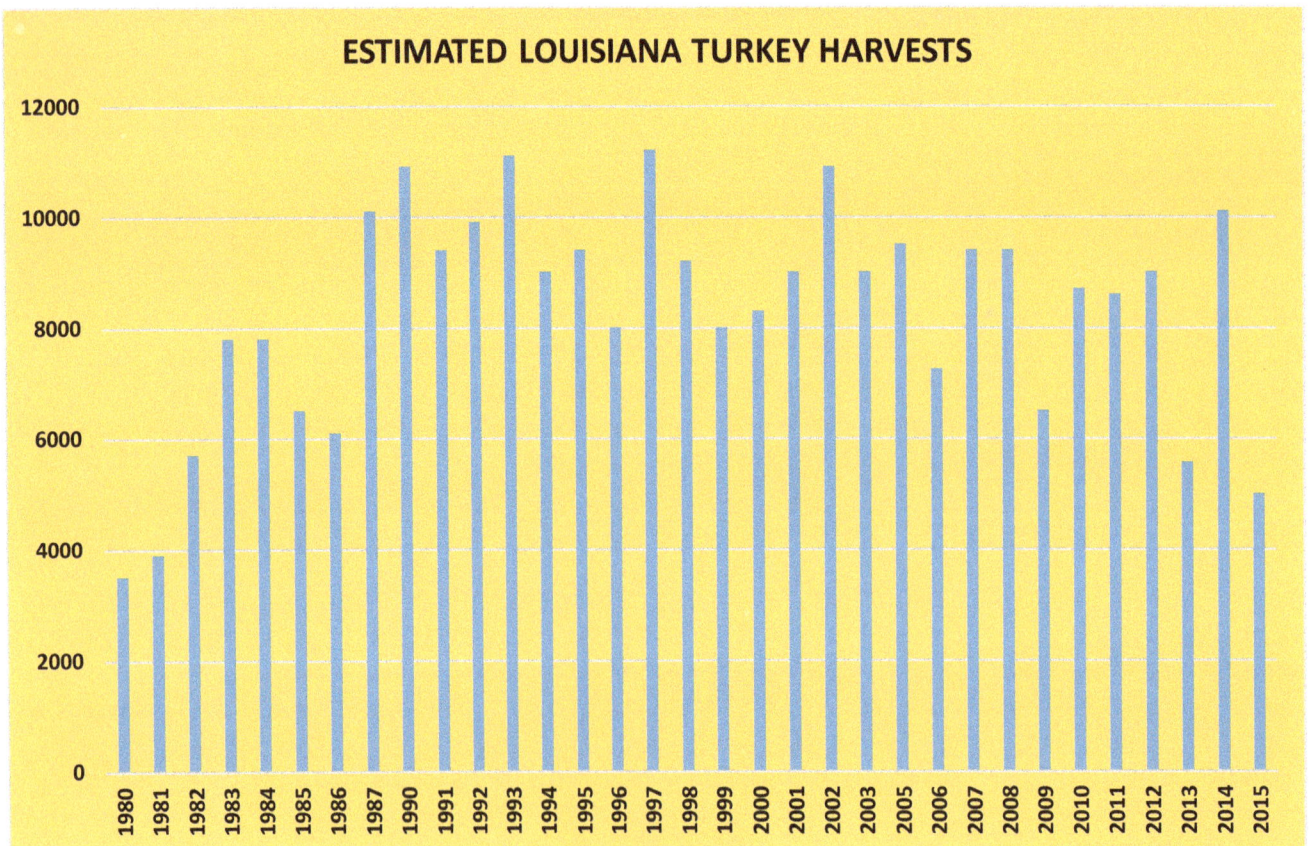

Figure 58 (LDWF)

116

This turkey harvest information seems to indicate a declining trend in annual harvests in Louisiana. Estimated hunters in Louisiana have also declined from a high of 25,800 hunters in 2003 to about 18,000 to 19,000 in 2015. These hunter estimates do not include youth hunters and until 2012 – 13, did not include lifetime license holders. Therefore, actual turkey hunter numbers may be 25% or greater than reported in the survey.

From 1988 – 2003 volunteer turkey check stations were established in every parish where turkeys were hunted. These volunteer check stations were located at country stores, sporting goods stores, LDWF offices, and other local sites. Some 1,000 to 1,700 turkeys were checked each year, representing about 10 – 20% of the estimated annual harvest in any given year. Despite drawings for shotguns donated by the Louisiana NWTF chapter, hunter participation slowly decreased over time and biologists suspected that a disproportionate number of adult gobblers were being checked compared to jakes. A determination was made that the biological data obtained was limited and the volunteer turkey check program was abandoned after the 2003 season.

In 2009 mandatory tagging was reinstituted for turkeys in Louisiana. In addition to tagging, hunters were required to validate each harvested turkey by reporting it within a specified time period. The percentage of harvested turkeys actually validated has to date been far less than expected. Based on a survey of hunters in 2013, only 19% of turkeys harvested were validated by reporting. Efforts to enforce this requirement have since increased. If too small a percentage of harvested turkeys are reported, tagging has little real value as a management tool. Table 4 illustrates the reported wild turkey harvest from 2009 – 2016.

Table 2: Validated turkey harvests 2009 – 2016 (LDWF)

Year	2009	2010	2011	2012	2013	2014	2015	2016
Adults	2,263	1,876	1,907	1,824	1,187	1,462	1,563	1,510
Jakes	323	345	673	217	384	223	214	240
Total Harvest	2,586	2,221	2,581	2,041	1,571	1,685	1,777	1,750

One useful result that tag reporting has accomplished is to provide a proportional representation of harvest data for all of the parishes where turkeys are hunted. Figure 59 illustrates the reported turkey harvest by parish during 2016. Reported harvest maps from 2009 – 2015 are found in Appendix D.

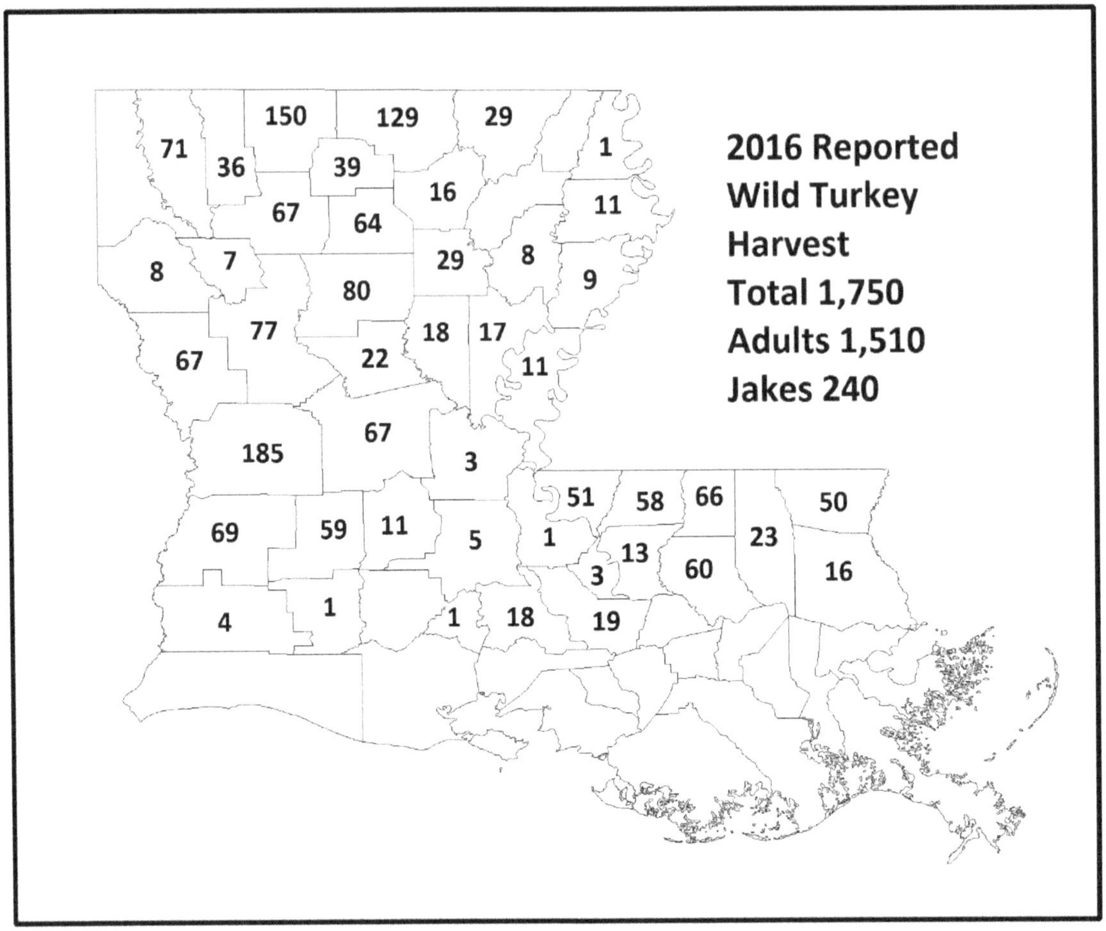

Figure 59 (LDWF)

In most years since tagging was reinstituted, the top 5 parishes for turkey harvests have been Vernon, Claiborne, Union, Beauregard, and Natchitoches with Rapides, Winn, and Bienville occasionally breaking into the top five. It is not surprising that Vernon tops the list each year with its 767,517 acres of forest (USDA Forest Inventory data 2007). Vernon has nearly twice the acres in forests as most other parishes. Beauregard has some 592,461 acres of forest, Claiborne 435,693 acres, Union 478,170 acres, and Natchitoches 559,577 acres of forest. Rapides has 562,213 acres, Winn has 546,508, and Bienville some 451,470 acres of forests. Generally speaking, these areas are less populated with people compared to other areas of the state. This is all the more evidence that large areas of sparsely populated forests are important to maintaining Louisiana's turkey population.

Hunter reported turkey harvests are an incomplete record of actual harvests. These data may also have additional biased information over time as reporting rates fluctuate. However, they can provide useful trend information especially when compared by ecoregion. Since 2009, the general trend for all Louisiana ecoregions is a decline in reported turkey harvests. The MAV bottomlands and UEGCP West Feliciana and Thompson Creek uplands have experienced the greatest declines while the west-central WGCP and northwest Louisiana UWGCP have experienced more modest declines (Figure 60). Regardless, in 8 short years, declines in reported harvests have been quite dramatic. Whether they are an accurate reflection of decreasing turkey numbers or reduced reporting compliance, if these declines continue into the future, there is considerable reason for concern.

Figure 60 (J. Stafford)

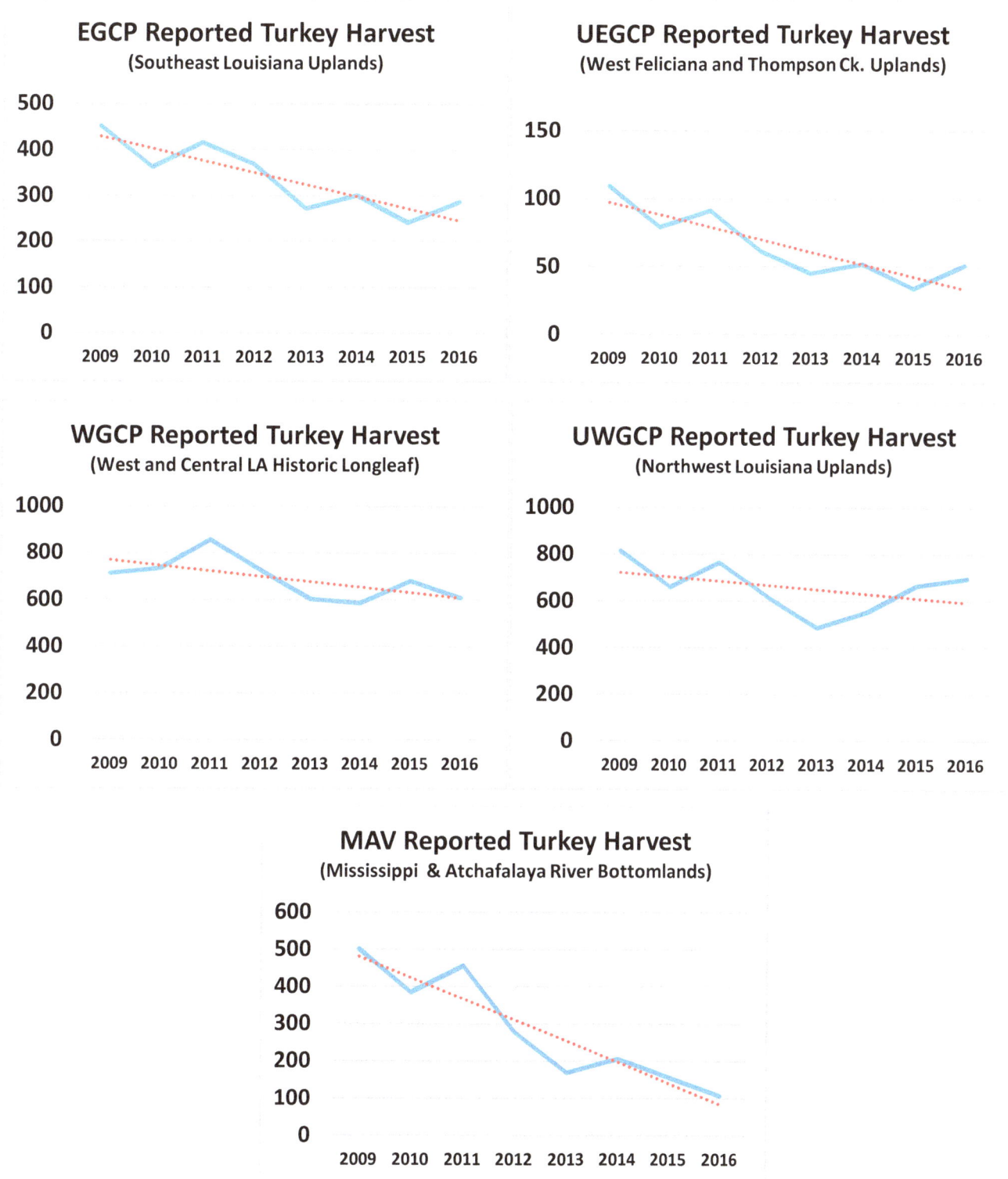

EGCP Reported Turkey Harvest
(Southeast Louisiana Uplands)

UEGCP Reported Turkey Harvest
(West Feliciana and Thompson Ck. Uplands)

WGCP Reported Turkey Harvest
(West and Central LA Historic Longleaf)

UWGCP Reported Turkey Harvest
(Northwest Louisiana Uplands)

MAV Reported Turkey Harvest
(Mississippi & Atchafalaya River Bottomlands)

(Note that harvest data from parishes containing portions of two or more ecoregions were grouped in the most appropriate ecoregion based on available turkey habitat acreage.)

119

Public Lands

Many experts believe that public lands today are the most important reservoir of wild turkeys. Public lands contain critically important large contiguous forest blocks that are virtually free from fragmentation caused by urbanization and non-compatible land management practices. In addition, public lands support turkey numbers on thousands of acres of smaller privately owned forests nearby. Without these large public land forests, these private lands would otherwise have far fewer turkeys. Without large forested public lands, turkeys would have long since disappeared in certain parts of the state. The presence of abundant public land holdings, managed in such a way to benefit turkeys, is essential to maintaining the wild turkey throughout Louisiana into the future. It is also of great importance to the future of turkey hunting.

Just a few years ago finding a place to hunt wild turkeys in Louisiana was not difficult. Most timber company lands were open access for anyone to hunt. Some timber companies even erected signs welcoming hunters (Smith 1959). Many private landowners would allow people to hunt their property with a simple request for permission. Today timber company lands and many large private land owner tracts are leased by hunting clubs. Although the leasing of land has in many cases contributed to increased turkeys due to added protection, leases have limited public hunter access and potential turkey hunting *"man-days"* per season statewide. Experience teaches that as hunting opportunities for a particular game species wain, such activity loses its value to society at large. Even those that hunt exclusively on private lands must understand that if the sport they love becomes relegated to a select few, it becomes vulnerable. Public lands are the last bastion of turkey hunting in Louisiana. These lands that offer *"open to all"* turkey hunting are of vital importance to the future of the sport. If the sport of turkey hunting is to be maintained over time, hunting access to public lands where turkeys occur is of vital importance. If hunting opportunities become too scarce hunters abandon the sport and other special interest activities are elevated, leading to the further decrease of turkey hunting. All effort must be made to maintain and expand public lands managed for turkeys as well as *"open to all"* turkey hunting.

On public lands within Louisiana, Wildlife Management Areas (WMA) have been at the forefront of turkey restoration and management for more than 60 years. WMAs were some of the first areas set aside for wild turkey restocking, propagation, and sources for restocking other lands. The LDWF is conducting active management for turkeys on many of its owned and leased properties. These areas have also been the sites for numerous wild turkey studies that have aided biologists in Louisiana and other states to better manage turkeys. It is on state WMAs where poult surveys to assess local reproductive success were refined in the 1980s and 1990s that have resulted in today's uniform statewide production survey.

There are 18 WMAs that offer a period of *"open to all"* public turkey hunting and 8 that are lottery hunt only. The LDWF, recognizing the importance of open to all to the sport of turkey hunting, has tried to offer as much hunting opportunity as possible while balancing resource concerns. Today, there are several WMAs that offer quality turkey hunting such as Big Lake, West Bay, Tunica Hills, Ft. Polk-Vernon, Peason Ridge, Bodcau, and Clear Creek. Several other WMAs have seen better turkey hunting in the past but have been in decline due to flooding, neighboring habitat degradation, and other limiting factors.

In recent years, the LDWF has lost several upland WMAs important to wild turkeys and hunters in Louisiana. More emphasis to maintain and grow the number of upland public access WMAs is needed to maintain turkey hunting in Louisiana. This push must first come from turkey hunters themselves and be directed toward large landholding companies and state officials, encouraging them to do what is necessary to lease or facilitate the purchase of new WMAs for the purpose of public hunting.

WMAs have maintained good turkey harvest records for many years in an effort to monitor trends. Figure 61 illustrates WMA harvest trends from 2006 – 2015. The 2016 results were not included in the graph since so many WMAs were closed due to extensive spring flooding. Specific WMA harvest data from 2006 – 2016 is found in Appendix G. For more information, contact ***www.wlf.louisiana.gov/wma***.

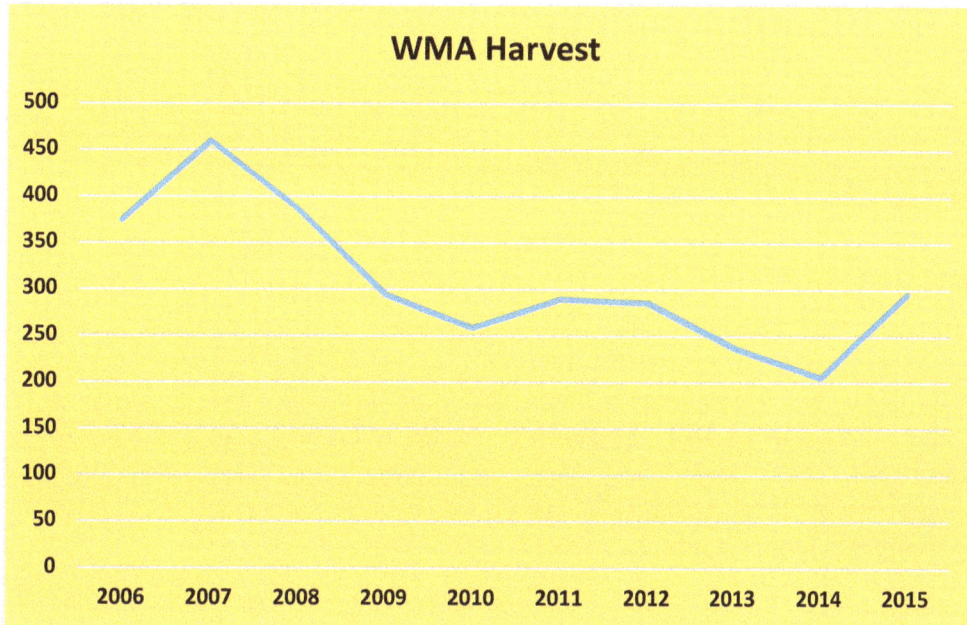

WMA Harvest

Figure 61

The Kisatchie National Forest (KNF) is another equally important public landholding for wild turkeys. KNF is comprised of 8 parcels of land within 5 ranger districts (RDs) located across 7 parishes and provides Louisiana turkey hunters with the largest public area of open to all access. KNF has been critically important as a large timbered reservoir for Louisiana turkeys. Much of the KNF was stocked with turkeys by the LDWF and some of these KNF sites later used to stock other parts of the state. The U.S. Forest Service, who manages KNF, works closely with the LDWF and considers the wild turkey a very important species as evidenced by its use of the wild turkey to represent KNF on the U. S. quarter in 2015.

To the north, the Caney Ranger District, at 32,000 acres, is the smallest and is comprised of 3 parcels: Caney Lake Unit, Middle Fork Unit, and Corney Lake Unit. This area contains mixed pine/hardwood forests of shortleaf pine, loblolly pine, and various hardwoods. Gobbler harvest studies conducted on this area by the LDWF in recent years have determined a 19% combined *"direct recovery (DR)"* rate. Direct recovery being the percent of banded gobblers harvested the first season after capture. DR rates over 35% are considered excessive. Wild turkey numbers remain relatively good in the more remote sections of this ranger district. After being absent for many years, the use of landscape scale prescribed fire is being returned to this RD and turkeys should respond favorably as more habitat is rehabilitated by fire.

The Winn Ranger District is comprised of some 164,000 acres of mixed pine/hardwood forests. Loblolly, longleaf, and shortleaf pines are common as are mixed hardwood hills and bottomland areas. This area has a long history of turkeys and turkey hunters. Part of the Catahoula National Wildlife Management Preserve is located within the Winn RD. In recent years, a hen nesting ecology study has been done on this area by the University of Georgia (UGA). The LDWF has also monitored gobbler harvests by banding gobblers. To date, a direct recovery rate of 24% has been determined on the Winn RD. Prescribed burning is a regular occurrence that maintains quality brood habitat aiding annual turkey production on Winn RD.

The Catahoula Ranger District is comprised of some 121,500 acres of pine and mixed pine/hardwood forests. Most of the area is in longleaf pine while other areas are a mixture of loblolly pine and hardwoods. As in all Kisatchie ranger districts, hardwood dominant bottoms with small streams traverse the area making for ideal turkey habitat. Much of the Catahoula National Wildlife Management Preserve is located on the Catahoula RD.

Prescribed burning is the primary management practice that helps turkey on this RD. Regular timber thinnings also aid in improving sites within the ranger district.

The Kisatchie Ranger District has some 102,000 acres of primarily longleaf pine mixed with scattered hardwoods. This area is characterized by rocky outcroppings uncommon to much of Louisiana. Several bottoms dominated by hardwoods also occur. The Red Dirt National Wildlife Management Preserve is located on this RD and has played an important part in Louisiana's deer and turkey programs. A gobbler mortality study has been conducted on Kisatchie RD and found a direct recovery rate of 20% from hunting. A hen nesting ecology study was also conducted on Kisatchie RD by UGA. Prescribed burning is regularly conducted on this RD which has helped maintain its growing turkey population.

The Calcasieu Ranger District is the southernmost ranger district comprised of two large parcels, the Evangeline Unit comprised of some 97,000 acres and the Vernon Unit comprising 85,000 acres. Evangeline is predominately longleaf and loblolly pine with scattered small hardwood bottoms. Prescribed fire is common on the area. The Vernon Unit, much of which is part of the Fort Polk-Vernon WMA, is longleaf pine dominant. Prescribed fire is often conducted more within this RD than many of the other RDs due to the increased occurrence of endangered red-cockaded woodpeckers and additional fires initiated during army training exercises. A gobbler mortality study conducted on the Vernon unit found a direct recovery rate of 18% from hunting.

Figure 62 shows each of the locations of Kisatchie National Forest land holdings. For more information, contact **www.fs.usda.gov/kisatchie.**

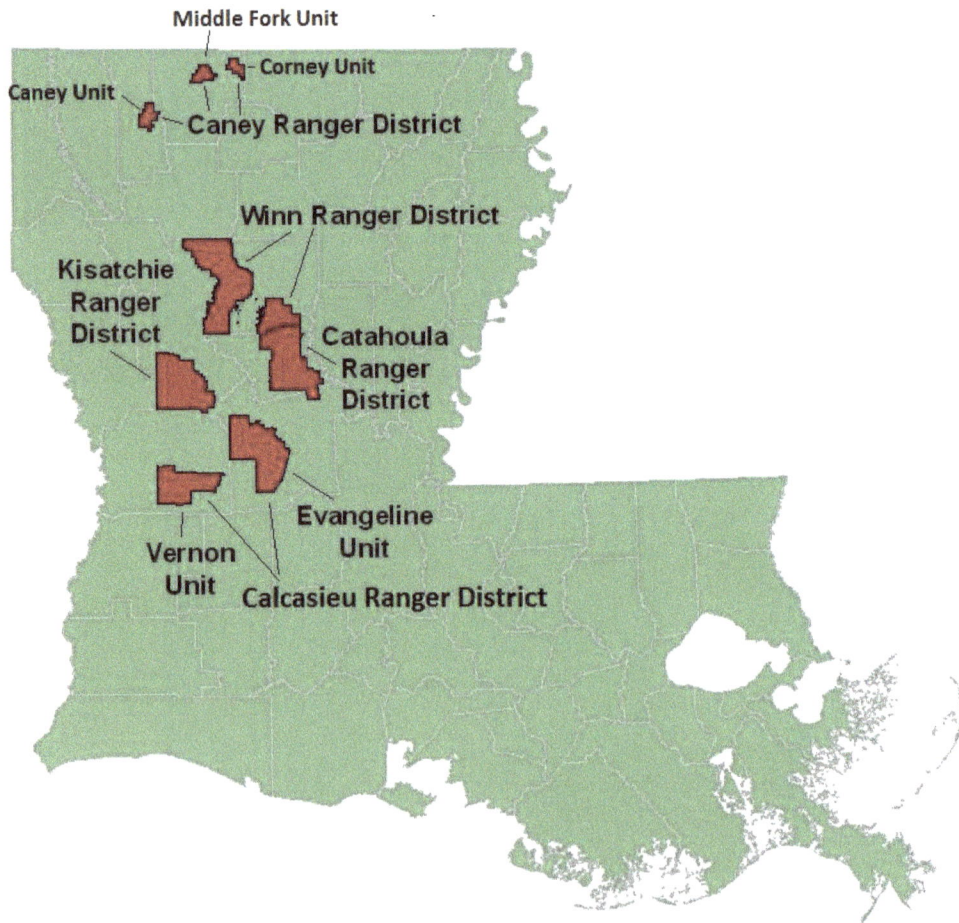

Figure 62: Kisatchie National Forest (U. S. Forest Service)

Louisiana has 23 National Wildlife Refuges (NWRs) encompassing some 550,000 acres. Only 4 offer open to all turkey hunting opportunities. Tensas River and Bogue Chitto NWRs offer hunting of Louisiana's original stock of native wild turkeys. These NWRs have very remote areas and each has unique challenges when hunting. Tensas River NWR has the greater population of turkeys and largest acreage while most hunting on the Bogue Chitto NWR is boat access only. This refuge is regularly subject to spring closure when flooding occurs. Atchafalaya NWR (part of the Sherburne WMA complex) and Lake Ophelia also offer turkey hunting. Both have additional youth hunting opportunities, some open to all and some lottery type hunting. Hopefully much needed turkey hunting opportunities will be expanded on Louisiana NWR public lands in future years where turkeys occur. For more information, contact ***www.fws.gov/refuges/refugeLocatorMaps/Louisiana***.

The U. S. Army Corps of Engineers (USACE) has scattered landholdings primarily within jurisdictional river bottoms. Some are included within WMAs while others, such as Indian Bayou Area USACE and Old River Control & Lock Area USACE, are standalone areas that offer public turkey hunting. Both areas have experienced turkey declines due to increased flooding in recent years. For more information, contact ***www.mvn.usace.army.mil/recreation***.

Other state, federal, and parish owned lands have in the past offered public hunting in Louisiana. Unfortunately, public hunting has been eliminated on most. Efforts should continue to return these public trust lands back to at least some form of public turkey hunting where feasible.

Louisiana Record Turkeys

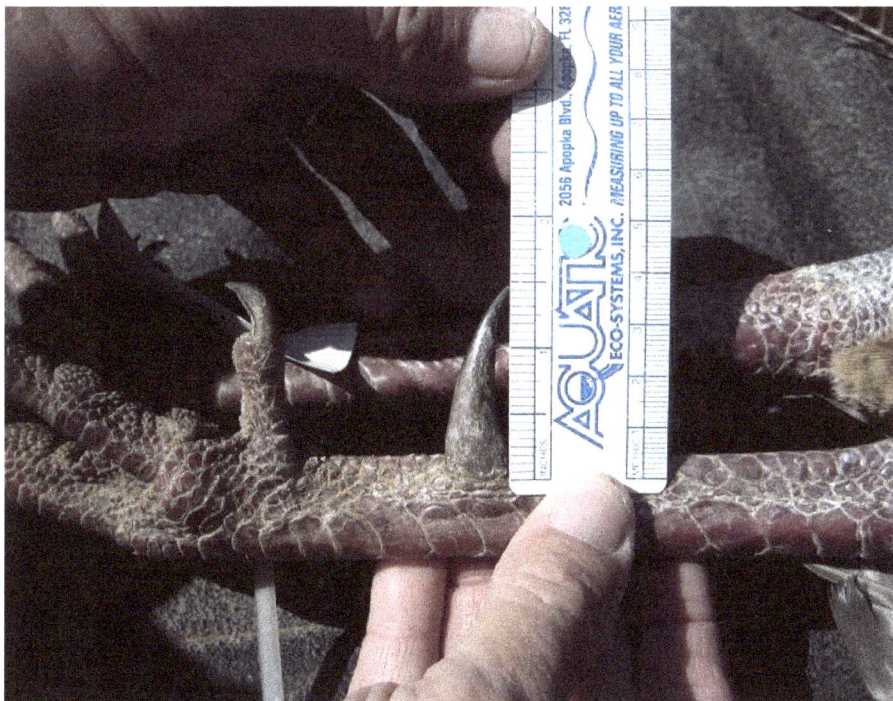

(L. Savage)

The LDWF maintains big game records for both white-tailed deer and wild turkeys. However, for wild turkeys spur length is the only trophy characteristic officially measured and recorded for this program. A minimum score of 40 is required to make the record book. Most 1 ¼" spurred turkeys will make this minimum score. Spurs must be officially measured by LDWF to qualify. To make the top tier of the big game record list, spurs need to score more than 50 points and be about 1 ½" long. Hunters can contact the LDWF at 225-765-2350 or email ***ccedotal@wlf.la.gov*** for more information.

INSTRUCTIONS FOR MEASURING WILD TURKEY SPURS FOR LOUISIANA BIG GAME RECORDS

Spurs must have dried for a minimum of 60 days.

Measurements must be taken with a flexible steel or tape ruler and calipers.

The length (in millimeters) of each spur must be taken along the centerline of the inside spur edge from the junction of the spur with the tarsus to tip of the spur. (Diagram A)

The width (in millimeters) of each spur must be taken at the junction of the spur with the tarsus at right angles to the inside centerline of the spur. (Diagram B)

Measurements of both spurs will be taken and the average lengths and widths will be used for scoring rather than individual spurs.

Total score is obtained by adding the average length and the average width of spur (in millimeters).

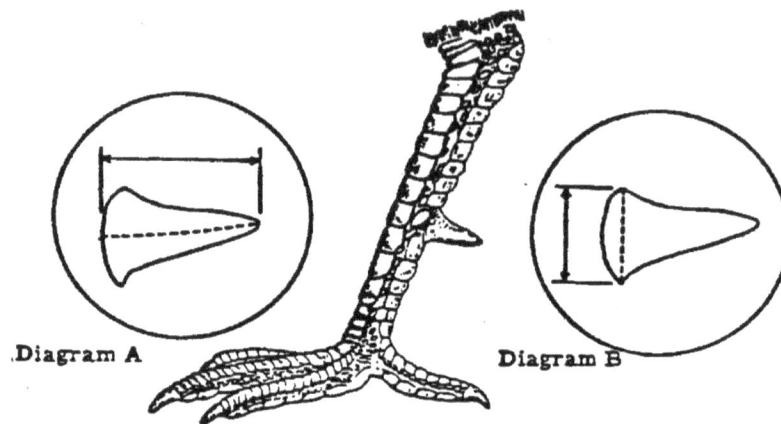

.Diagram A   Diagram B

The NWTF maintains its own trophy turkey records for each state. The NWTF system considers weight, spurs, and beard. To enter a turkey under NWTF guidelines simply contact *www.nwtf.org/hunt/records*.

Union parish "limb hanger" scoring 48 points (L. Savage)

Louisiana Turkey Hunting Tactics

If it were not for its hunting, the wild turkey would miss its greatest purpose and be just another beautiful bird species among thousands. The hunting of wild turkeys is like nothing else. Unlike most other game species, the wild turkey boldly announces his presence and location with each thunderous gobble. Upon hearing this announcement, the hunter then cautiously enters the gobbler's domain to do battle with an adversary that possesses skills of observation far greater than his own. It is a game of moves and counter moves. The experience and skill of either will weigh heavily on the day's outcome. Most often the prey (gobbler) will outwit or simply out maneuver the predator (hunter). However, depending on the skill of the hunter and the actions or inactions he or she selects, sometimes the master of the game, *"Ole Tom"*, can be outwitted.

In the game of hunting turkeys, experience is truly the best teacher. One who spends much time afield with turkeys will gain the most experience and better understand their language and habits. There is no real replacement for this firsthand experience. Unfortunately, few have the time or opportunity to gain such extensive firsthand experience. The best substitute for personal experience is seeking knowledge from those who have spent considerable time with turkeys and have been successful hunters for many years. As a boy I spent hours listening to experienced turkey hunters like my dad, local turkey hunting legends Tommy Arthur, William Russell, Carey Bateman, and others. Mr. Tommy, originally from Mississippi where turkeys were more plentiful in the early days, was making homemade mouth calls decades before they were commercially available. Mr. William's successful strategy was to enter the most remote Louisiana swamps by small boat while Mr. Carey, always the keen listener, seemed to know exactly where every single turkey was within a five parish area. Each of these men first stressed the importance of staying well-hidden and using good camouflage. Prior to the 1970s, camouflage clad hunters in Louisiana were uncommon. Most would simply wear dark or forest neutral colored clothing while turkey hunting. Some of the more fortunate had old military clothing issued during the World War II, Korean, or Vietnam era. It was often olive drab green in color or one of the few military camo patterns. As the first widely available commercial camouflage patterns appeared, hunters had a new tool that increased hunting success. I remember acquiring my first store bought camouflage jumpsuit in the 1970s and thinking that I would now be invisible to turkeys. Since that time camouflage patterns have continued to evolve, making concealment much more effective.

Staying out of sight is one thing, but convincing a gobbler to come close enough to kill is another. Accomplishing this is the true essence of being a turkey hunter. Turkeys killed by mere happenstance will never be as meaningful as one drawn into gun range by a call.

Learning to speak the wild turkey's language is of great importance. Knowing what to say and when to say it is of greater importance. If one traveled to Spain, having perfected the pronunciation of a handful of Spanish words without knowing their meaning or use, when spoken would perplex the Spanish speaking recipient rather than communicate effectively. The same happens when a turkey hunter sends out a series of turkey sounds with no regard for their meaning or when such sounds should be deployed. Using such *"turkey babble"* can even raise suspicion in an older turkey causing it to quietly vacate the area.

Spending thousands of hours sitting in turkey blinds while trapping, sometimes mere inches from turkeys, helped this author learn much about their communication. Listening to the calls of actual wild turkeys has always been the best method to learn turkey sounds and their meanings. Listening to experienced turkey hunters make turkey sounds will always be second best. Lovett Williams, Jr. (1991) documented 31 distinctive calls of wild turkeys and suspected more. This author has heard most of the calls that Williams described. Turkeys also communicate through posture, head movements, walking pace, and wing movements. The efforts of the late Lovett Williams Jr. to document turkey calls is the best that this author has found and are thoroughly described in his many books. In brief, this book will examine some 15 useful calls/sounds for hunting and associated turkey behaviors. There are several devices that hunters use to mimic turkey sounds that include one's natural voice, green leaves, peg and slate calls, peg and other materials (aluminum, acrylic, & etc.), box type calls, wing bone calls, tube type calls, diaphragm mouth calls, gobble tubes, striker box calls, and many more. Like the game of chess where each move is carefully considered before execution, each turkey sound deployed by a hunter should be thoroughly considered before being executed. Throwing a series of haphazard turkey calls to the wind is as foolish as moving chess pieces with no thought to the consequences. The most important turkey sounds for a hunter to understand are described below, as are their uses.

"*Kee Kee*": The kee kee call is performed by juvenile turkeys, most often in the summer and fall, to locate one another or the parent hen. This call, earlier in life vocalized as a whistle, has now matured into more of a squeal sound. The sound is just as spelled, "*Kee Kee*". It is most often a two or three note call. Sometimes a kee kee can be heard in the spring and can best be emulated by a diaphragm type mouth call. Its hunting use might be to rally a scattered group of jakes or lure closer a hen that has an adult gobbler in tow.

"*Kee Kee Run*": This call starts just like the kee kee but transitions into a crude yelp. It starts with two or three kee kee notes then finishes with two or three yelps. It reminds one of a teenage boy whose voice is changing into a man's voice. This call can also be successfully used in the same way as the kee kee. Good hunters will often mix a little kee kee run into a series of normal yelps to emulate a young hen. Sometimes this call is the trigger that brings birds closer when nothing else will work.

"*Plain yelp*": The plain yelp is probably the most used and most productive call deployed by hunters. Yelps usually come in properly rhythmed series of 3 to 8 calls. A yelp makes a "yawnk-yawnk-yawnk-yawnk" sound. I once had a Cajun friend that described the sound as "Peeyak-peeyak-peeyak-peeyak". Both hens and gobblers yelp, the gobbler having a coarser yelp. To perfect this call, the rhythm and space between each yelp must be correct. Yelps should have a sharp end to each note so that each does not bleed into the next. This call should be a hunter's "*go to*" call for most situations. It can be used very liberally near fly down time but then sparingly as the day progresses. There are exceptions to this when very vocal gobblers are encountered mid-day, under such circumstances more aggressive yelping sometimes works well.

"*Assembly yelps and lost yelps*": Assembly yelps are often done by the mother hen to rally her separated young. Assembly yelps may have 6 to 20 yelps in a row. Assembly yelps are sometimes quite loud. Hens without young will also use this call when members of their group are separated. The social structure of turkey flocks is very dynamic, but at times groups that have been together for extended periods will become very uneasy when members are missing. This author has often witnessed as groups of turkeys would come to a baited trapping site every day and voraciously consume all of the bait, but on a day when one member of their group is missing, they would walk past the bait as if it were not there, frantically assembly yelping for their lost friend. Many times they would leave without feeding only to return minutes or hours later with their lost companion, at which time they then feed contently as a group. Lost yelps may be interchangeable with assembly yelps but are more frantic in sound and are often performed by the one that is lost or separated. Both gobblers and hens will use lost/assembly calls. Hunters can have success using these calls on scattered birds or on dominant hens that may be accompanied by a gobbler. Since hens form a pecking order within a given area just like male turkeys, a key hunting tactic is to ignore the gobbler and focus calling on getting the hen interested or agitated. Often during the spring, where the hen goes so does the gobbler.

"*Tree Yelps*": The tree yelp is a 3 to 5 note series of yelps at the same cadence as all types of yelps, except that these yelps are very quiet. Turkeys tree yelp very softly as if whispering, "*good morning, I survived the night without being eaten or flushed. How about you?*". They do this usually expecting some sort of reply. If no reply comes, the turkey may become more cautious fearing a problem. There is no urgency projected in tree yelp notes. It is often the first call made in the morning while still on the roost and can seldom be heard by a hunter more than 50 yards away. In the absence of "*shock noises*", those sounds that startle a gobbler like an owl's hoot or a crow's call, a hen's tree yelp can often instigate the first gobble of the morning. Having judged turkey calling contests, this author has found that many participants will replicate the tree yelp far too quietly to be heard by a turkey beyond 50 yards. Depending on the situation and acoustics of the day, I have projected tree yelps at higher volumes to cover longer distances but soft enough that an old gobbler thinks the hen is only a few yards away from him. Using more than 3 sets of tree yelps will sometimes prove excessive, as it may cause the gobbler to stay in the tree much longer. A single three note tree yelp if answered by a gobbler is often sufficient for the early morning. Other successful hunters that I know will completely refrain from calling to a roosted gobbler until he has flown to the ground; however, this author has found no ill effect from using one or two tree yelps while the gobbler is still roosted. Hens on the ground will occasionally make a similar soft yelp to collect her wide foraging friends, coax a nearby gobbler closer, or signal that it is time for her group to move on. This very soft yelp can also be used on a gobbler that stops just out of gun range and refuses to budge.

"Plain Cluck": This call is a single short note that sounds somewhat like a large drop of water falling into a pond. The cluck, in turkey language, most often means *"where are you?"* or *"I am over here."* This simple call is hard to perfect and if improperly executed, can send the wrong signal to the gobbler one wishes to attract. It is a great tool for use in heavily hunted areas, where birds are scattered, or when a turkey has stopped just out of gun range. Using a single cluck or two to three clucks spaced about 2 seconds apart can work well, although sometimes using more can also be effective.

"Alarm Putt": The alarm putt is a cluck on steroids. It is the call that a very disturbed turkey makes, often just before fleeing. It has little practical use for a hunter to attract turkeys, although this author has used it to encourage an already alarmed gobbler to hesitate a few seconds before flight to facilitate a clear shot. All too often novice hunters think that they are making a *"cluck"* when actually they are making an *"alarm putt"* sound. Such hunters eat very little wild turkey.

"Alarm Pit-Pit": This call has little hunting application but should be understood by hunters. Alarm pitting happens when a predator has been seen but is not an immediate threat. It warns all members of the flock and is often echoed by all members. The pit-pits become more frequent and louder as the threat grows. Lovett Williams believed that this echoing of pits might confuse a predator as to the specific location of birds. If a hunter hears the pit-pit alarm it does not necessarily mean his hunt is over. I have replicated this call in an attempt to slow the group pit-pit cadence and lessen the group anxiety level. A similar pit-pit call can be heard as turkeys fly to roost or fly down from roost communicating urgency, but not alarm. Turkeys will also make an occasional single *"pit"* sound periodically when going about normal daily activities. This sound is made when a bird of prey passes overhead, a stick pops, a dead tree limb falls, or any other minor alarm occurs.

"Cut": The loud *"cack"* sound of a cut is a versatile call that, if mastered, can help bag many turkeys. It is a call of excitement, aggression, or urgency to gather and usually occurs in rapid 2 to 3 note flurries. It must be used in its proper context and generally is executed at the beginning or end of a building series of yelps. It is used by many experienced hunters to locate gobblers, but with its use a hunter may be forced to seek cover quickly if a gobbler responds close by. Using such a call to locate turkeys will also divulge the hunter's location to any turkey in sight.

"Cackle/Fly Down Cackle": The cackle, a rapid succession of about 6 to 8 *"cack"* sounds, is most often performed by hens or young males and is a call of extreme excitement sometimes done while flying to or from the roost. Its sound carries for great distances and may serve the purpose of helping turkeys know where other nearby flocks are near dawn and dusk. During the 1980s this call became somewhat of a fad. To that point in time cackling had seldom been used, but quickly became the *"go to"* locator call for many hunters. It was great at making a turkey gobble, but not so great for calling one in. Before long, especially on heavily hunted public lands, turkeys got wise to this sound and gobbled less at its use. This call can be used to culminate a series of excited cuts and yelps producing occasional success, but might best be deployed in early mornings to encourage a roosted Tom not to linger in the tree. It can also be used to tell an evening roosted gobbler that *"I am roosted over here and will see you in the morning"*. Timing is everything in one's use of a fly up or fly down cackle. Experienced turkey hunters know that a turkey will usually fly to roost when the sun hits the horizon (sunset) and fly down just before the sun

first becomes visible (sunrise). In most cases, the cackle call should be used once at those exact times for best results.

"*Gobble*": The gobble is the most common vocal male turkey call during the spring. LSU researchers studying recorded spring sounds have determined that the intense sound created by a wild turkey gobble looks similar to that of a gunshot blast on a spectrograph. The gobble announces the presence and sometimes social status of a gobbler to other males and hens. As a lure used by hunters, use of the gobble call can often reduce chances for success. In other states where more turkeys occur, use by hunters of the gobble call can be more effective. In Louisiana this author has found about 1 in 10 gobblers can be called in using a gobble call. The remaining 9 will usually vacate the area or quit gobbling. Its effectiveness can be increased if you know the position of dominance of the bird being called. The most dominant gobblers are more likely to respond to a gobble call. I have tricked subdominant adult Toms by deploying a jake and a hen decoy then making a rather poorly executed gobble to a gobbler that is in sight of both of the decoys. However, this tactic does not always work. In addition, extreme caution must be used both on public and private lands when using a gobble call due to the ever present threat of hunters who fail to properly identify their target before shooting. Such people who tarnish the name of "*hunters*", all too often end up on news headlines after some tragedy has occurred.

"*Fighting Rattle/Purr*": This call can bring some gobblers running in while others respond with total indifference. It is a call of loud purring similar to sounds made when two raccoons fight. When turkeys fight this sound can last for a few seconds or several minutes. Incidentally, this can be a good time to approach closer as fighting gobblers have more pressing issues at hand than watching out for pesky hunters. I have experienced little success using this call except when hunting with another hunter after one gobbler from a group of gobblers is shot; another can sometimes be immediately called back into gun range for a second kill using the fighting purr call.

"*Feeding Purr*": This sound is a near constant call made by contented feeding hens. Its volume is very low and can seldom be heard by a hunter beyond 20 yards. It sounds almost like a purring cat but at a higher pitch. It is a good tool for hunters that have gotten a gobbler close, but not close enough. Most hunters that I have observed do not know how to successfully replicate this call or its volume because they have never heard it in the wild. Unknowingly, most attempting a feeding purr, are actually replicating a fighting purr or aggression purr.

An adult female "hen" wild turkey. Understanding her vocabulary can mean the difference between success or failure for a turkey hunter. (D. Moreland)

Adult gobbler strutting on Pearl River WMA. (J. Stafford)

"*Chump-Hum (Spitting & Drumming)*": Being able to recognize this non-vocal sound can improve hunting success tremendously. The first time I heard this sound as a boy I mistakenly thought it was someone working on an old truck a half mile away. I was convinced that this person was cranking his truck, giving it gas, then allowing it to die. Later, I found strut marks in a trail where the gobbler had been within gun range of me for some 30 minutes, just beyond some thick brush. The first time I took my wife to hunt a roosted gobbler one started drumming an hour before daylight within 30 yards of us. When I pointed out the sound to her in the predawn darkness, she replied "*there is no way on earth that sound is coming from a turkey. That sound is an oil well pumping far away*". After daylight when gobbling was heard from the exact same spot, she realized that I was right. No one really knows what process makes the first (spit) sound during strutting. Some have speculated that it is made by the rapid movement of the feathers cocked taunt just before the drumming sound. This author believes that the sound originates internally from the rapid inhalation or exhale of air from the lungs. Sometimes full or partial strutting turkeys will make this spitting sound without the accompanying drumming sound. The hum (drumming) believed to be an internal sound, reverberates in all directions. This author once witnessed a dying adult gobbler make this drumming sound for nearly 20 seconds as it exhaled its last breath. Within 3 feet of the bird, the sound was amazingly loud and I began frantically looking around as it sounded like a large truck was about to run over both of us. When hunting it is nearly impossible to course the exact location of the drumming sound, as it is a low frequency soundwave. This sound may have survival benefits as a non-verbal communication, especially in dense cover areas. No known replications of this sound are manufactured as a hunting call, nor is it clear if such a call would attract gobblers.

"*Wing Flap*": This sound is commonly heard when turkeys fly to and from the roost and if replicated correctly, can aid a hunter. Wing flapping can also be used by a hunter in conjunction with the fighting purr call to imitate a turkey fight. The frequency of wing beats (flaps) can communicate to other turkeys if the flight is urgent or routine. The volume can indicate the sex of the bird, with louder flapping indicating the heavier male. Learning when and how to replicate this sound can bring hunting success. To make such a call one can use an old turkey wing (the outer 10 primary feathers only), commercial wing flappers, a piece of canvas material, or simply use a hat against one's side. At sunrise this author has used wing flapping sounds many times, especially in heavily hunted areas to successfully bag turkeys. A purest might argue that this method is not *"calling"* a turkey, but I argue that a sound was made and the turkey responded favorably.

'Leaf Scratching/Footsteps": This too is a non-vocal sound used to attract turkeys. It simulates the sound of a feeding turkey. Experienced turkey hunters know that when a turkey scratches it often makes two scratches then a third to clear the leaves from a spot. This makes a *"scratch-scratch"* (pause) *"scratch"* sound with the first two scratches simultaneously followed by the last, after a one second pause. This can be repeated several times as needed. In very dry leaf conditions, one can also add a few walking steps by making smaller scratch sounds at the cadence of a man's normal walk. Using 4 to 6 steps at a time is likely enough.

Locator calls: There are any number of sounds and calls that will make a turkey *"shock gobble"*. From peacock calls to logging chains dropped in the bed of a truck, doves cooing to chainsaws, when turkeys are primed for gobbling, they will gobble at nearly anything. Many people use owl, hawk, pileated woodpecker, and crow calls. Owl calls work great in most areas but can be overused at some sites, making gobblers less responsive. I have seen other areas where hawk calls worked best. But both hawks and owls are predators of adult turkeys so don't be surprised if after using such the gobbler will be reluctant to come to that exact spot when you later begin to make turkey sounds. If using a hawk or owl call it is best to move several yards to another location before replicating turkey sounds. Using a crow call or pileated woodpecker call shocks, but is less threatening to turkeys. It is also this author's belief that turkeys occasionally follow crows to food sources and vice versa. Understanding and replicating the immensely complex crow vocabulary is daunting, but if one could master the crow food location call it could prove useful to turkey hunters.

A turkey's **posture and movements** speak volumes. Most hunters know that a strutting gobbler is slightly less aware of a hunter's movement than one not strutting. Experience teaches that there is a big difference in the level of awareness of a feeding turkey that lifts its head about once every 30 seconds compared to another that stands erect for 30 seconds. The first is likely to stay put for a while and the second will likely soon leave. An erect turkey that cranes his head over its back has seen something disturbing, while nearly every turkey hunter has witnessed the double wing tuck when a gobbler smells a trap, signaling his immediate departure from the scene. Even when not alarmed, turkeys will stand on their toes stretching their wings as a signal to the flock that it is time to move to another location. A dominant gobbler will walk quickly towards a subdominant bird if he gets too close to one of his hens. If the subdominant bird does not move away quickly enough, he will be reprimanded with spur or wing slaps. Williams (1991) reported males with slightly raised beaks as showing dominance, but this author has witnessed this behavior also in gobblers that have not yet become the dominant male of a group. Being observant of these subtle signs can increase one's understanding of the complex behavior of wild turkeys.

A hunter does not have to be masterfully skilled at making turkey sounds to be successful. Each day turkeys hear all sorts of strange sounds. If a poor call occurs or some other noisy mistake is made, simply cover the bad sound with another more skillfully executed call and always remember to be patient. Turkeys often move slowly and deliberately. My brother Bill once said the most useful turkey hunting advice I ever gave him was to wait as long as he could physically tolerate sitting at a single calling spot then wait 30 minutes longer.

Hunting turkeys in each Louisiana habitat region has its own unique challenges. Tactics can be similar and/or very different. Let's face it, in most cases hunting unmolested turkeys on private land can be much easier than chasing them on public land. On private land where there is little or no hunting competition, there is no urgency to rush turkeys by using high pressure tactics. Yet on other private lands where there may be considerable hunting pressure, turkeys can prove just as difficult to harvest as those on public lands. The following sections will address both public and private land hunting issues for each ecoregion.

Hunter Gene Miller using a wing bone turkey call. (L. Lewis)

East Gulf Coastal Plain Turkey Hunting Tactics

Southeast Louisiana's EGCP has experienced significant changes in the last few decades that make hunting turkeys more difficult than just a few years ago. In many areas the habitats where turkeys occur have become smaller and in some cases hunting pressure has greatly increased. Much of the remaining EGCP habitat today is found on large timber company hunting leases. These leases offer turkey hunting opportunities to its members, but short rotation timber management and lack of prescribed burning has reduced turkey carrying capacity compared to years past. Nonetheless, where river or creek bottom hardwoods remain relatively intact and timber activities create ample openings, turkeys have persisted. Within the planted pine forests of the EGCP, areas thinned produce relatively good brood habitat for the immediate nesting season post-thinning. In past years such areas would remain good turkey habitat in successive years with the regular use of prescribed fire.

Open hunting lands that once were common in the EGCP are all but gone. Current public lands within this habitat ecoregion have low turkey numbers that cannot satisfy current demands for turkey hunting. Relatively small private tracts where turkeys still exist require "*low impact*" hunting. This means subtle tactics with the intention of not pushing turkeys away from the property. Low impact hunting includes greatly limiting ATV use, parking vehicles on the edges of the property, and walking longer distances rather than taking a chance on spooking a turkey. Using binoculars before entering fields, staying out of interior forest where turkeys lounge during the day, and limiting exploratory jaunts during the hunting season, all aid in low impact hunting. Exploring is something better done during deer season and not during turkey season or the days leading up to turkey season. Listening for preseason gobbling is warranted but one should stick to main roads and trails while avoiding detection by turkeys at all cost. Absolutely no preseason calling should be done on small landholdings. Doing such will increase the likelihood of detection by turkeys and decrease later hunting success.

In more upland pine and mixed pine/hardwood areas of Washington, Tangipahoa, northern St. Tammany, St. Helena, East Feliciana, and northern Livingston parishes, turkeys will often be found near hardwood and pine transition zones at roosting time. Early in hunting season turkeys are still looking for residual acorns but begin

131

visiting openings more often. The cooler it is on a given morning, the greater their need for carbohydrates found in acorns. On warmer and inclement weather days, turkeys will spend more time in fields eating flowers, grass seed heads, grasses, forbs, and insects. During hot mid-day periods, they will seek somewhat open, shaded areas to lounge and cool down. Eight to 10-year-old pine plantations that have shaded out most of the underbrush are sometimes selected for this purpose due to their shade value. This is an example of how a small amount of a particular habitat feature, not usually considered desirable for wildlife habitat can serve a useful purpose. Another example might be a 10 acre, overstocked, 35-year-old pine stand in need of a thinning, but useful as a roosting area. Knowing where these unique and useful habitat features occur can help a hunter know where to hunt. Random calling should be limited on small EGCP private tracts as each call exposes the hunter to being spotted by a silent turkey. Every year hunters spook thousands of turkeys across the state unknowingly which makes those spooked turkeys much more difficult to hunt. Using a few leafy branches to create a blind at spots where turkeys can be expected to visit then calling with purpose can be more effective than moving about on such small acreage sites. Depending on how turkeys have historically reacted to decoys in your area will determine their value. I have found decoys to help and hinder depending on the situation. In very open places decoys can sometimes be less effective, while in more confined openings they seem more useful. When hunting with kids or inexperienced hunters, decoys are indispensable at diverting a wary gobbler's attention.

Knowing where turkeys gather after they leave the roost can greatly increase a hunter's odds of early morning success. Turkeys using *"small habitats"* can be very predictable in where they go and at what times during the day they visit such places. Game cameras and preseason *"listening"* can aid in determining these patterns. Limited habitat resources such as roost sites, food sources, and openings, limit options for turkey use. Remaining undetected while hunting small tracts is critical so as not to alter these predictable resource use patterns. It is better to allow turkeys to walk away on one day's hunt than to chance spooking birds off of the property. As long as habitat use patterns remain uninterrupted, the patient hunter has the advantage and will eventually bag his prize.

Within small habitats in the EGCP, using a locator call is often better than using a turkey call to locate gobblers. Most experienced hunters can recall at least one occasion of calling in the open to locate a gobbler then having one immediately appear from nowhere, only to spook. Especially in areas with low turkey numbers, one cannot afford *"buggered"* turkeys. With each foiled encounter that causes a turkey to fly or run away at top speed from a hunter, they become more difficult to call in. As a result, by mid-season many gobblers have become *"call proof"*. Once, while hunting with the late Kenny Morgan who had a rather unique sense of humor, he sent me to a large field in East Feliciana parish where I was guaranteed to see a gobbler. At 7 o'clock his promise came true and a big gobbler stepped into the field some 300 yards away. As I executed the most beautiful yelp ever heard, the gobbler turned and ran from the field as if shot at. When Kenny returned later that morning he simply smiled and said, *"I guess I should have told you I had an encounter or two with that bird already this season."*

Upper East Gulf Coastal Plain Turkey Hunting Tactics

Although the UEGCP ecoregion in West Feliciana and Thompson Creek uplands has experienced recent declines in habitat quality and turkey numbers, it still remains one of the best turkey hunting areas in the state. To the west the UEGCP skirts the food rich Mississippi River bottoms that transition sharply into loess bluffs. The bluff soils are highly fertile and the woods filled with abundant hardwoods mixed with other food sources. In spite of its good turkey numbers, the UEGCP can be difficult to successfully hunt. Two factors confound success, the widespread availability of good habitat and higher turkey numbers themselves. Turkeys of this area are not as subject to site fidelity issues of other regions of the state and they will range on any given day in any number of directions making hunting more difficult. The terrain also offers seclusion just over every hill, and increased turkey numbers make luring a Tom quite difficult at times. The severe terrain limits hunter access further giving turkeys the advantage. If this author were a turkey, the UEGCP is where I would choose to live due to the fact that this habitat works more to the turkey's advantage than any other I have seen in the state, with the possible exception of similar habitats found on Sicily Island Hills/J. C. "*Sonny*" Gilbert WMA area.

Public turkey hunting is limited in the UEGCP to the Tunica Hills WMA, most of which is lottery hunt only. Private lands are where the bulk of this region's habitat lies. Small, intensively managed hunting clubs populate the UEGCP where turkeys are highly prized.

As to tactics, calling can be deployed more frequently, since turkeys in the UEGCP may not hear calls at certain times of day due to the steep hills that limit the distance that sounds travel. Hunter movement is also more warranted in such habitats in an effort to locate turkeys. Turkeys may seek openings during the mid-day or simply feed in the hardwoods from dawn to dusk. However, during the early to mid-spring as temperatures warm gobblers will follow hens into more open habitats. Hunting near log roads, trails, dusting spots, cutovers, and fields can pay off. As in most areas throughout the state, rain will cause turkeys to seek fields, right of ways, or recently logged areas within the UEGCP. If a hunter does not mind getting wet, hunting in such conditions can pay off.

An often successful UEGCP tactic is to hunt oak ridges during dry mid-day periods, listening for scratching in the leaves. Food habit studies of this area indicate that turkeys seek out residual acorns throughout the hunting season. Finding and listening near oak feeding areas can help put a hunter close to a flock during mid-day hours when birds are often more likely to be lured by calling. At dawn and dusk, pressured turkeys are often conditioned to be wary of calling. Anytime that a midday gobble is heard, the hunter should know his odds of calling success are usually increased.

Setting up to hunt along food plots of clover or wheat can put a hunter where turkeys want to forage. This may seem to some as "*bushwhacking*", but it is really no different than hunting a favorite scratched-over oak ridge. Any hunter riddled with guilt can simply use his call periodically to clear his conscience.

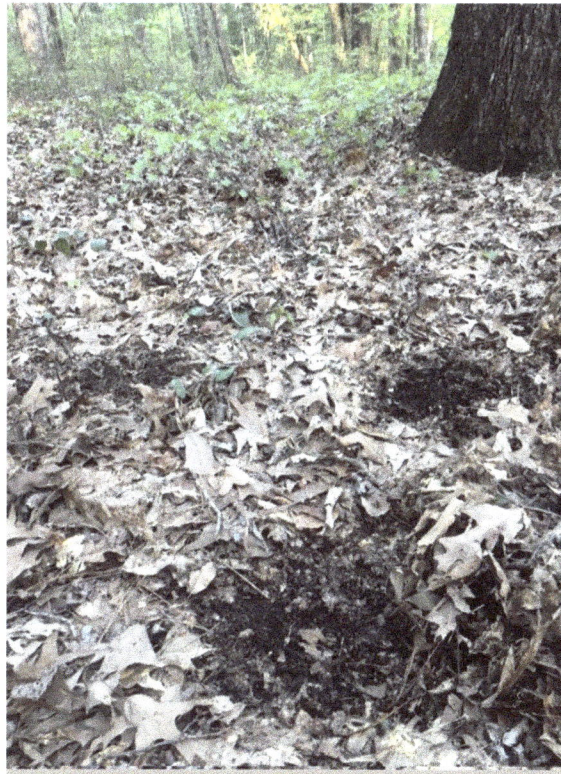

Turkey scratching sign under a cherrybark oak tree. Turkey scratching is often circular in shape and seldom disturbs the soil like certain other wildlife species such as squirrels, armadillos, and feral hogs. (J. Stafford)

133

Mississippi River Alluvial Plain Turkey Hunting Tactics

Similar to the UEGCP, the MAV bottomland forests can be a difficult place to be successful at hunting turkeys. Food sources usually abound during the spring and habitat features are often so similar that turkeys can be anywhere at any time. Within the MAV there are a few habitat features that hunters should take note of. Roosting habitat will often be in association with flooded timber. Although not always the case, turkeys in the MAV often roost over water. Oxbow lakes with cypress-lined edges make perfect roost sites. Forest-lined sloughs, bayous, rivers, ponds, streams, and wet areas are also common roosting spots and strategic locations to hunt at dawn.

Within the MAV, palmetto densities can influence where turkeys spend time. During dry periods, formerly flooded flats which are free of palmetto may be hot spots for turkeys even though the nearby ridges are choked with dense palmetto. These same sites may be void of turkeys during high water. One of the primary factors determining where turkeys will be in the MAV is how thick or how open the habitat is. Either extreme is not optimal. As a rule, areas that have 50% palmetto or other dense underbrush coverage are beginning to diminish as useful habitat. By 75% dense coverage, turkeys are at high risk of predation if relegated to using such sites. While hunting, a hunter should look for areas within hardwood forests with scattered palmetto and brush covering less than 50% of ground space. An exception to this is when hunting pressure or other disturbances cause turkeys to seek out the heavier palmetto/brush areas for refuge. MAV LDWF biologist and avid turkey hunter John Hanks reports that turkeys will inhabit low growing palmetto plant areas more often than tall growing palmetto plant areas; the lower growing palmetto allowing greater visibility for turkeys to avoid predators.

MAV sites are very fertile and can grow dense herbaceous groundcover such as goose grass, yellow-top, stinging nettle, and other plants growing as tall or taller than an adult turkey. Such dense groundcover can put a hunter at a great disadvantage. Setting up to hunt along more open dry sloughs, ridges, trails, or other openings will help improve the odds of hunting success. Food habit studies within the MAV indicate turkeys heavily use sweet pecans, acorns, vetch, clover, hackberry, American elm, and poison ivy seeds. Finding and hunting near such food sources can lead to success. The flatter and more open the habitat, the less movement hunters can make after dawn. Staying at a single location for longer periods will often result in hunting success within such open habitats. Hunters should be reminded that gobblers can easily pinpoint calling but may be very slow and deliberate on their approach. Longtime MAV LDWF ecoregion manager and turkey hunter Tony Vidrine jokingly told the author that his secret to successful turkey hunting along the Atchafalaya basin was to get to a good spot and set up his decoy, then call a while, sleep a while, wake up, and look for a turkey, then repeat these steps until a kill is made. Joking or not, Tony usually gets his bird.

Due to flooding, some sites close to major rivers within the MAV can lack ground cover and mid-story trees that provide hunters, as well as turkeys, with much needed concealment. Patience, camouflage, and sometimes a little trickery can be the ticket to success in such habitats. The late John T. Lincecum, MAV LDWF biologist and avid turkey hunter, once told the author that he climbed a tree, then wrapped himself completely in leafy vines to bag one old gobbler that several other good hunters had failed to kill in the open woods of Tensas parish. *"John T."* and other wildlife professionals working on the front lines of wild turkey restoration, became some of the first hunters to become infatuated by the challenge of wild turkey hunting as numbers increased.

A frequently flooded MAV forest lacking concealment cover (J. Stafford)

The MAV should soon see turkeys showing up in older CRP/WRP forested areas especially as they begin producing acorns and are managed through timber thinning. Savvy hunters first to take note of these expanding populations will be greatly rewarded.

West Gulf Coastal Plain Turkey Hunting Tactics

The WGCP in western and central LA. is the most reliable turkey hunting ecoregion in the state as it offers the largest and most secure habitat base of public lands. This quality habitat base feeds surrounding smaller private landholdings where turkeys also thrive. On private lands, hunting tactics mirror those described for southeast Louisiana EGCP and UEGCP ecoregions but on the larger WGCP public land base, tactics are slightly different.

The public lands of Kisatchie and various WMAs can be a challenge to hunt but have good turkey numbers, that make a gobbler encounter very likely. Pressured turkeys can quickly become *"call proof"*. This does not mean they become impossible to call but rather extremely difficult to call into gun range. Being observant of every sound that turkeys in the area are making gives a hunter clues to what is happening in the flock. It helps if the hunter attempts to imitate a separated member of the flock, calling only when appropriate for the time of day and member status of a given flock. Hunters can call at sunrise most days without causing alarm, however calling during later periods of the day on public land should have a clear purpose or doing such may actually prevent turkeys from traveling to your location. While hunting public land, I have sometimes in disgust referred to my old box call as my *"ETWD"* (Early Turkey Warning Device), meaning that turkeys hunted that day were more often repelled by my calling than attracted. If a public land flock has become scattered and a bird is nearby gobbling to recollect his hens, calling is definitely warranted. The key is paying close attention to calls made by other turkeys. Joining a turkey conversation can sometimes be better than trying to initiate a new conversation on public land. If the woods are quiet, calling should be very limited. Clucks and 2 to 3 note yelps, sporadically performed throughout the day, can sometimes be productive in high pressured areas. Assembly yelping just before roosting time can sometimes attract a silent gobbler, but as actual fly up time nears gobblers often become unreceptive as they seek a tree in which to roost for the night.

Locating gobblers on the roost the evening before helps the odds of success the next morning. Moving to within 100 yards of the roosted gobbler before dawn can put a hunter on public land in the game. Hunters should think like a turkey when selecting where to set up to hunt on a roosted gobbler. Considering the direction that he is likely to go that morning and the specific spot where he might land when flying from the tree can increase the likelihood of success. Turkeys often land in an opening or on a slight ridge where visibility is good during early morning low light conditions. It is not wise to set up to hunt in the opening itself or on the ridge top, but rather on the edge least you be forced to shoot the turkey as he tries to land in your lap. If birds are pressured, one can simply cluck or tree yelp just before fly down time then flap a wing several times and wait. This move often yields results within 1 to 30 seconds so be ready. If another hen begins to call at the gobbler, match her call for call. This sometimes aggravates the hen to the point of confrontation, leading a nearby gobbler into the fray.

Upper West Gulf Coastal Plain Turkey Hunting Tactics

In recent years the northwest Louisiana UWGCP has experienced some of the best turkey poult production found anywhere in the state. From the mixed hardwood/pine forests of east Morehouse parish to Natchitoches parish and north to Caddo, turkeys occur in varying densities. Relatively large forested blocks of mostly private and industrial forest lands, interspersed with numerous hardwood areas where openings abound, have resulted in good hunting in recent years. This area's habitat is much like the EGCP during the 1990s when it led the statewide turkey harvest. Parts of the UWGCP may still be in the post-restocking population expansion phase. Many years ago, I was concerned about potential problems facing a very large turkey population site hunted in Mississippi so I asked noted Mississippi State University turkey researcher Dr. George Hurst what management techniques would he recommend to prolong this bounty? Expecting some cutting-edge research based advice, George simply responded, *"Have fun shooting them."* He proceeded to explain that, *"you cannot stockpile turkeys"*. George pointed out that at some point a density dependent factor, outside of our control, would eventually reduce this turkey population. Not enjoying the day's bounty would be like watching fruit from a tree fall to the ground and rot. Today's good times in certain high population sites of the UWGCP should be taken advantage of, today.

The UWGCP has some public hunting but there are fewer areas now open than in past years and those open simply do not meet the large public demand for turkey hunting. With the recent loss of yet another popular turkey hunting WMA in this ecoregion, hunting pressure will likely increase on the remaining public lands. Gobbler mortality studies from 2000 – 2010 on private lands within the UWGCP indicated low gobbler harvest rates (low hunting pressure) but also indicated that harvest rates were gradually increasing with time.

Much of this ecoregion is covered with a substantial number of oil, gas, and electric rights-of-ways. Such openings, often used by turkeys make long distance (low impact) scouting easy. Further examination of such rights-of-ways for droppings and heavily tracked spots will indicate regular use by turkeys. Male droppings are most often linear in shape, about ½ inch in diameter, and up to 3 inches long. Many will have the classic "J" shape (Figure 63-left). While hen droppings are often deposited in small concise piles (Figure 63-right). Sometimes hen droppings can be linear but the diameter will be closer to 1/4 to 3/8 inch and seldom exceed 2 inches long. Such linear hen droppings usually lack the "J" shape. When having recently fed in clover, ryegrass, or other green fall/winter plantings, droppings of both sexes will have little shape and be the constancy of pudding. The size of the pile helps determine sex with the larger piles being more likely made by males. Hens can produce extremely large droppings during incubation recesses but this usually occurs late- to post-hunting season.

Figure 63: The drawing on the left is the typical shape of male droppings and on the right, female droppings.

Finding strutting sign indicates gobbler use of an area and many such spots are used repeatedly. The author has found that strutting spots are somewhat like bread, the fresher the better. Figure 64 is a drawing that illustrates wing markings found on the ground typical of a strutting gobbler.

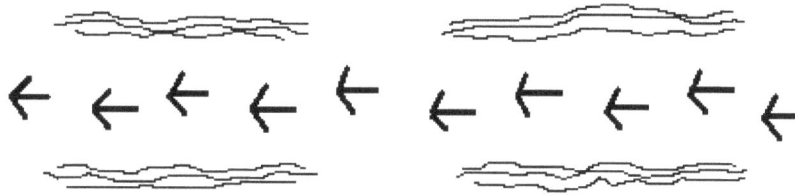

Figure 64: Drawing of wing drag marks left by a strutting gobbler.

Turkeys can be very transient in nature, moving over large areas. Since habitat in much of the UWGCP is good for turkeys over much of the landscape, site fidelity may be low. Again, low impact hunting tactics described earlier should be employed in this ecoregion to reduce turkey movement away to other lands. Limiting ATV and vehicle traffic is a good year around management tool also. Using gates or other barriers to further restrict access can increase turkey use of an area.

Since this part of the state can have more rigorous winters, green planted areas, especially in years of acorn mast failures, can be an asset to turkeys and hunters. Clovers and wheat attract best, but keep in mind that high deer densities may decimate such plantings for turkeys. Having larger acreages planted will help mitigate this competition for food. High hog numbers found in the UWGCP are more difficult to deal with and may render plantings of little value in certain areas. Aggressive hog control should be practiced wherever hogs occur.

Regardless of the ecoregion hunted, tactics can mean the difference between success or failure. Novice hunters emulating TV turkey hunting programs will often set up to hunt beside a tree in the wide open along a trail, field, or food plot. This does not often end well with Louisiana's keen-eyed wild turkeys. Remember, you are hunting in the turkey's living room and must blend seamlessly into the surrounding cover to avoid detection. Taking a few extra seconds to consider where to hide and where turkeys are likely to approach from, can mean everything. Building even a modest hunting blind can change the outcome of the day's hunt.

Throughout this writing a great deal has been said about achieving *"success"* or *"harvest"* while hunting. Yet even with success there can be a moment of sadness as we kneel beside a freshly harvested gobbler that dueled with honor. However, we should never feel guilt for harvesting a turkey, for it is the culmination of our labor. Often it is the unsuccessful or hypocritical turkey hunter who says, *"I don't hunt turkeys for the kill"*. If true, let that hunter leave his gun at home the next time he gets up at 3 AM to head to the turkey woods. The *"kill"* is not the sole reason we hunt nor should we consider our day a failure if it does not result in a harvest, but it is a primary goal. Nevertheless, I am reminded of a wise quote by Tom Kelly from the book *Tenth Legion*, *"Killing turkeys is fun. But there is a far more satisfying feeling in driving home, drinking the last cup of coffee you have saved from daylight, and knowing he is still out there in the early sun, feathers gleaming as if he were freshly oiled, light and quick and wild, rather than a bundle of meat and feathers stiffening on the floor in the back seat."* (Kelly 1973).

Respect of the Bird

Edward A. McIlhenny often referred to the wild turkey as a *"Noble Bird"* in his 1914 book about turkey hunting. This no doubt born out of his respect of this greatest of game birds. Most who have long pursued the wild turkey have great respect for it. Each hunting season wild turkeys in Louisiana are a finite resource and in some areas quite rare. Being blessed to harvest one is very special and most hunters I know, including the author, offer a prayer of thanks each time they lay hands on a freshly taken bird. Some new to the sport have not yet matured to this level of respect for the bird. Maybe they think that the wild turkey is no different than every other game species they have hunted or maybe they have not yet had an old Tom gobble in front only then to sneak to within 10 feet behind and flush. This, quicker than anything, will grow one's respect of the wild turkey. Such novice hunters may also be encouraged to heed shameful ammo advertisements that tout their products to kill turkeys at 70 yards or more. Encouraging hunters to shoot turkeys at such long ranges has caused many to be crippled only later to be eaten by predators hours or days following the ill-advised shot. Just because one's gun can poke holes in a paper target at 70 yards does not mean that the pellets have the energy to penetrate deep enough to consistently make clean kills. When hunting with most 12 gauge shotguns, turkeys should be shot at 35 yards or less. If on target, shooting at this range is effective almost 100% of the time. It has been this author's experience that with each 5-yard increase in distance, one's chance of a kill drops by about 10% (Figure 65). Shooting a turkey at any range beyond 90% effective range is not giving this precious resource the respect it is due.

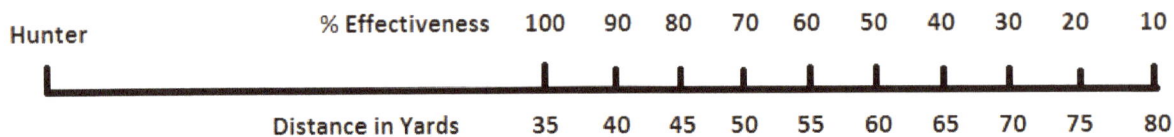

Hunter	% Effectiveness	100	90	80	70	60	50	40	30	20	10
	Distance in Yards	35	40	45	50	55	60	65	70	75	80

Figure 65: Effective turkey harvest range percentages based on the author's experience using various 12 gauge 3 ½" turkey loads

Passing up a long shot is not only the ethical thing to do, but it is the smart thing to do also. A crippled bird is likely out of the game for the entire season but a passed bird is there to hunt the very next day. That single bird can continue to provide enjoyment for many people for many hunts until harvested if not wasted with a bad shot.

It also goes without saying that a hunter must never shoot at a turkey through brush where it is not clearly identifiable. This can cause other turkeys to be killed in the same shot and even worse, an unidentified target can result in another hunter being shot. Louisiana has had a fairly good turkey hunting safety record in recent years, but when accidents occur, it is almost always one hunter shooting at a target that has not been clearly identified.

I once heard it said that *"a sportsman is simply a hunter with a good place to hunt"*, meaning that one with many opportunities to kill is more likely to be more *"sporting"*. There is some truth to this statement, but a genuine sportsman or sportswoman is one who does not stoop to nefarious tactics even when game is scarce.

Any time that this author starts talking about hunter ethics, I get a little uncomfortable as I am reminded of John 8: 7. *"…He who is without sin among you, let him cast the first stone…"* (KJV *Holy Bible*). If it is a legal tactic, however dastardly, this author has used it in the past. From roost shooting to bushwhacking I have done it all during a lifetime of hunting turkeys. However, if we respect the bird, each of us must always be maturing in the practices of fair chase and good sportsmanship. Experience has taught me that those turkeys harvested through nefarious methods have little meaning compared to the memories of those harvested (or not) when I acted as a true sportsman. May we all continue to grow in respect of The Bird.

Let us also guard against harvesting turkeys for the sheer trophy value. It saddens me to see hunters harvest a gobbler, then immediately roll it over to see if its beard and spurs measure up to trophy status. Even worse is when they think less of a bird that does not meet these standards even though mere seconds earlier it provided them with an exhilarating rush of excitement. Each harvest is a blessing from God and should be treated as such regardless of its chest and leg ornaments.

We must also respect one another. When another hunter is first to a gobbling bird, it is our responsibility to give that hunter space to work the bird without interference. If he manages to harvest the bird, we should be happy for his success and acknowledge such as a fellow participant of this great sport. We must also respect property boundaries as we would have others respect ours.

A big part of respecting the bird is abiding by game laws. This means following daily and season bag limits designed to share this great resource with others and ensure that there are plenty of older birds around during those poor hatch years. Not hunting around bait goes without saying, as only a pathetic excuse for a turkey hunter would stoop to such tactics. Tagging and reporting all harvested turkeys is the duty of every turkey hunter in order to help biologists better manage the resource. Today, Louisiana has a glaring weakness in both the baiting law and the tag validation law that allows many to skirt the system to the detriment of wild turkeys. The *"200 yards from the bait"* rule in effect today allows turkeys to be killed by the aid of bait. It is the opinion of this author that bait should be completely prohibited in all turkey hunting areas from March – April. As for tagging and tag validation, this should at a minimum come with much greater penalties if violated. Louisiana could learn much from other states that require harvested turkeys to be checked in on the same day of harvest. This would close a huge loophole in law enforcement of tag validation compliance.

Out of respect for every turkey ever harvested, my desire would be to have each one mounted as a lasting tribute to the hunting experience and the individual beauty of each bird. The reality is, however, that financial limitations and a wife with very different home decorating tastes prevents this from becoming reality. Nonetheless, finding ways to utilize every turkey after the harvest is just one more way to give it the respect it is due. First and foremost is to fully utilizing the meat. Often among those who have never eaten wild turkey I hear it said, *"wild turkey is not as tasty as domestic turkey"*. I strongly disagree. While domestic turkey can sometimes taste somewhat bland, wild turkey has much more flavor. It can be prepared in numerous ways from frying to smoking, each appealing to differing pallets. Hunters should utilize all edible portions of every turkey harvested as any form of waste diminishes its value.

Besides the retention of beards and spurs by most turkey hunters, utilizing feathers is another form of respect. Feathers can be used for a variety of purposes including wall decorations, wreaths, jewelry, arrow fletchings, and countless other purposes. Figure 66 is an example of a very inexpensive method for hunters to preserve the feathers of a harvested wild turkey. It involves simply cutting a line from the major caruncles to the anal vent then another perpendicular cut from wing to wing. Removing the head, carefully separate the skin from the flesh. The wing bones are maintained but are stripped of muscle and fat. Then tack the feather-side down tightly against a plywood board, using borax, salt, or commercial taxidermy preservative to treat all of the exposed under skin. Once the skin is dried, simply reverse and tack onto a smaller board for display. The following display is 25 years old yet still preserves the memory of the hunt and the full beauty of this turkey's feathers.

Figure 66 (J. Stafford)
139

Hunter Chad Bowen tags and later validates a Winn parish gobbler. (L. Lewis)

The Future of Wild Turkeys in Louisiana

Wild turkey numbers are strong at several sites across the state. A hunter can still find places in Louisiana where a half dozen or more gobblers can be heard on a clear spring morning. But could the wild turkey ever go the way of the bobwhite quail in Louisiana? The simple answer is yes. Bobwhite quail, which were once very common, are still present across the state but in numbers generally too small and scattered to draw hunters to the sport. Their demise was the result of widespread habitat degradation over time. In many places where quail still occur in reasonable numbers today, the few quail hunters remaining no longer have free hunting access to such areas. Currently, turkey habitats are also suffering widespread degradation and access to hunting areas are rapidly diminishing in much of the state. Recent harvest information indicates declining trends in turkey population monitoring indices throughout much of the state. Louisiana turkeys are highly dependent on large contiguous forest blocks that are slowly being carved away in many areas where declines have been observed. Louisiana's alluvial bottomland forests have also diminished in value to turkeys due to increasing flood frequency. If turkeys are to be hunted in Louisiana well into the future, we must find new ways to restore and maintain large forested blocks of timber. These forests cannot simply be restored and left idle, but must be managed by practices friendly to turkeys. Wildlife managers must also identify connective corridors important to turkeys where additional enhancement and maintenance emphasis can be prioritized. Improved hydrological considerations of leveed areas, waterways, and transportation projects, must be considered to reduce bottomland hardwood flooding. Without deliberate actions to restore the quality of turkey habitats across the state, incremental declines will continue, which will result in further decreases in wild turkey numbers.

It is of vital importance for the perpetuation of the sport of turkey hunting that more public lands be secured for turkey management and turkey hunting. In recent years the LDWF has lost multiple leased WMAs that once provided great public turkey hunting opportunities. Another need is for more USFWS lands to be opened to turkey hunting opportunities. The ecoregions most in need of upland turkey hunting grounds are southeast Louisiana's EGCP, UEGCP, and northwest Louisiana's UWGCP. Other ecoregions, such as the MAV bottomlands, would benefit from more public hunting areas which would further enhance black bear restoration corridors. West-central Louisiana's WGCP could use more LDWF owned lands to offset the lack of management control on leased and federal lands. However, the ECGP, UEGCP, and UWGCP are in direst need of public hunting lands to act as wild turkey reservoirs and proximal turkey hunting areas within these landscapes that are becoming increasingly fragmented. The rational for acquiring new public lands is further justified to the general public by the suite of imperiled species that would also benefit from such well managed upland habitats. If possible these lands should be purchased by LDWF and not leased. Only by combining the interests of wild turkeys with other state species of concern can such large expenditures for public land acquisition gain widespread support. Pittman-Robertson (PR) funds raised through excise taxes on sporting equipment help fund state wildlife agencies. These funds have produced more money than ever in recent years. Although *"PR"* funds cannot be used for land purchases, they can, if matched with 25% state funds, be used for the management expenses of new WMAs. Other funds are set aside for wild turkeys through the special turkey hunting license and the wild turkey specialty vehicle license plate. These funds have within their dedicated language that they may be used for land acquisition. Current funds in this dedicated account are insufficient to buy significant acreage. It is vital that Louisiana politicians refrain from raiding these *"dedicated"* accounts in times of general fund shortages. Wild turkey conservationists must be on guard for such misusage of dedicated turkey funds and hold elected officials accountable. These important wild turkey funds, if coupled with other more substantial funding sources, can make new land acquisitions for turkey management a reality. Should leasing of critical turkey habitat prove the only near-term option, then such an option should be employed without delay.

With the purchase of a wild turkey specialty license plate, funds are raised for wild turkey land acquisition, research, restocking, and management (Figure 68).

Figure 68: Louisiana wild turkey specialty license plate (LDWF)

Local, state, federal, industrial, and private groups must work together to solve the many issues facing wild turkeys and other species of concern today. This requires partnerships that in the past may have been avoided. All partners must be honest and willing to be flexible for the greater good of wildlife. We must be forever vigilant that turkey management efforts focus on HABITAT and net large acreage results.

Another consideration today is that turkeys are pursued with an ever evolving technological arsenal of tools compared to just a few decades ago. Hunters use decoys, some of which now move by automation and are covered with real turkey feathers. We use Ghillie suits, iPhones, GPS, 2 way radios, mirror blinds, thermal imaging, night vision, battery powered UTVs, 3 1/2" shotgun shells, and drones. Rather than simply turkey hunting, it seems as if we are more equipped to take out some high level terrorist. Turkey managers must be vigilant in monitoring technology and its efficacy in conservation. There may come or may have already come a point where a line should be drawn in the sand to maintain traditional fair chase principles and protect the resource from overexploitation.

It is important for turkey hunters to stay involved in conservation. This can be in the form of membership and active service in non-governmental organizations that advance science based conservation practices. One organization at the forefront of wild turkey conservation is the National Wild Turkey Federation. Supporting the NWTF and other science based conservation groups can help place limited funding for wildlife where it is most beneficial. Keeping abreast of governmental agency policies and their effect on wild turkeys and the tradition of turkey hunting, as well as participating in the public comment process when needed, helps the cause of wild turkey conservation. Last but not least, simply sharing the turkey hunting experience with others can mean a great deal for the future of the sport. The following emblem and slogan of the NWTF is quite appropriate for wild turkey enthusiasts.

Turkey hunters sometimes act selfishly by not encouraging others to join the sport since the resource is quite limited. The thought being that there are already too many turkey hunters in the woods pursuing too few turkeys, so w*hy add more?* Unfortunately, a sport that does not recruit new users is destined to fade away. Sharing our sport, especially with the young or inexperienced hunter, is one of the greatest actions we can take to ensure its future. Based on a recent survey, recruiting younger people into hunting increases hunter avidity and hunter retention (Responsive Management/National Shooting Sports Foundation 2008). The increase in youth hunting opportunities in Louisiana during recent years has been one of the most important steps taken in preserving the sport of turkey hunting for the future. Besides the lifetime benefits offered youths, the rewards gained by those who take youths hunting are priceless (Figure 67). In 1959 a turkey hunter named Ted Williams from Bush, Louisiana shared his time and experience with a young school teacher named James Stafford who later shared turkey hunting with his two sons and many others. The details of this first turkey hunt in 1959 were recorded by my Dad shortly after the event. This story is found in Appendix H.

Figure 67

Left Danny and Dustin Neilson, center Brandon and Jimmy Stafford, and right Anna and Robert Helm (J. Stafford and LDWF file photo).

Turkey populations exist in a precarious state of existence based on habitat conditions. Their existence is greatly influenced by the activities of man and is highly dependent on annual production. If we take for granted that good hatch years will always occur to bolster numbers, we are fooling ourselves. Managers must take into consideration that successive poor hatch years will come. If enough such years follow one another in succession, turkey numbers can decline dramatically to critical lows that may not rebound. Failing to anticipate and manage appropriately for such inevitable occurrences can have disastrous results. Today diminishing habitat quality would likely render any new restocking efforts far less effective than past restoration efforts. Therefore, it is essential that we take care of the turkey resources we have now. The turkey hunting public should stay involved and support sound biologically based wild turkey management decisions aimed at sustaining quality hunting through both the good and bad times.

A future hunter with his first turkey call at an NWTF "JAKES" event. (Loyd Stafford)

<u>What Matters Most</u>

God and Country

Wild turkeys are a special bird and turkey hunting a total thrill to experience, but in the end like any other favorite activity, simply a wonderful game that we enjoy in this short life. As author, I debated whether or not appropriate to bring that which is spiritual into a book about wild turkeys. However, this debate was brief, as I consider it inexcusable not to write about that which is so important. Some might find it unusual that a biologist (scientist) could be influenced by that which cannot be seen, but I am not alone. *"For His invisible attributes, namely, His eternal power and divine nature, have been clearly perceived, ever since the creation of the world, in the things that have been made…"* Romans 1:20 (ESV *Holy Bible*). Today, one can find other scientists, as well as sportsmen and sportswomen all over the world, that unashamedly profess one God and one Savior. For it is among those who spend the greatest amount of time afield, observing how nature interacts so perfectly, who most clearly recognize God's glory. There would be no love for our fellow man if we kept this knowledge to ourselves.

Mankind has an inherent desire to seek truth. It is this quest for truth that leads one to God. Yet sometimes our pride and intellectual arrogance prevents us from seeing the simplest truth. After living for a few years, which in fact is but a single grain of sand in time, man tries to use human reasoning to rationalize that which is so much greater than our brief existence. In Matthew 11: 25 Jesus said, *"I praise you, Father, Lord of heaven and earth, because you have hidden these things from the wise and learned, and revealed them to little children"* (NIV *Holy Bible*). There are many world *"religions"* that point to past individuals for direction. Many of these religions encourage rituals, obedience, and zealotry. Some share similarities, while others go in very strange directions. I have and continue to seek the truth, and have found that deep truth recorded in only one place, the *Holy Bible*. There are millions of books in the world but none like this one. Though exposed to this book's words in brief passages during childhood, it was not until years later that its primary truth was revealed. The truth being that God has a plan not just for the world, but for each human life. In my quest for truth and its wisdom, I have been amazed by how words written thousands of years ago are alive and true today. Only God could inspire such accurate and insightful words. And if His words are true, then there is but one path to His grace: Jesus Christ. Acts 4:12 states, *"Salvation is found in no one else, for there is no other name under heaven given to men by which we must be saved."* (NIV *Holy Bible*). Jesus himself said *"I am the Way, the Truth, and the Life. No one come to the Father except through me"* (John 14: 6 ESV *Holy Bible*). If you have not read this book called the *Holy Bible*, you are missing the pathway to the greatest gift in life. Jesus instructed, *"Come unto me, all ye that labor and are heavy laden, and I will give you rest"* (Matt. 11:28 KJV *Holy Bible*). This call remains open to all who seek Him today.

One can see in nature God's perfection. In nature, even that which we as humans see as imperfect has perfection as its final result. God is sinless and flawless, while man is fallen by his own pride and sin. God's plan for the redemption of mankind and to show his love came in the form of His son. Jesus Christ lived as a man on earth yet He was still God. Proof of his deity came in the words he spoke and the many miracles he performed. He was tempted like us, yet never sinned. He willingly allowed himself to be put to death by men as payment for our sins, while his many followers hid during his tortuous death on the cross. But in 3 days, as prophesized hundreds of years earlier, he arose to life showing himself to his disciples and more than 500 people. Much of the New Testament of the *Holy Bible* was written by these changed men who documented what they saw, heard, and experienced firsthand. None sought to elevate themselves and most were martyred for their testimonies, yet each continued to unashamedly profess Jesus as Lord to the end. To not read these recorded words and deeds of Jesus Christ, if for no other reason than curiosity, is unconscionable.

"Behold, I stand at the door and knock: If anyone hears my voice, and opens the door, I will come in to him, and sup with him, and he with Me" (Rev. 3: 20 KJV *Holy Bible*).

In my youth, I mistakenly thought that the greatness of our country was in the superiority of *"American know how"*. That Americans were just somehow smarter than the rest of the world. As a kid I watched as the United States put Neil Armstrong on the moon. I later found out that without scientists and technology from other countries, this would not have been possible. As an observer of world history's successes and failures, I now know that what makes this country great is freedom and God's blessing. Freedom ordained by God and penned in the Constitution by our founding fathers is the basis for America's greatness. For without this guarantee of freedom, the many great minds that have come to this country would have never sought refuge here, nor would they have had the freedom to think and act independently. Freedom is the impetus of innovation, not some attitude or self-determined superiority. This great Constitution inspired by God's precepts also granted us freedom of choice to worship Him or not. When this country has freely sought to emulate God's character and follow His will, it has prospered. When it has not, the country has rapidly declined. The *Holy Bible* and *Constitution* should be known and followed if freedom is to be maintained. *"But whenever anyone turns to the Lord, the veil is taken away. Now the Lord is the Spirit, and where the Spirit of the Lord is, there is freedom"* (2 Cor. 3: 16 – 17 ESV *Holy Bible*).

Family, Friends, and Fun

Turkey hunting is most often *"A One Man Game"* as the late Kenny Morgan's first book titled it. Although hunting alone can be rewarding, the many rewards from enjoying that one-man game with others, can be even greater. For no one but a fellow participant will regale the experience of a particular hunt through time with equal fondness. The bond that occurs while hunting with someone else is like no other. A unique understanding and trust comes from regularly hunting with a friend or family member. Conversations among hunters rarely contain social pretense, but rather express an earthy common purpose. While hunting we share each other's triumphs and failures, all the while learning what is most important in life to one another. These hunting experiences forever sear into our memory like no others. And as one matures we find that it is not where one travels, what one hunts, or what one does in life that makes it most memorable, but rather the precious time spent with those we care most about. The following snapshots capture such priceless memories of pure enjoyment hunting and spending time with close friends and family.

Figure 69 (J. Stafford, D. Moreland, S. Bible, L. Savage, J. C. Davis, & L. Lewis)

Author & Dad.   Author's wife Tina   Sons David & Brandon.

Mark Bible & author

Tony Vidrine & author

Dave Moreland

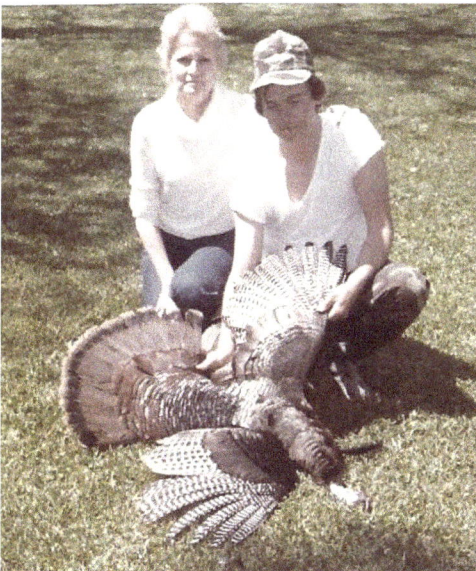

Author's Mom Lillian & author

Larry Savage

Len Bennett, author, & Cody Cedotal

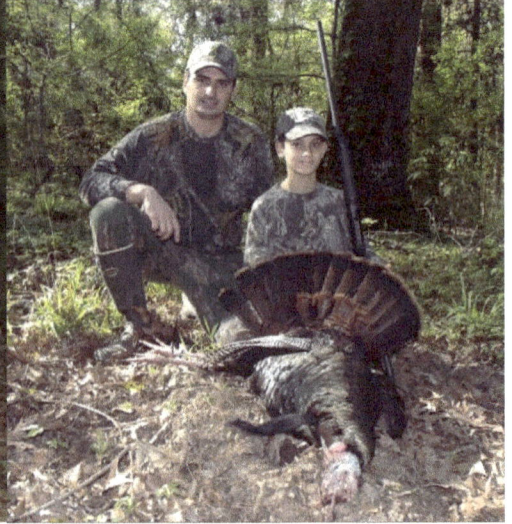

Author's daughter-in-law Jasmine   James "Chris" Davis   Randy & Connor Myers

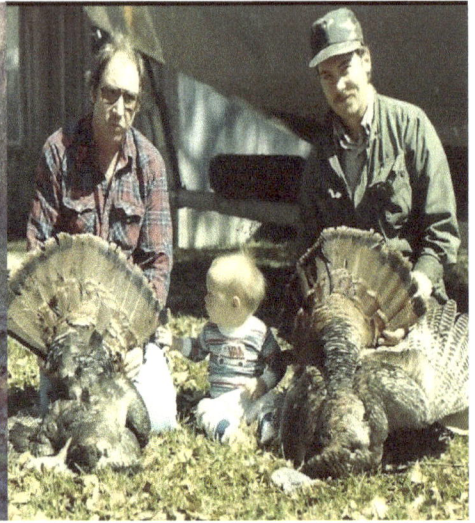

Author's Dad & Carey Bateman   Luke Lewis   Danny Timmer, Jason Bible, & author

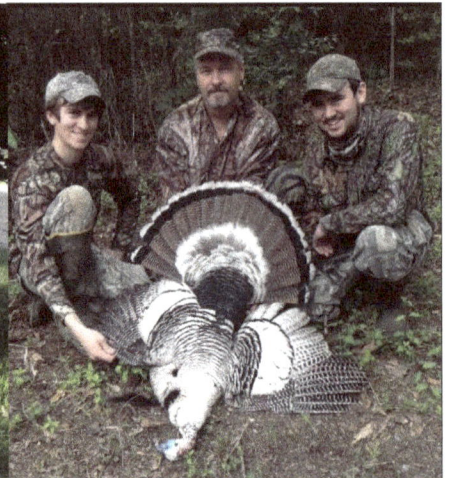

Tommy Arthur, author, Thomas Arthur,   Author & Dad   Son David, author, & son Brandon

& James Arthur.

Closing Remarks

The perfect spring day means different things to different people in Louisiana. To a bass fisherman, it might mean sunrise on Toledo Bend casting lures to spawning largemouth bass. To a baseball fan, it could be watching an LSU batter at Alex Box stadium having just hit a grand slam in the ninth inning for a come from behind win. While to a Louisiana turkey hunter it is first light near a cypress lined bayou as birds awaken, the cardinal's song leading the way, followed by an ever growing chorus of other birds. For a moment, one enamored by this great production might forget the primary purpose of the day. Then far in the distance a barred owl hoots and the thunder of a gobbler's reply less than 100 yards away reminds the hunter why he came. Suddenly, the mind races with thoughts of a lifetime of turkey encounters. Decisions of strategy are then intermingled with hopes for a close encounter. As the sun rises to illuminate the forest floor, skillfully placed calling and patience elicits the gobbler's appearance in full strut at 30 yards. It is this unforgettable heart pounding experience that turkey hunters of this generation and the next will hopefully enjoy in Louisiana for years to come.

Many game species are pursued, but few elicit the fanaticism exhibited by wild turkey hunters. The sport brings with it more excitement and reward than any other I have found. Those that are not members of this elite clan simply do not understand its allure. Until one has engaged in battle at close quarters with this respected adversary called the wild turkey, he or she can never fully appreciate the experience. I have witnessed strong men tremble uncontrollably and women tear up with joy at the close encounter of a Louisiana wild turkey. I challenge those that might consider such reactions nonsense to simply give turkey hunting a try!

There is probably no more eloquent nor accurate a description of the thoughts and feelings a turkey hunter experiences when encountering a wild gobbler at close range than that given by noted author Tom Kelly in his book *Tenth Legion*. It is most fitting to end this writing with his insightful words.

"The first turkey that ever came to me on the ground did it a long time ago. I sat there with my hands shaking and my breath short and my heart hammering so hard I could not understand why he could not hear it. The last turkey that came to me last spring had exactly the same effect, and the day that this does not happen to me is the day that I quit. The last one that ever does come to me will call forth the same emotion that the second one did. I will sit there waiting, gun up and heart thundering, and say to myself what I have said on every single occasion since the second one, 'I'm glad I lived to see it one more time.'" (Kelly 1973)

(D. Moreland)

Appendix

Appendix A: Turkeys trapped in Louisiana and out-of-state 1962-2016. (LDWF)

Year	Louisiana Source	Other State Sources	Totals
1962	1		1
1963	24		24
1964	9		9
1965	50	Florida 47	97
1966	39	Alabama 9; Mississippi 4	52
1967	58	Florida 64; Mississippi 10	132
1968	6	Mississippi 32	38
1969	45	Florida 26; Mississippi 27	98
1970	146	Mississippi 13	159
1971	150		150
1972	179		179
1973	127		127
1974	66	Arkansas 15	81
1975	57		57
1976	56		56
1977	45		45
1978	68		68
1979	5	South Carolina 6	11
1980	82		82
1981	180	Mississippi 2	182
1982	34	South Carolina 19	53
1983	70	South Carolina 23; Arkansas 12	105
1984	12		12
1985	105		105
1986	13		13
1987	124	Missouri 23	147
1988	202		202
1989	183	South Carolina 18	201
1990	203		203
1991	134	Alabama 18	152
1992	59		59
1993	201	Wisconsin 88; Arkansas 10; Alabama 11	310
1994	119	Connecticut 17; Arkansas 5; Alabama 21	162
1995	67	Alabama 24; Iowa 12	103
1996	45	Iowa 97	142
1997	49		49
1998	29		29
1999	10		10
2000	14	South Carolina 60	74
2001		South Carolina 40	40
2004	14	South Carolina 20	34
2007	21		21
2008	7		7
2014	19		19
2015	6		6
2016	7		7
Totals	**3,160**		**753**

Appendix B

Louisiana Turkey Seasons 1902-2017 (H. D. Hollis & J. Stafford)

Year	Area	Season Dates	Season Length	Season Limit	Comments
1902		Nov.-March	151 days	none	No daily or season limit-either sex
1903		Nov.-March	151 days	none	No daily or season limit-either sex
1904		Nov.-March	152 days	none	No daily or season limit-either sex
1905		Dec.-March	121 days	none	Daily bag limit=25-gobblers only
1906		Dec.-March	121 days	none	Daily bag limit=25-gobblers only
1907		Dec.-March	121 days	none	Daily bag limit=25-gobblers only
1908		Dec.-March	122 days	none	Daily bag limit=25-gobblers only
1909		Nov. 15-April 15	151 days	none	Daily bag limit=25-gobblers only
1910		Nov. 15-April 15	151 days	none	Daily bag limit=25-gobblers only
1911		Nov.-April 15	166 days	none	Daily bag limit=1-gobblers only
1912		Nov.-April 15	167 days	none	Daily bag limit=1-gobblers only
1913		Nov. 15-March	136 days	none	Daily bag limit=1-gobblers only
1914		Nov. 15-March	136 days	none	Daily bag limit=1-gobblers only
1915		Nov.-Feb. 15	107 days	none	Daily bag limit=1-gobblers only
1916		Nov.-Feb. 15	107 days	none	Daily bag limit=1-gobblers only
1917		Nov.-Feb. 15	107 days	none	Daily bag limit=1-gobblers only
1918		Nov. 15-March	136 days	none	Daily bag limit=1-either sex
1919		Nov. 15-March	136 days	none	Daily bag limit=1-either sex
1920		Nov. 15-March	137 days	none	Daily bag=1-gobblers only Feb. 15-March
1921		Nov. 15-March	136 days	none	Daily bag=1-gobblers only Feb. 15-March
1922		Nov. 15-March	136 days	none	Daily bag=1-gobblers only Feb. 15-March
1923		Nov. 15-March	136 days	none	Daily bag=1-gobblers only Feb. 15-March
1924		Nov. 15-March	137 days	none	Daily bag=1-gobblers only Feb. 15-March
1925		Dec.-Jan.	62 days	12	Daily bag limit=1-either sex

1926		Dec.-Jan.	62 days	12	Daily bag limit=1-either sex
1927		March	31 days	5	Daily bag limit=1-either sex
1928		March	31 days	5	Daily bag limit=1-either sex
1929		March	31 days	5	Daily bag limit=1-either sex
1930		March	31 days	5	Daily bag limit=1-either sex
1931		March	31 days	5	Daily bag limit=1-either sex
1932		March	31 days	5	Daily bag limit=1-either sex
1933		closed			
1934		closed			
1935		closed			
1936		closed			
1937		closed			
1938		closed			
1939		closed			
1940		closed			
1941		closed			
1942		closed			
1943		closed			
1944		closed			
1945		April 1-15	15 days	1	Gobblers only from this season forward
1946		April 1-15	15 days	1	
1947		April 1-15	15 days	1	
1948		April 1-15	15 days	1	
1949		closed			
1950		closed			
1951		closed			
1952		closed			
1953		closed			
1954		closed			
1955		April 1-6	6 days	1	St. Tammany., St. Helena., Livingston., Tensas, Madison & part Washington parishes
1956		March 31-April 6	7 days	1	added Franklin & part East Feliciana
1957		April 5-7	3 days	1	
1958		March 29-April 2	5 days	1	reported harvest = 89
1959		April 2-8	7 days	1	
1960		April 2-8	7 days	1	other areas included as well as part of Morehouse

1961		April 8-16	9 days	1	
1962		April 7-15	9 days	1	
1963		April 6-21	16 days	1	
1964		April 4-19	16 days	1	
1965		April 3-18	16 days	1	
1966		April 2-17	16 days	1	
1967		April 1-23	23 days	1	
1968		March 30-April 21	23 days	2	
1969		March 29-April20	23 days	2	
1970		March 28-April 19	23 days	2	rifles prohibited for hunting turkey
1971		March 27- April 18	23 days	2	
1972		March 25-April 16	23 days	2	
1973		March 24-April 22	30 days	2	
1974		March 23-April 21	30 days	2	
1975		March 15-April 27	44 days	2	
1976	ABFG	March 27-April 25	30 days	3	
	C&D	March 20-April 25	37 days		
	E,I,&J	April 3-11	9 days		
	H&K	March 20-April 11	23 days		
1977	AB&C	March 26-April 24	30 days	3	
	D	March 12-April 17	37 days		
	E&G	March 26-April 10	16 days		
	F&H	March 19-April 10	23 days		
1978	ABCE	March 25-April 23	30 days	3	
	D	March 18-April 17	37 days		
	F&H	March 18-April 9	23 days		
	G	March 25-April 16	23 days		
	I	March 25-April 30	37 days		
1979	AB&C	March 24-April 22	30 days	3	
	D	March 17-April 22	37 days		
	E&I	March 24-April 30	38 days		
	F	March 17-April 8	23 days		
	GH&J	March 23-April 15	23 days		
1980	A,B,&C	March 22-April 20	30 days	3	
	D	March 15-April 20	37 days		
	E	April 5-30	26 days		

	F&G	March 22-April 13	23 days		
	H	March 22-April 30	40 days		
	I	April 5-13	9 days		
1981	A&B	March 28-April 26	30 days	3	
	C	March 21-April 19	30 days		
	D	March 14-April 19	37 days		
	E	April 4-30	27 days		
	F&G	March 21-April 12	23 days		
	H	March 21-April 26	37 days		
	I	April 4-19	16 days		
	J	March 21-April 5	16 days		
1982	AB&C	March 20-April 25	37 days	3	
	D	March 13-April 18	37 days		
	E	April 3-30	28 days		
	F&G	March 20-April 11	23 days		
	H	March 20-April 4	16 days		
1983	A,B&C	March 19-April 24	37 days	none	Season limit 1 gobbler per day entire season
	D	March 12-April 17	37 days		
	E	April 2-30	29 days		
	F,G&H	March 19-April 10	23 days		
	I	March 19-April 3	16 days		
1984	A	March 31-April 22	23 days	3	
	BC&J	March 17-April 22	37 days		
	D	March 10-April 15	37 days		
	E	March 31-April 30	31 days		
	FG&H	March 17-April 8	23 days		
	I	March 17-April 1	16 days		
1985	ABCH	March 23-April 21	30 days	3	
	D&F	March 16-April 21	37 days		
	E	March 30-April 28	30 days		
	G	March 23-April 14	23 days		
1986	ABGH	March 22-April 20	30 days	3	
	C	March 29-April 30	33 days		
	D&F	March 15-April 20	37 days		
	E	March 29-April 27	30 days		
1987	ABGH	March 21-April 19	30 days	3	
	C	March 21-April 26	37 days		
	D&F	March 14-April 19	37 days		
	E	April 4-30	27 days		

1988	ABGH	March 26-April 24	30 days	3	
	C	March 19-April 24	37 days		
	D	March 12-April 17	37 days		
	E	April 2-30	29 days		
	F	March 12-April 17	37 days		
	I	April 23-30	8 days		
1989	A	March 25-April 23	30 days	3	
	B	March 11-April 16	37 days		
	C	March 18-April 23	37 days		
	D	April 1-30	30 days		
	E	April 15-23	9 days		
1990	A	March 31-April 29	30 days	3	
	B	March 17-April 22	37 days		
	C	April 21-29	9 days		
1991	A	March 30-April 28	30 days	3	
	B	March 23-April 28	37 days		
	C	April 20-28	9 days		
	D	April 13-28	16 days		
1992	A	March 28-April 26	30 days	3	
	B	March 21-April 26	37 days		
	C	Closed			
	D	April 11-26	16 days		
1993	A	March 27-April 25	30 days	3	
	B	March 20-April 25	37 days		
	D	April 10-25	16 days		
1994	A	March 26-April 24	30 days	3	
	B	March 19-April 24	37 days		
	D	April 9-24	16 days		
	E	March 26-April 3	9 days		
1995	A	March 25-April 23	30 days	3	
	B	March 18-April 23	37 days		
	D	April 8-23	16 days		
	E	March 25-April 2	9 days		
1996	A	March 16-April 21	37 days	3	
	B	April 6-21	16 days		

	C	March 16-April 24	40 days		
1997	A	March 22-April 27	37 days	3	
	B	April 12-27	16 days		
	C	March 22-30	9 days		
1998	A	March 21-April 26	37 days	3	
	B	April 11-26	16 days		
	C	March 21-29	9 days		
1999	A	March 27-April 25	30 days	3	
	B	April 3-18	16 days		
	C	March 27-April 4	9 days		
2000	A	March 25-April 23	30 days	3	
	B	April 1-16	16 days		
	C	March 25-April 2	9 days		
2001	A	March 24-April 22	30 days	3	
	B	March 31-April 15	16 days		
	C	March 24-April 1	9 days		
2002	A	March 23-April 21	30 days	2	
	B	March 23-April 14	23 days		
	C	March 23-March 31	9 days		
2003	A	March 22-April 20	30 days	2	
	B	March 22-April 13	23 days		
	C	March 22-March 30	9 days		
2004	A	March 27-April 25	30 days	2	first private lands youth hunt-weekend before
	B	March 27-April 18	23 days		
	C	March 27-April 4	9 days		
2005	A	March 25-April 24	31 days	2	
	B	March 25-April 17	24 days		
	C	March 25-April 3	10 days		
2006	A	March 25-April 23	30 days	2	
	B	March 25-April 16	23 days		
	C	March 25-April 2	9 days		
2007	A	March 24-April 22	30 days	2	
	B	March 24-April 15	23 days		
	C	March 24-April 8	16 days		
2008	A	March 21-April 20	31 days	2	voluntary tagging instituted

	B	March 21-April 13	24 days		mandatory tagging instituted
	C	March 21-April 6	17 days		
2009	A	March 28-April 26	30 days	2	
	B	March 28-April 19	23 days		
	C	March 28-April 12	16 days		
2010	A	March 20-April 18	30 days	2	Plus 7 day fall hunt on Peason Ridge WMA
	B	March 20-April 11	23 days		
	C	March 20-April 4	16 days		
2011	A	March 19-April 17	30 days	2	youth lottery hunt on KNF Vernon unit
	B	March 19-April 10	23 days		
	C	March 19-April 3	16 days		
2012	A	March 24-April 22	30 days	2	Season changed back to opening day on 4th Sat. in March
	B	March 24-April 15	23 days		youth lottery hunts on Calcasieu Ranger District of KNF
	C	March 24-April 8	16 days		
2013	A	March 23-April 21	30 days	2	
	B	March 23-April 14	23 days		
	C	March 23-April 7	16 days		
2014	A	March 22-April 20	30 days	2	Open youth hunts on Caney, Calcasieu, & Kisatchie Ranger Districts of KNF
	B	March 22-April 13	23 days		
	C	March 22-April 6	16 days		
2015	A	March 28-April 26	30 days	2	Open youth hunts on all KNF Ranger Districts
	B	March 28-April 19	23 days		
	C	March 28-April 12	16 days		
2016	A	March 26-April 24	30 days	2	
	B	March 26-April 17	23 days		
	C	March 26-April 10	16 days		
2017	A	March 25-April 23	30 days	2	
	B	March 25-April 16	23 days		
	C	March 25-April 9	16 days		

Appendix C

Estimated Wild Turkey Nest Initiation Periods 1990-2004 in Southeast Louisiana
(J. Stafford 2004)
(268 BROOD OBSERVATIONS VISUALLY AGED 10 WEEKS OR LESS)

WEEK of HATCH	BROODS
1 FEB.-7 FEB.	1
8 FEB,-14 FEB.	2
15 FEB.- 21 FEB.	–
22 FEB.- 28 FEB.	3
1 MAR.- 7 MAR.	12
8 MAR.- 14 MAR.	6
15 MAR.- 21 MAR.	20
22 MAR.- 28 MAR.	22
29 MAR.- 4 APR.	35
5 APR,- 11 APR.	38
12 APR.- 18 APR.	31
19 APR.- 25 APR.	22
26 APR.- 2 MAY	24
3 MAY- 9 MAY	18
10 MAY- 16 MAY	9
17 MAY- 23 MAY	12
24 MAY- 30 MAY	9
31 MAY- 6 JUNE	2
7 JUNE – 13 JUNE	1
14 JUNE- 20 JUNE	1

*Note nest initiation dates determined by backdating 40 days from estimated hatch date.

Appendix D: Reported Turkey Harvest 2009 – 2015 (LDWF)

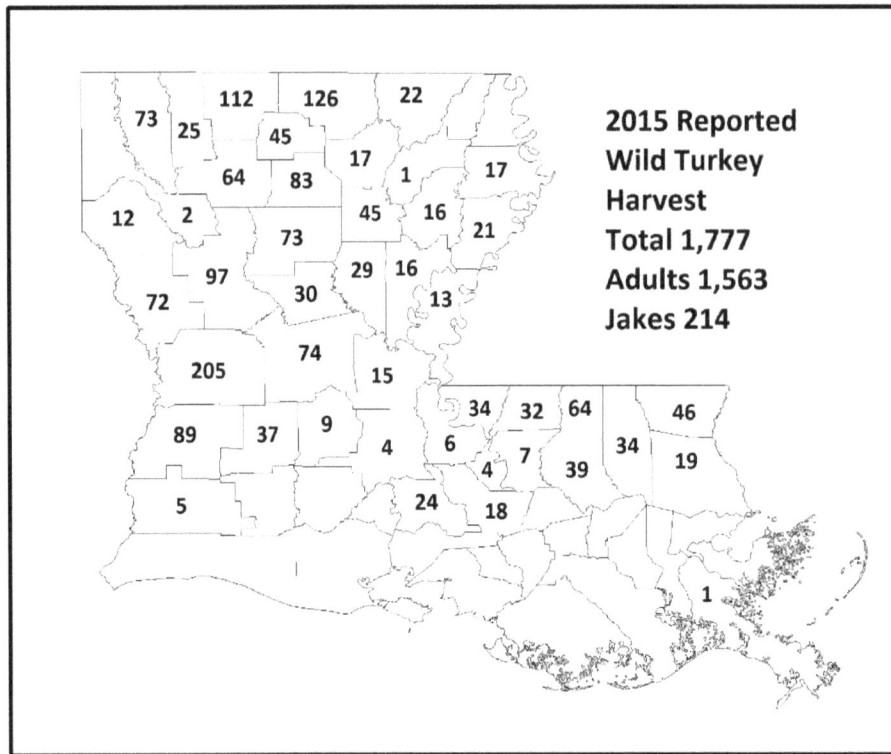

2015 Reported
Wild Turkey
Harvest
Total 1,777
Adults 1,563
Jakes 214

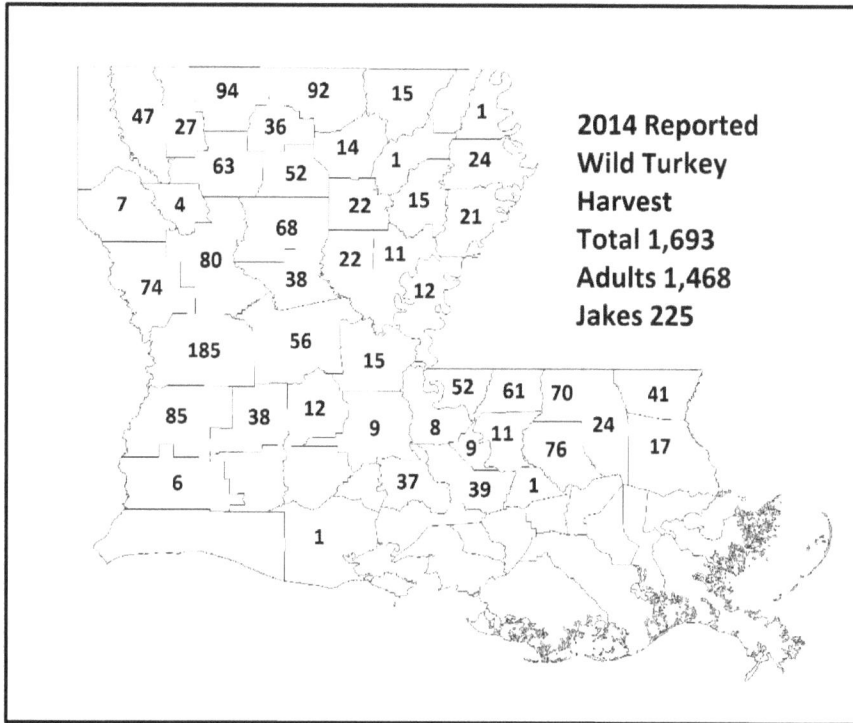

2014 Reported
Wild Turkey
Harvest
Total 1,693
Adults 1,468
Jakes 225

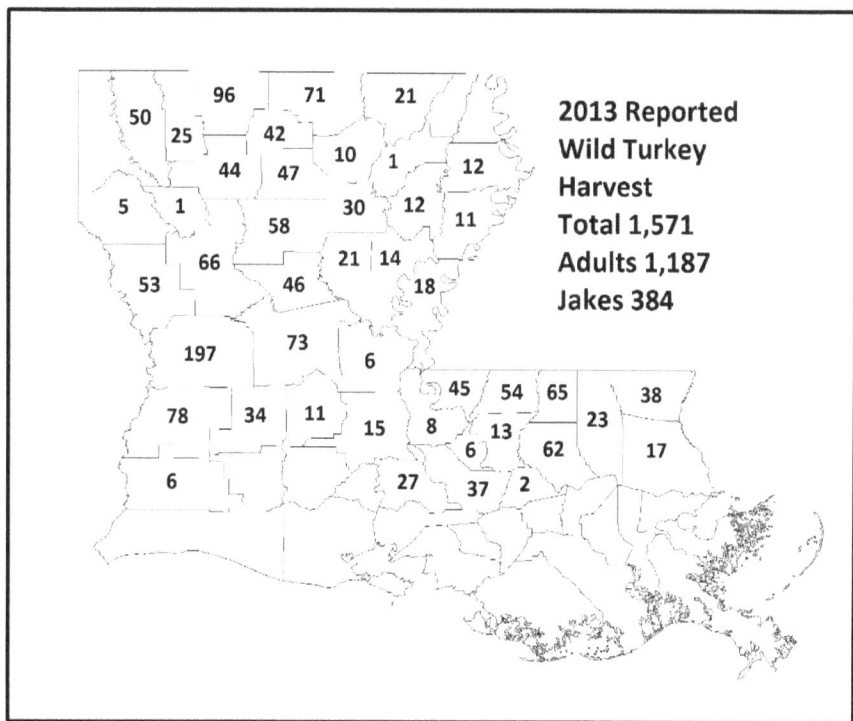

2013 Reported
Wild Turkey
Harvest
Total 1,571
Adults 1,187
Jakes 384

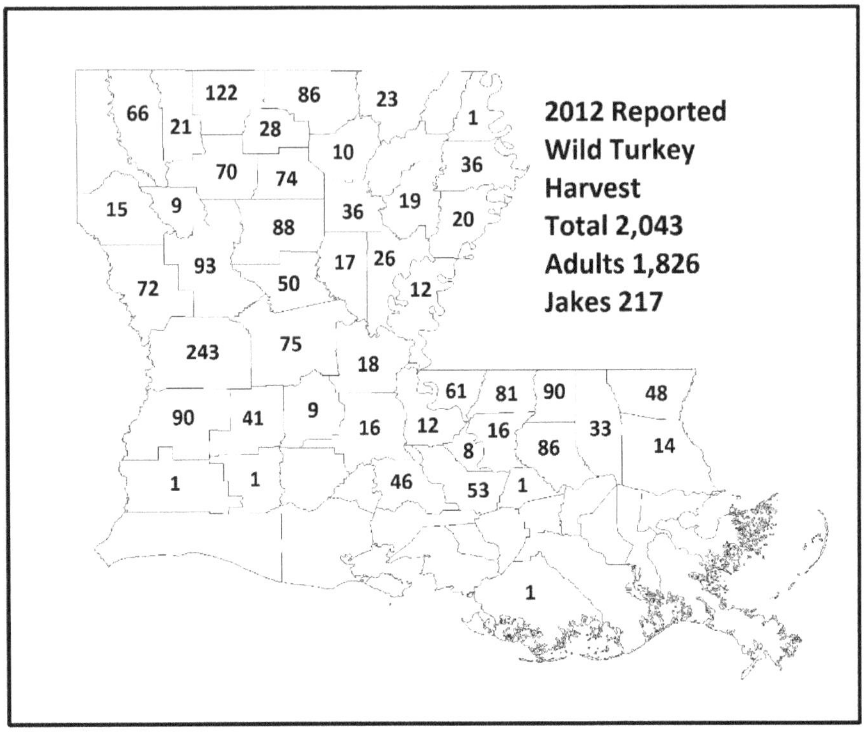

2012 Reported
Wild Turkey
Harvest
Total 2,043
Adults 1,826
Jakes 217
66
21
122
28
86
23
1
10
36
70
74
15
9
88
36
19
20
93
72
50
17
26
12
243
75
18
61
81
90
48
90
41
9
16
12
16
33
8
86
14
1
1
46
53
1
1

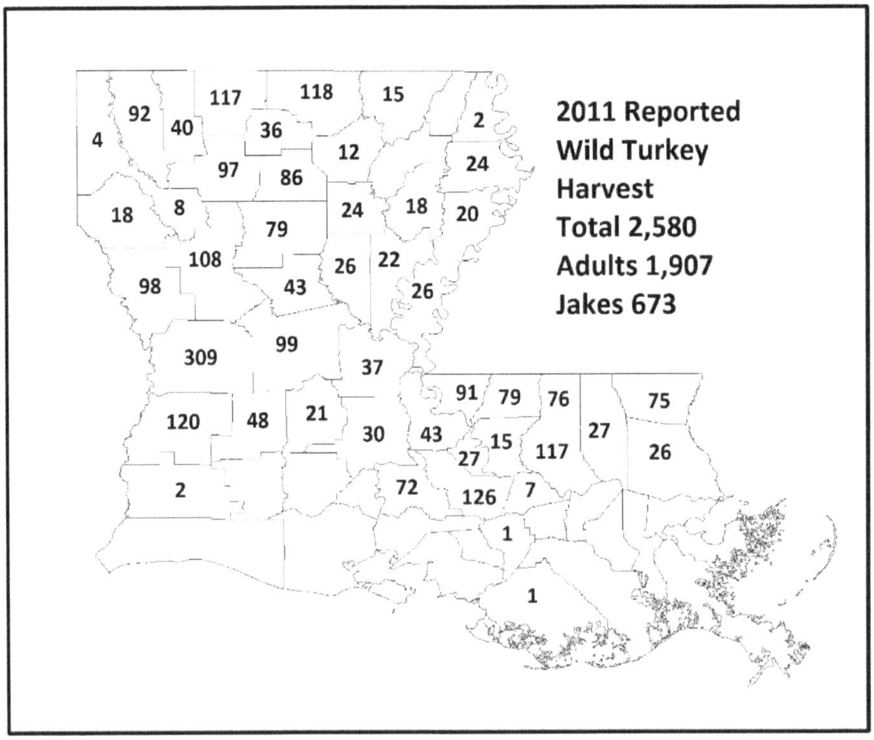

2011 Reported
Wild Turkey
Harvest
Total 2,580
Adults 1,907
Jakes 673
92
4
40
117
36
118
15
2
12
24
97
86
18
8
79
24
18
20
108
98
43
26
22
26
309
99
37
91
79
76
75
120
48
21
30
43
15
117
27
27
26
2
72
126
7
1
1

2010 Reported Wild Turkey Harvest Total 2,221 Adults 1,876

2009 Reported Wild Turkey Harvest 2,586 Total 2,263 Adults 323 Jakes

Appendix E: Habitat Evaluation Form

Turkey Habitat Evaluation

Wildlife biologist/manager: _____Parish_____. Date: _____

Size of property managed_____acres. (<1000ac. = limiting, 1000 – 2000 = moderate, & <2000 = good)   **RATING** _____

Acres of contiguous usable mature forest_____ (<3000 ac. = limiting, 3000 – 4000 = moderate, & >4000 = good) **RATING**_____

Are turkeys present on the site?_____(none = limiting, very few = moderate., & fair - good = good)   **RATING**_____

Turkey Harvest History (Last 5 years): _____

Percent of Property in Hardwood_____%, Pines_____%, Mixed Pine/Hardwoods_____%, Cypress/tupelo_____%, and openings_____%.

Hardwoods_____acres. (inadequate hardwoods = limiting, some hdw. = moderate, & abundant hdw. = good.) **RATING**_____

 Dominant hardwood tree species: _____

(forest dominated by primary turkey foods = good., modest availability of foods = moderate., & few foods = limiting) **RATING**_____

Average age of hardwood trees_____.(age <30 = limiting, 30 – 50 = moderate, & >50 = good)   **RATING**_____

Hardwood Timber Management History: _____ _____
(active timber mgt. every 8 years or less = good., infrequent 8 – 20 years = moderate., & seldom >20 years = limiting) **RATING**_____

Pines_____acres. Average age of pine _____.(age <26 = limiting, 26 – 35 = moderate, & >35 = good) **RATING**_____

Pine Timber Management History:_____
(active timber mgt. every 8 years or less = good., infrequent 8 – 15 years = moderate., & seldom >15 years = limiting) **RATING**_____

Burn History:_____

(patch burned every 1-3 years = good, burned every 4 – 5 years = moderate, & burned >5 years = limiting)   **RATING**_____

Mixed Pine/Hardwood_____acres. Average age of trees_____. Timber Management History: _____

(age <30 = limiting, 30 – 45 = moderate, & >45 = good)   **RATING**_____

(active timber mgt. & regular burning every 5 yrs. or less = good., infrequent 5 – 15 yrs. = moderate., & seldom >15 yrs. = limiting)
.   **RATING**_____

Cypress/tupelo_____acres. Average age of trees_____. Timber Mgt. History: _____
(<20% of forested area in cypress/tupelo = good, 21% - 50% = moderate., & > 50% = limiting)   **RATING**_____

Openings/fields_____acres. Plants growing in openings: _____
(0% - 5% or >50 % openings = limiting, 6% - 9% or 30% - 50% = moderate, & 10% - 29% = good)   **RATING**_____

Predators, poaching, flooding, thick palmetto, lack of burning, etc._____
(rate good, moderate, or limiting as warranted)   **RATING**_____

 Other Limiting Factor(s). for turkeys _____ _____

Issues on surrounding lands that limit turkeys:_____
(rate good, moderate, or limiting as warranted)   **RATING**_____

(ALL FACTORS RATED AS *"LIMITED"* SHOULD BE ADDRESSED WHERE POSSIBLE-THOSE RATED MODERATE ADDRESSED SECONDARY)
(Note that all rating percentages and timelines are general and may be ignored if onsite evidence justifies otherwise)

General Habitat recommendations: _____
_____
_____
_____
_____
_____
_____

Appendix F: Louisiana Poult Production Index (Poults per Hen) 1994 – 2015. (LDWF)

Year	N Mississippi Delta	NW Lob/Sh/HdWood	S Atch/L Mississippi Delta	SE Loblolly Pine	W Longleaf Pine
1994	0.9	1.5	1.8	2.6	3.1
1995	0.0	2.0	3.6	1.1	2.8
1996	1.1	4.1	2.2	1.5	4.7
1997	3.4	2.4	1.4	1.6	3.4
1998	5.5	3.0	2.9	0.8	3.1
1999	3.8	3.6	3.4	1.3	3.0
2000	3.7	3.1	0.7	1.0	1.9
2001	7.0	2.9	1.3	1.2	2.9
2002	5.3	2.9	0.6	1.4	5.1
2003	3.3	1.4	0.6	2.1	2.9
2004	1.9	2.4	1.2	0.6	1.1
2005	2.0	2.6	3.0	2.0	2.1
2006	1.2	1.4	1.4	1.4	2.0
2007	1.9	1.5	1.2	1.9	1.3
2008	0.5	1.7	0.2	1.6	1.3
2009	0.7	0.8	1.2	2.1	1.7
2010	1.6	1.7	0.6	1.6	1.7
2011	1.3	2.5	0.2	1.3	0.8
2012	2.2	2.3	1.7	2.0	2.7
2013	0.8	3.0	2.0	1.6	1.4
2014	1.0	1.7	0.9	1.1	1.5
2015	1.0	2.7	2.9	1.5	2.5

Appendix G: **Specific WMA Harvest Data (2006 – 2016 LDWF)**

Attakapas

Year	Days	Effort	Bag	Effort/Harvest	Acres	Comments
2016	9	0	0		27,930	open
2015	9	0	0		27,930	open
2014	9	1	0		27,930	open
2013	9	0	0		27,930	open
2012	9	1	0		27,930	open
2011	9	0	0		27,930	open

Bayou Macon

Year	Days	Effort	Bag	Effort/Harvest	Acres	Comments
2016	2	7	0		6,919	2-day lottery (8 hunters)
2015	2	9	0		6,919	2-day lottery (8 hunters)
2014	2	10	1	10	6,919	2-day lottery (8 hunters)
2013	2	11	1	11	6,919	2-day lottery (8 hunters)
2012	2	11	3	3.7	6,919	2-day lottery (8 hunters)
2011	2	11	3	3.7	6,919	2-day lottery (8 hunters)
2010	2	10	4	2.5	6,919	2-day lottery (8 hunters)
2009	2	9	2	4.5	6,919	2-day lottery (8 hunters)
2008	2	13	2	6.5	6,919	2-day lottery (8 hunters)
2007	2	12	4	3	6,919	2-day lottery (8 hunters)
2006	2	12	1	12	6,919	2-day lottery (8 hunters)

Big Lake

Year	Days	Effort	Bag	Effort/Harvest	Acres	Comments
2016					19,231	Closed due to flooding
2015	17	797	27	29.5	19,231	1-day youth lottery, open
2014	17	402	20	20.1	19,231	1-day youth lottery, open
2013	17	649	23	28.2	19,231	1-day youth lottery, open
2012	17	632	45	14.0	19,231	1-day youth lottery, open
2011	17	421	6	70.2	19,231	1-day youth lottery, open
2010	17	762	21	36.3	19,231	1-day youth lottery, open
2009	17	909	27	33.6	19,231	1 day youth lottery, open
2008	17	807	42	21.0	19,231	1-day youth (10)
2007	16	845	58	16.5	19,231	1-day youth (10)
2006	9	749	36	27.8	19,231	1-day youth (10)

Bodcau

Year	Days	Effort	Bag	Effort/Harvest	Acres	Comments
2016	20	291	12	24.3	34,355	open
2015	20	255	18	14.2	34,355	open
2014	20	291	8	36.4	34,355	open
2013	20	318	10	31.8	34,355	open
2012	20	324	20	16.2	34,355	open
2011	18	364	18	20.2	34,355	open
2010	16	320	8	40.0	34,355	open
2009	16	512	13	39.4	34,355	open
2008	17	412	9	45.8	34,355	open
2007	16	409	11	37.2	34,355	open
2006	16	344	16	21.5	34,355	open

Bouef

Year	Days	Effort	Bag	Effort/Harvest	Acres	Comments
2016					50,967	closed due to flooding
2015	9	90	5	18	50,967	open
2014	9	95	1	95	50,967	open
2013	9	145	8	18.1	50,967	open
2012	9	131	11	11.9	50,967	open
2011	9	111	4	27.8	50,967	open
2010	9	34	2	17	50,967	open
2009	9	115	14	8.2	50,967	open
2008	10	155	12	12.9	50,967	open
2007	9	152	14	9.6	50,967	open
2006	9	67	4	6.3	50,967	open

Clear Creek

Year	Days	Effort	Bag	Effort/Harvest	Acres	Comments
2016	26	725	16	45.3	48,500	4-day lottery, 21 open, & 1 lottery youth
2015	26	728	13	56	48,500	4-day lottery, 21 open, & 1 lottery youth
2014	26	833	27	31	48,500	4-day lottery, 21 open, & 1 lottery youth
2013	26	711	23	30.9	55,672	4-day lottery, 21 open, & 1 lottery youth
2012	26	748	38	19.7	55,672	4-day lottery, 21 open, & 1 lottery youth
2011	26	352	12	29.3	55,672	4-day lottery, 21 open, & 1 lottery youth
2010	26	791	27	29.3	55,672	4-day lottery, 21 open, & 1 lottery youth
2009	25	891	26	34.3	55,672	4-day lottery & 21 open
2008	26	847	29	29.2	55,672	5-day lottery & 21 open

Year	Days	Effort	Bag	Effort/Harvest	Acres	Comments (**Clear Creek Cont.**)
2007	25	636	12	53.0	55,672	two 2-day lottery(poor comp. self-clr)
2006	21	725	23	31.5	55,672	two 2-day lottery

Camp Beauregard

Year	Days	Effort	Bag	Effort/Harvest	Acres	Comments
2016	9	92	0		12,500	open
2015	9	130	7	18.6	12,500	open
2014	9	72	1	72.0	12,500	open
2013	9	95	2	47.5	12,500	open
2012	9	84	2	42.0	12,500	open
2011	9	56	2	28.0	12,500	open
2010	9	43	1	43.0	12,500	open
2009	9	113	3	37.7	12,500	open
2008	10	112	2	56.0	12,500	open
2007	9	56	0	0.0	12,500	open
2006	16	119	2	59.5	12,500	open

Dewey Wills

Year	Days	Effort	Bag	Effort/Harvest	Acres	Comments
2016	4	0	0		63,901	2-2 day lottery (5hunters/hunt)
2015	4	11	0		63,901	2-2 day lottery (5hunters/hunt)
2014	4	5	0		63,401	2-2 day lottery (5hunters/hunt)
2013	4	5	0		63,401	2-2 day lottery (5hunters/hunt)
2012	4	0	0		63,401	2-2 day lottery (5hunters/hunt)
2011	4	7	1	7.0	60,276	2-2 day lottery (5hunters/hunt)
2010	4	13	2	6.5	60,276	2-2 day lottery (5hunters/hunt)
2009	4	9	2	4.5	60,276	2-2 day lottery (5hunters/hunt)
2008	2	2	1	2.0	60,276	2-day lottery (5hunters)
2003-07	Closed					

Fort Polk-Vernon

Year	Days	Effort	Bag	Effort/Harvest	Acres	Comments
2016	30	1374	44	31.2	105,545	no youth hunt
2015	30	1338	48	27.9	105,545	no youth hunt
2014	30	1195	24	50	105,545	no youth hunt
2013	30	1270	29	43.8	105,545	no youth hunt
2012	30	1047	28	37.4	105,545	no youth hunt
2011	30	1043	31	33.6	105,545	no youth
2010	30	1100	35	31.4	105,545	no youth

Year	Days	Effort	Bag	Effort/Harvest	Acres	Comments (**Ft. Polk-Vernon Cont.**)
2009	30	1299	19	68.4	105,545	1-day youth(20)/significant military closure
2008	31	295	16	18.4	105,545	1-day youth(20)/significant military closure
2007	30	1028	34	30.2	105,545	1-day youth(20)/significant military closure
2006	30	535	31	17.2	105,545	1-day youth(20)/significant military closure

Grassy Lake

Year	Days	Effort	Bag	Effort/Harvest	Acres	Comments
2016					12,983	closed due to flooding
2015	10	101	11	9.0	12,983	9 day open & 1 day lottery youth
2014	10	163	6	27.0	12,983	9 day open & 1 day lottery youth
2013	10	147	3*	70.5	12,983	9 day open & 1 day lottery youth
2012	10	175	5	35.0	12,983	9 day 0pen & 1day lottery youth
2011	9	78	7	11.0	12,983	9 day open
2010	9	117	6	19.5	12,983	9 day open
2009	9	258	8	32.3	12,983	9 day open -Reduced due to 2008 water
2008	17	385	17	22.6	12,983	16 day open
2007	16	256	26	10.0	12,983	16 day open
2006	16	201	17	11.8	12,983	16 day open

Hutchinson Creek

Year	Days	Effort	Bag	Effort/Harvest	Acres	Comments
2016	30	35	0		129	open
2015	30	28	1	28.0	129	open
2014	30	19	0		129	open
2013	30	30	0		129	open
2012	30	17	0		129	open
2011	30	18	1	18.0	129	open
2010	30	21	0		129	open
2009	30	17	0		129	open
2008	31	15	1	15.0	129	open
2007	30				129	open
2006	30				129	open

Lake Ramsay

Year	Days	Effort	Bag	Effort/Harvest	Acres	Comments
2016	16	40	3		796	open
2015	16	6	0		796	open
2014	16	8	0		796	open
2013	16	9	0		796	open

Year	Days	Effort	Bag	Effort/Harvest	Acres	Comments (**Lake Ramsay Cont**.)
2012	16	6	0		796	open
2011	16	4	0		796	open
2010	16	3	0		796	open
2009	16	6	0		796	open
2008	17	10	0		796	open
2007	16	4	0		796	open
2006	16	13	0		796	open

Little River

Year	Days	Effort	Bag	Effort/Harvest	Acres	Comments
2016	16	2	0		3,911	
2015	16	22	0		3,911	
2014	16	17	1	17.0	3,911	
2013	16	53	4	13.5	3,911	
2012	16	12	2	6.0	3,911	
2011	16	29	0		3,911	
2010	16	26	3	8.6	4,727	
2009	16	18	2	9.0	4,727	
2008	16	23	0		4,727	
2007	16	22	1	22.0	4,727	
2006	16	39	0		4,727	

Loggy Bayou

Year	Days	Effort	Bag	Effort/Harvest	Acres	Comments
2016	5	0	0		6,381	2-youth-3 lottery
2015	5	1	0		6,381	2-youth-3 lottery
2014		4	1	4.0	6,381	2-youth-3 lottery
2013		9	1	9.0	6,381	2-youth-3 lottery
2012	5	10	1	10.0	6,381	2-youth-3 lottery
2011	4	6	0		6,381	1-youth-3 lottery
2010	3	8	1	8.0	6,381	1-day youth lottery (5), 2-day lottery
2009	3	14	0		6,381	1-day youth lottery (5), 2-day lottery
2008	3	4	1	4.0	6,381	1-day youth lottery (5), 2-day lottery
2007	3	13	2	6.5	6,381	1-day youth lottery (5), 2-day lottery
2006	3	21	1	21.0	6,381	1-day youth lottery (5), 2-day lottery

Pearl River

Year	Days	Effort	Bag	Effort/Harvest	Acres	Comments
2016					35,031	closed due to flooding
2015	3	16	1	16.0	35,031	2 reg. lottery & 1 youth lottery
2014	2	3	1	3.0	35,031	2 lottery youth days only
2013	2	8	0		35,031	2 lottery youth days only
2012	1	4	2	2	35,031	1 lottery youth day only
2011	1*	2	1	2	35,031	1 lottery youth day only
2010	Closed				35,031	
2009	Closed				35,031	
2008	Closed				35,031	
2007	Closed				35,031	
2006	Closed due to low population/hurricane damage					

Peason Ridge

Year	Days	Effort	Bag	Effort/Harvest	Acres	Comments
2016	31	669	15	44.6	51,004	1youth/limited days
2015	31	704	22	32	51,004	1youth/limited days
2014	31	388	12	32	33,010	1youth/limited days
2013	31	470	19	24.7	33,010	1-youth/limited days
2012	31	617	19	32.5	33,010	No youth hunt-fall kill not included
2011	30	372*	17*	21.9	33,010	1-youth day-fall hunters/harvest not inc.
2010	31	622	24	25.9	33,010	1-youth & open
2009	31	20	1	20.0	33,010	1-youth all other closed due to military activity
2008	31	n/a	n/a	n/a	33,010	
2007	30	119	15	7.9	33,010	Significant military closure
2006	30	144	10	14.4	33,010	Significant military closure

Pomme de Terre

Year	Days	Effort	Bag	Effort/Harvest	Acres	Comments
2016	6	24	1	24	6,434	1 day youth lottery-5 days open
2015	6	36	4	9	6,434	1 day youth lottery-5 days open
2014	6	70	3	23	6,434	1 day youth lottery-5 days open
2013	1	0	0		6,434	1 day youth lottery
2012	1	2	0		6,434	1 day youth lottery
2011	1				6,434	1 day youth lottery
2006 - 2010	Closed				6,434	

Richard K. Yancey (Red River/Three Rivers)

Year	Days	Effort	Bag	Effort/Harvest	Acres	Comments
2016	17	353	13	27.2	71,725	open
2015	17	243	23	10.6	71,725	open
2014	16	413	20	21	71,725	open
2013	16	684	26	26,3	71,725	open
2012	16	446	16	28	71,725	open
2011	16	576	33	17	71,725	open
2010	16	742	24	31	71,725	open
2009	16	1007	47	21.4	71,725	open
2008	17	814	78	10.4	71,725	open
2007	16	1332	87	10.4	71,725	open
2006	9	590	59	7.7	71,725	open

Sabine

Year	Days	Effort	Bag	Effort/Harvest	Acres	Comments
2016	6	19	5	3.8	7,554	2-3 day lottery
2015	6	10	3	3.3	7,554	2-3 day lottery
2014	6	16	4	4	7,554	2-3 day lottery
2013	6	18	1	18	7,554	2-3 day lottery
2012	6	11	3	3.7	7,154	2-3 day lottery
2011	6	12	2	6	13,706	2-3 day lottery
2010	4	12	2	7	13,706	2-2 day lottery
2009	4	18	3	6	13,706	2-2 day lottery
2008	5	29	3	9.7	13,706	3-day & 2-day lottery
2007	4	23	5	4.6	13,706	2 2-day lottery
2006	4	31	5	6.2	13,706	two 2-day lottery

Sandy Hollow

Year	Days	Effort	Bag	Effort/Harvest	Acres	Comments
2016	16	235	4	58.8	4,174	open
2015	16	197	5	39.4	4,174	open
2014	16	164	2	82	4,174	open
2013	16	173	6	28.8	3,696	open
2012	16	85	2	42.5	3,696	open
2011	16	92	3	30.7	3,696	open
2010	16	157	3	52	3,696	open
2009	16	105	1	105	3,696	open
2008	17	105	2	52.5	3,696	open

Year	Days	Effort	Bag	Effort/Harvest	Acres	Comments (**Sandy Hollow Cont**.)
2007	16	85	2	42.5	3,696	open
2006	16	136	1	136.0	3,696	open

Sherburne

Year	Days	Effort	Bag	Effort/Harvest	Acres	Comments
2016	6	144	6	24	43,618	1-youth(10),3-open,& 2-lottery
2015	6	116	7	17.0	43,618	1-youth(10),3-open,& 2-lottery
2014	6	194	8	24.0	43,618	1-youth(10),3-open,& 2-lottery
2013	6	176	10	17.6	43,618	1-youth(10),3-open,& 2-lottery
2012	9	178	13	13.7	43,618	2-youth,2-open,& 5-lottery
2011	11	743	77	10.0	43,618	2-day youth(20)5 lottery & 4 open
2010	11	660	34	19.0	43,618	2-day youth(20)5 lottery & 4 open
2009	11	753	38	19.8	43,618	2-day youth(20)5 lottery & 4 open
2008	12	929	78	11.9	43,618	2-day youth(20)/6- lottery & 5-open
2007	11	591	92	6.0	43,618	2-day youth(20)/3 2-day & open
2006	9	574	55	10.4	43,618	2-day youth (20)/2-day& 3-day lot.

J. C. "*Sonny*" Gilbert (Sicily Island Hills)

Year	Days	Effort	Bag	Effort/Harvest	Acres	Comments
2016	17	169	16	10.6	7,504	1-day youth/16 days lottery
2015	17	140	9	15.6	7,504	1-day youth/16 days lottery
2014	17	123	4	30.8	7,504	1-day youth/16 days lottery
2013	17	158	5	31.6	7,504	1-day youth/16 days lottery
2012	17	173	13	13.3	7,504	1-day youth/16 days lottery
2011	17	165	2	82.5	7,504	1-day youth/16 days lottery
2010	17	149	8	18.6	7,504	1-day youth/16 days lottery
2009	17	199	9	22.1	7,504	1-day youth/16 days lottery
2008	17	171	12	14.3	7,504	1-day youth/16 days lottery
2007	17	161	12	13.4	7,504	1-day youth/16 days lottery
2006	9	129	13	9.9	7,504	three 3-day lottery hunts

Spring Bayou

Year	Days	Effort	Bag	Effort/Harvest	Acres	Comments
2016	2	4	0		12,506	1-day youth
2015	1	4	0		12,506	1-day youth
2014	1	3	0		12,506	1-day youth
2013	1	0	0		12,506	1-day youth
2012	1	4	1	4	12,506	1-day youth
2011	1	3	0		12,506	1-day youth

Year	Days	Effort	Bag	Effort/Harvest	Acres	Comments (**Spring Bayou Cont.**)
2010	1	4	0		12,506	1-day youth
2009	1	5	3	1.7	12,506	1-day youth
2008	1	4	2	2.0	12,506	1-day youth
2007	1	3	0		12,506	1-day youth
2006	1	3	1	3.0	12,506	1 day youth - First turkey season

Tangipahoa School Board

Year	Days	Effort	Bag	Effort/Harvest	Acres	Comments
2016	30	75	1	75	1,643	open
2015	30	46	2	23	1,643	open
2014	30	61	1	61	1,643	open
2013	30	62	0		1,643	open
2012	30	61	0		1,643	open
2011	30	54	0		1,643	open
2010	30	35	1	35	1643	open
2009	30	82	1	82	1,643	open
2008	31	93	0		1,643	open
2007	30		1	30	1,643	open
2006	30	20	2	10.0	1,643	open

Tunica Hills

Year	Days	Effort	Bag	Effort/Harvest	Acres	Comments
2016	14	171	10	17.1	5,906	1-day youth (6) / 6 lottery & 7 open
2015	14	201	12	16.8	5,906	1-day youth (6) / 6 lottery & 7 open
2014	14	210	10	21	5,906	1-day youth (6) / 6 lottery & 7 open
2013	14	276	17	16.2	5,906	1-day youth (6) / 6 lottery & 7 open
2012	14	270	16	16.9	5,906	1-day youth (6) / 6 lottery & 7 open
2011	14	224	18	12.4	5,783	1-day youth (6) / 6 lottery & 7 open
2010	14	301	14	21.5	5,783	1-day youth (6) / 6 lottery & 7 open
2009	14	280	24	12.0	5,783	1-day youth (6) / 6 lottery & 7 open
2008	14	287	20	14.0	5,783	1-day youth (6) / 6 lottery & 7 open
2007	13	257	17	15.1	5,783	3 2-day lottery & 7 days open
2006	13	256	15	17.0	5,783	6-day lottery (15/wk)/7-day open

West Bay

Year	Days	Effort	Bag	Effort/Harvest	Acres	Comments
2016	7	185	36	5.1	60,000	1-youth 3-2-day lottery hunts
2015	7	123	22	5.9	60,000	1-youth 3-2-day lottery hunts
2014	7	184	19	10.0	60,000	1-youth 3-2-day lottery hunts
2013	7	142	17	8.4	60,000	1-youth 3-2-day lottery hunts
2012	7	157	15	10.5	60,000	1-youth 3-2-day lottery hunts
2011	5	211	10	21.1	60,000	1 youth 2-2 day lottery hunts
2010	5	144	6	24.0	60,000	1 youth 2-2 day lottery hunts
2009	4	145	11	13.2	60,000	2 2-day lottery hunts
2008	5	150	12	12.5	60,000	2 2-day lottery hunts
2007	4	92	14	6.6	60,000	2 2-day lottery hunts
2006	4	135	11	12.2	60,000	4-day lottery hunt

(J. Stafford)

Appendix H   **My First Turkey Hunt**

By Norman James Stafford, Jr. (With commentary added by son Jimmy Stafford)

Few events in man's life will prompt him to put to pen a record of the happening. Perhaps past war memories, a significant family experience, or some monumental world changing event could justify such. For my dad, his first wild turkey hunt in 1959 was such an event. This story recounts a hunt where an experienced turkey hunter decided to take a novice hunting. This experience occurred at a time in history when turkey sightings were very rare. When seen, wild turkeys were often the subject of barber shop conversations for months. From 1933 thru 1954 (except for a brief four-year period) Louisiana's turkey season was closed for lack of turkeys. Cautiously, the season was reopened in 1955 for a brief 6-day season within a limited 8 parish area. The season was expanded to 7 days in 1958 but only 89 turkeys were reported as harvested statewide. At the time of Dad's first turkey hunt in 1959, he was a young vocational agriculture teacher in southeast Louisiana. A lifelong squirrel, duck, quail, and dove hunter, he was not without hunting skills-but then he went turkey hunting. The following story was written by Norman James Stafford, Jr. shortly after this first turkey hunt.

I grew up hunting small game in an area devoid of wild turkeys but was blessed to sign a teaching contract in eastern St. Tammany Parish where turkey season had recently been reopened. The Pearl River and Bogue Chitto river swamps had always maintained a sprinkling of wild turkeys that outlaws and subsistence hunters never could completely wipe out. When it came to turkeys, I was a complete greenhorn but I heard about a local turkey hunter named Ted Williams. Mr. Ted was probably as famous in eastern St. Tammany Parish as the other great Ted Williams that was knocking baseballs out of Fenway Park.

One day, I worked up the courage to visit this local legend that I had never met before in hopes of the visit developing into a turkey hunt. As I knocked on the door Mrs. Williams answered then directed me to Mr. Ted in the kitchen. Mr. Ted stood tall and appeared the rugged woodsman that everyone had spoken of. I felt rather awkward, walking into a man's house that I did not know seeking a hunt, but I quickly got right to the point. *"Mr. Williams I have never been turkey hunting but was told that you were the best and might consider taking a greenhorn like me on a hunt."* He paused for what seemed like an hour then said: *"Well I know where some turkeys were yesterday. They move around a lot and tomorrow they may be a mile away. But you meet me here tomorrow (Saturday) morning at 4 am and we will go after them."* I confessed to him that I knew nothing about turkey hunting and asked him to share some of his knowledge with me. He proceeded to fill me in with what I call wild turkey hunting 101. He replied, *"I suppose that I have killed about as many as anybody around here. Sometimes I believe they are as sharp as a human. A man don't see a turkey every time he goes hunting. They sneak around feeding on acorns, pine mast, grasshoppers, and berries. Turkeys fly up to roost every evening usually landing in big pine trees. On a still evening you can hear their flapping up to a quarter mile away. Then the next morning you know the general area to hunt. About March the gobblers begin gobbling. Their gobble is sharper and quieter than a tame turkey. Sometimes they will gobble a couple of times before they fly down off of the roost. They will often fluff their feathers and stretch their wings before flying down. When they fly down you can use your yelper to call at them a time or two but you being a novice I don't advise you doing that. One sour note and you may never see that bird again. Now me, I sometimes just call with my mouth but that takes a few years to pick up."* I then asked Mr. Ted, *"How can I tell a gobbler from a hen?"* He replied, *"By their size. Gobblers are twice as big as hens and if you are close you can see their beard."* Ted went on to say, *"I have hunted for a long time and never killed a hen. Any man that deliberately destroys the female of the species should never be given a hunting license after convicted."* I could see that he spoke these words with great conviction and I dare not disappoint him. I then asked *"where do I aim at a turkey?"* He replied, *"At the head. If you shoot one in the body it will likely fly off, die, and you will never find it."* I asked *"how far do they fly when spooked?"* Ted replied, *"when they bail out they can fly much faster than you think usually not stopping for at least 300 yards. And don't even think about running one down on foot."* He then proceeded to tell me a couple of turkey hunting stories as I sat on the edge of my seat. After this brief but ever critical tutorial I thanked Mr. Ted and rushed out to attend an agriculture teacher's meeting in neighboring Tangipahoa Parish. As I closed the front gate to his yard, he yelled *"Oh, be sure not to wear any loud colors especially blue. Turkeys can spot blue a mile away."* I returned *"No problem, I have a closet full of old green Army clothes.*" At this point I was walking 10 feet off of the ground in excitement. Even at the meeting, my mind was on turkeys. I jokingly told a fellow teacher that I was going to get a gobbler in the morning. He laughed and said *"Stafford, I have been hunting all of my life and never killed a turkey. You have to be part Indian to sneak up on one of those critters."* When I arrived home, my wife's confidence in me bagging a turkey was no better. She reminded me of those 3 deer hunts last winter that resulted in nothing added to the freezer. This didn't sway my enthusiasm as I proceeded to ready my hunting gear. Before I knew it, it was 10 pm time to hit the bed for a good night's sleep. 3:15 am seemed to come in seconds after falling asleep. As I arrived at Mr. Ted's house he was ready to go. After a 5 minute drive to the hunting spot we quietly exited the truck. Ted gave me two high brass number 2 shot 12 gauge shells that he said worked well on turkeys. I had brought a hand full of low brass number 6 squirrel loads thinking the odds 1000 to 1 that I would fire a shot. Ted headed in the direction of a creek bottom some ¼ mile away. All of the sudden he stopped and whispered *"Did you hear that?"* I replied *"hear what?"* Then he said, *"A deer just got up and ran off."* Surely this man was half Indian as I never heard a peep. As we crossed a small creek, an owl sounded off. Still dark Ted asked, *"Exactly where was that owl?"* I said, *"to our right but that was not a turkey."* He reported, *"That is where you are wrong, that is our turkey! Owls are curious animals and will sometimes fly up to a turkey and hoot till he gobbles."* Not sure if this was a tall tale or fact I followed the master in the direction of the owl. At some point Ted instructed me to wait where I was until daylight while he circled to the back side of where the owl-turkey was. This plan sounded as good as any to me. But before we parted company, he said *"This old bird has out smarted me for 3 seasons so I have named him Old Smarty. I have spooked him off the roost several times but have only laid eyes on him twice. He is a heavy bird. Last year one day, he circled me twice then came up behind and spotted me. Once you spook a bird like this it is near impossible to get close to him again. Now this old bird is likely up the creek today in one of those big pines. When it gets daylight I will cross the reed cane thicket and get on his other side. If he spots us, one may get a shot as he flies from the other."* Ted then slipped into the darkness and once he was 10 feet away I never heard another sound as he entered the thick creek bottom. If any man could sneak up on Old Smarty, Ted could. *(During the early days of turkey hunting a harvest was so rare that nearly any method of harvest was considered sporting.)* As day broke, I began scanning the big pines along the creek bottom. Then I saw this dark object about ¾ of the way up a tree. This was my chance at Old Smarty. Being a Cracker Jack squirrel hunter, I knew to place something between me and my quarry. After several minutes of silent maneuvering, I had stalked to within gun range. With my safety off and heart racing, I peered around the brush ready to fire. As I took aim, this turkey of my dreams had somehow transformed into a simple squirrel nest. Surely this elusive turkey possessed some magical powers or maybe I just let my imagination get the best of me. I quickly left the area extremely embarrassed hoping that Mr. Ted was far enough away not witness my folly.

At about 7am, and I was daydreaming about all that Ted had taught me regarding turkey hunting, when all of the sudden I hear a clear sharp gobble just like Ted had described. The sound sent a chill thru my veins that was like no other hunting experience I had ever encountered. It couldn't have been more than 300 yards ahead of me. At last, I was now in the game. For a moment I stood motionless to consider my options. If this was Old Smarty, my approach would have to be flawless. I began moving in his direction ever so slowly with the determination of a lion seeking its prey. I carefully scanned the group of large pines some 200 yards ahead of me. Suddenly the silence was broken with the sound of loud flapping followed by steady wing beats that were getting louder. Instinctively, I dropped to one knee and spotted this large bird flying like a jet straight in my direction. He looked as if his wingspread was 8 feet wide. As he entered my Browning automatic shotgun's range, I fired. I knew my shot was true but the turkey kept flying. As I settled in on my second shot the turkey was directly over my head. By now it looked like an elephant too big to miss. This shot had more effect and caused Old Smarty to drop a leg. But his wings kept beating. As I whirled around firing my third and last shot of squirrel load, Smarty kept going. But he was losing altitude as he cleared the hill some 200 yards away. As I turned to head his way, I heard the now familiar voice of Mr. Ted yelling *"Did you get him?"* I yelled back, *"Not sure but I know he is carrying a lot of lead in him."* We topped the hill where the turkey had been last seen, guns at the ready. Every tree stump we approached with caution as each looked like a turkey but to our disappointment none were. My despair grew with each minute searching. I began to wonder if Old Smarty even went down or if he simply kept flying. Mr. Ted remained silent. No doubt his thoughts being that this greenhorn had just missed or worst yet crippled this bird he had hunted for more than 3 years. At this point I respectfully said *"Mr. Williams, based on my experience as a quail hunter, I think that wherever this turkey landed, he died."* Maybe this was youthful optimism but it sounded good at the time. Nonetheless, experience had taught me in circumstances like this, to go back to the scene of the crime and reexamine what exactly happened. So I headed back to where I had fired my shots. Finding all three empty shells, I visualized where the bird came from as well as each of my shots. I pictured him as he flew over the hill and got a good bearing on where he went. Again I walked over the hill but this time continued on a truer course. Some 70 yards ahead I spotted another black object but this one was different than the stumps witnessed earlier. As I got closer it looked more like a turkey. Suddenly there was no doubt Old Smarty was dead his legs pointing straight up. I let out a yell that could be heard over the entire area. *"I've got him!"* I continued to yell until Mr. Ted topped the hill heading my way. *"Yep that's Old Smarty"* he said. *"Boy he is heavy, about 19 lbs."* I said.   With a smile Ted asked *"Well, what does it feel like to get a turkey on your first hunt?"* *"Wonderful"* I exclaimed. *"I wouldn't trade this bird for a hundred dollars!"* Ted then said *"let's head to the house cause I'm hungry."* I was not hungry in the least but quite eager to get to my own house to show my wife. But ever so grateful to Mr. Ted I followed his lead.

We entered the Williams home with our prize. The bathroom scales confirmed the weight as 19 lbs. which he told me was exceptionally large for a turkey. I then told Mr. Ted that we would split the turkey. But he simply laughed and said *"Son, you don't split turkeys. Besides I will have another in my deep freezer before the season ends."* *"Thanks a million"* was all I could say which seemed so inadequate and off to my house I went.

After pulling into my driveway, I yelled to my wife *"come see this big rabbit I shot"*. *"Rabbit"* in fun she said *"you are a poor excuse for a turkey hunter."* As she approached the truck I pulled out Old Smarty. Smiling from ear to ear she exclaimed *"what a nice gobbler."* I then went on what some would later describe as *"the tour of turkey"*. I traveled some 60 miles to show my dad and mom as well as my in-laws, friends, neighbors and anyone else in the community that wanted to see what a wild turkey looked like. It was rumored that the turkey had spoiled prior to my returning home that evening but I assure you we ate it with no ill effect.

The next day, I returned to drink coffee with Mr. Ted after church and to again relive the previous day's events. Somewhere during our conversation, I asked Mr. Ted *"Just what made that turkey fly towards me?"* Ted smiled and said *"I did. You see I crept within gun range of the bird and he saw me. I had earlier spotted you on the side of the hill and when he flew straight in your direction I figured I would let you have a little fun with him. Had he flown back my way he was going to get both barrels. Besides I got more of a kick seeing you kill him than me. And I will bet money that come next year you will be ready to hunt turkeys again."* He was absolutely right about that!

(Born in 1905, Ted Williams continued to hunt wild turkeys in St. Tammany parish for many years. He was known throughout the Bush, Louisiana community as a master woodsman. This man's simple act of introducing a young agriculture teacher to turkey hunting would later be paid forward in this same passion being passed on to Stafford's children, grandchildren, great grandchildren, and many others who themselves would introduce others to the thrill of turkey hunting. For the love of turkey hunting and other outdoor pursuits, one son and two grandsons of Stafford would later pursue careers in wildlife conservation.

In 1983 Ted's small fishing boat was found floating in the Bogue Chitto River without him in it. Sadly, days later his body was recovered. Many that came to know the excitement of the outdoors thru Ted knew that he died with his boots on enjoying the outdoors to the very end.

James Stafford has hunted wild turkeys every year since this first trip with Ted. For years his skills improved later manifesting in a stretch of 36 consecutive years bagging a Louisiana gobbler. Age now limits his mobility in the woods but it has never dampened his enthusiasm as each spring turkey season returns. At age 83, he called up and bagged a Louisiana turkey during the 2016 season. It is this kind of enthusiasm about wild turkey hunting that he has shared like Ted with so many others.)

References Cited

Adkins, Gerald 1988. From a little acorn... Louisiana Conservationist. January February edition pp. 4 – 7.

Aldrich, J. W. and A. J. Duvall 1955. Distribution of American gallinaceous game birds. U. S. Department of Interior U. S. Fish and Wildlife Service. Circ. 34. pp. 30.

America's Longleaf 2009. Range-wide conservation plan for longleaf pine. By Regional Working Group for America's Longleaf. P. 1.

Austin, J. 2012. A turkey hunting dilemma: Should you shoot a jake? **http://www.turkeyandturkeyhunting.com/turkeyscratchings/brian-lovett-blog/a-turkey-hunting-delimma-should-you-shoot-a-jake**. Access 9 February 2015.

Bick, George H. 1947. The journal of wildlife management. Volume II, No. 2 April 1947 pp. 126-139.

Bittner, S. R. 1973. Wild turkey food habits, movements and populations on winter quarters hunting club, Tensas parish, Louisiana. M. S. Thesis, Louisiana State University, Baton Rouge La., pp 89.

Byrne, Michael E. and Michael J. Chamberlain 2013. Nesting ecology of wild turkeys in a bottomland hardwood forest. The American Midland Naturalist. 170: 95-110.

Byrne, Michael E., Michael J. Chamberlain, James G. Dickson, Larry Savage, and Norman J. Stafford, III 2014. Survival and recovery rates of male wild turkeys on private lands in north-central Louisiana. Journal of the Southeast Assoc. of Fish and Wildlife Agencies, 1: 110 – 114.

Byrne, Michael E., Michael J. Chamberlain, and Bret A. Collier 2016. Potential density dependence in wild turkey productivity in the southeastern United States. Proceedings of the National Wild Turkey Symposium 11: 329 – 351.

Byrne, Michael E. and Michael J. Chamberlain 2016. Using behavioral space use of raccoons to indirectly assess the nature of nest predation. Proceedings of the National Wild Turkey Symposium 11: 283 – 293.

Byrne, Michael E., Bret A. Collier, and Michael J. Chamberlain 2016. Roosting behavior of male Eastern and Rio Grande wild turkeys. Proceedings of the National Wild Turkey Symposium 11: 175 – 185.

Chamberlain, Michael J., Michael E. Byrne, Norman J. Stafford, III, Kevin L. Skow, and Bret A. Collier 2013. Wild turkey movements during flooding after opening of the Morganza Spillway, Louisiana. Southeastern Naturalist, 12 (1): pp 93-98.

Chamberlain, Michael J., Blake A. Grisham, Jennifer L. Norris, Norman J. Stafford, III, Frederick G. Kimmel, and Michael W. Olinde 2012. Effects of variable spring harvest regimes on annual survival and recovery rates of male wild turkey in Southeast Louisiana. The Journal of Wildlife Management 76(5): 907 – 910.

Cohen, Bradley S., Thomas J. Prebyl, Norman J. Stafford, III, Bret A. Collier, and Michael J. Chamberlain 2016. Space use, movements and habitat selection of translocated eastern wild turkeys in northwestern Louisiana. Proceedings of the National Wild Turkey Symposium 11: 165 – 173.

Conley, Mason D., Nathan A. Yeldell, Michael J. Chamberlain, and Bret A. Collier 2016. Do movement behaviors identify reproductive habitat sampling for wild turkeys? Ecology and Evolution. In Press.

Cope, E. B. 1932. The wild turkey, its hunting and future in Louisiana. La. Conservation Review 2 (10): pp 5-7, 32.

Cooper, Susan M. and Tim F. Ginnett 2000. Potential effects of supplemental feeding of deer on nest predation. Wildlife Society Bulletin 28 (3) pp 660 – 666.

Davidson, William R., Emmett B. Shotts, Jeff Teska, and David W. Moreland 1989. Feather damage due to mycotic infections in wild turkeys. Journal of Wildlife Diseases, 25 (4): 534-539.

Davidson, William R. 2006. Field manual of wildlife diseases in southeastern United States (Third edition). Southeast Cooperative Wildlife Disease Study. University of Georgia pp 253-273.

Dennett, Dan 1997. A guide to managing the wild turkey in Louisiana. Published by the Twin City Longbeards of the National Wild Turkey Federation. Monroe, Louisiana pp 1 – 33.

Dennett, Dan and McFadden Duffy 1982. Turkey talk. Louisiana Conservationist. January February edition. Pp. 22 – 24.

Dickson, James G. 1992. The wild turkey biology and management. Published by Stackpole Books pp. 8-9.

Duffy, McFadden 1974. Traveling turkeys. Louisiana Conservationist. Louisiana Dept. of Wildlife and Fisheries magazine March-April issue. pp 19 – 20.

Dupratz, La Page, 1758. Histoire de la Louisiana, Vols. I-III, 1758 (Oiseaux, Vol. II pp. 109-150.) New Orleans Public Library.

Dutrow, George F. and Hugh A. Devine 1981. Economics of forest management for multiple outputs: Timber and turkeys. Proceedings of the Symposium: Habitat Requirements and Habitat Management for the Wild Turkey in the Southeast. Richmond, Va. p 114 – 121.

Everett, D. D., D. W. Speake, and W. K. Maddox. 1980. Natality and mortality of a north Alabama wild turkey population. Proc. National Wild Turkey Symposium 4:117 – 126.

Exum, J. H., J. A. McGlincy, D. W. Speake, J. J. Buckner, and F. M. Stanley. 1987. Ecology of the eastern wild turkey in an intensively managed pine forest in southern Alabama. Tallahassee, FL: Tall Timbers Research Station Bulletin 23: pp 70.

Gill, F. B. 1994. Ornithology. Second Edition. W. H. Freeman and Co., New York, NY.

Grigg, G. W., 1957. The structure of stored sperm in the hen and the nature of the release mechanism. Poultry Science 36(2): 450-451.

Gross, John T., Bradley S. Cohen, Thomas J. Prebyl, and Michael J. Chamberlain 2015. Movements of wild turkey hunters during spring in Louisiana. Journal of the Southeastern Association of Fish and Wildlife Agencies 2: 127 – 130.

Gross, John T., Andrew R. Little, Bret A. Collier, and Michael J. Chamberlain 2015. Space use, daily movements and roosting behavior of male wild turkeys during spring in Louisiana and Texas. Journal of the Southeastern Association of Fish and Wildlife Agencies 2: 229 – 234.

Gross, John T., Bradley S. Cohen, Bret A. Collier, and Michael J. Chamberlain 2016. Influences of hunting on movements of male wild turkeys during spring. Proceedings of the National Wild Turkey Symposium 11: 259 – 268.

Healy, W. M., R. O. Kimmel, and E.J. Goetz. 1975. Behavior of human imprinted and hen-reared wild turkey poults. Proc. National Wild Turkey Symposium 3:97-107.

Healy, William M. 1981. Habitat requirements of wild turkeys in the southeastern mountains. PP 24 – 34 in P. T. Bromley and R. L. Carlton, eds., Proc. Symposium: Habitat requirements and habitat management for the wild turkey in the southeast. Ellison: Virginia Wild Turkey Foundation. PP 180.

Herring, Joe L., 1959. Wild turkey in Louisiana. Louisiana Conservationist. November pp. 23 – 24.

Hollis, F. D. 1950. The present status of the wild turkey in Louisiana. Louisiana Department of Wild Life and Fisheries. Pittman-Robertson pp. 1 – 78.

Holmes, William S. 1920. Division of Game Fourth Biennial Report, Louisiana Dept. of Conservation 1918-20: pp 71-75.

Hyde, Kenneth M. and John D. Newsom 1973. A study of a wild turkey population in the Atchafalaya River basin of Louisiana. Proceedings Annual Conference of Southeast Association of Game and Fish Commissions 27: 103-113.

Hughes, Thomas W., Jennifer L. Tapley, James E. Kennamer, and Chad P. Lehman 2005. The impacts of predation on wild turkeys. The Proceedings of the Ninth National Wild Turkey Symposium Pp 117 – 126.

Jones, Jeanne C., Jessica Tegt, B. Nicole Hodges, and Adam B. Butler 2015. Invasive non-native species and wild turkey in the southeastern United States. The Proceedings of the Ninth National Wild Turkey Symposium Pp 89 - 103.

Kelly, G. 1975. Indexes for aging eastern wild turkeys. Proceedings of the National Wild Turkey Symposium. 3: 205 – 209.

Kelly, Tom, 1973. Tenth legion. Wingfeather Press. Spanish Fort, Alabama pp. 118 – 119.

Kimmel, Frederick G. 1984. Habitat use by wild turkey hens in the Mississippi river floodplain. Master thesis Louisiana State University Baton Rouge, Louisiana pp 1 – 116

Latham, R. M., 1956. Complete book of the wild turkey. Harrisburg, PA: The Stackpole Co. pp 265.

Little, A. R., M. M. Streich, M. J. Chamberlain, L. M. Connner, and R. J. Warren 2014. Eastern wild turkey reproductive ecology in frequently-burned longleaf pine savannas. Forest Ecology and Management. 331: 180 – 187.

Louisiana wildlife conservation review 1934. Louisiana Dept. of Conservation Bulletin No. 25: pp. 189 – 200.

Lucas, A. M., and P. R. Stettenheim. 1972. Avian anatomy: integument. Parts I & II. U.S. Dept. of Agriculture, Agriculture Handbook 362. Pp 750. Michigan State University, East Lansing.

Marsden, S. J., and J. H. Martin 1955. Turkey management. Sixth ed. Danville, Il.: The Interstate. Pp. 999.

Martin, James A., William E. Palmer, S. Michael Juhan Jr., and John P. Carroll 2012. Wild turkey habitat use in frequently burned pine savanna. Journal of Forest Ecology and Management. 285: pp 179 – 186.

Mayell, Hillary 2004. National Geographic News March 2004. Report from meteorologist Michael Garstang University of Virginia Charlottesville.

McIlhenny, Edward A. 1914. The wild turkey and its hunting. Published by Doubleday, Page & Company pp. 1-245.

Mosby, H. S., and C. O. Handley 1943. The wild turkey in Virginia: its status, life history and management. Richmond: Virginia Division of Game, Commission of Game and Inland Fisheries. P-R Projects. 281 pp.

Murry, Robert 1963. Wildlife research. 10th Biennial Report. Louisiana Wildlife and Fisheries Commission. Pp 95 – 98.

National Wild Turkey Federation (NWTF) 2003. Behavioral, attitudinal, and demographic characteristics of spring turkey hunters in the United States. Presented at the Conference of Outdoor Writers of America. Columbia, Missouri.

Newsom, John D. 1962. Turkey season results: *"Best in Years"*. Louisiana Conservationist July-August 1962. Pp 16 – 17.

Olinde, M. and Danny Timmer 1997. Louisiana's wild turkey restoration program 1962-1997. Pittman-Robertson project. Louisiana Department of Wildlife and Fisheries. Funding for publishing provided by the Louisiana Chapter of the NWTF.

Owen, C. N. 1976. Food habits of wild turkey poults (*Meleagris gallopavo silvestris*) in pine stands and fields and the effects of mowing hayfield edges on arthropod populations. M. S. thesis. Mississippi State University, Mississippi State pp 62.

Responsive Management/National Shooting Sports Foundation 2008. The future of hunting and shooting sports: Research-based recruitment and retention strategies. Produced for the U. S. Fish and Wildlife Service. Grant CT-M-6-0. Harrisonburg, Va. Pp. 1 – 261.

St. Amant, Lyle 1959. Louisiana wildlife inventory and management plan. Published by Pittman-Robertson and the Louisiana Wild Life and Fisheries Commission. Pp. 142-157.

Savage, J. Larry 1977. Status and habitat selection of two introduced turkey populations in bottomland hardwoods of Louisiana. M. S. Thesis, Louisiana State University, Baton Rouge pp 1 - 122

_____1999. Aflatoxin testing in Louisiana. LDWF unpublished report.

Savage, John Larry 2008.   Louisiana wild turkey nesting chronology. Combined LDWF research studies. Unpublished LDWF research.

Schaffer, Bradley A. 2002. Nesting chronology and its influences on reproduction for eastern wild turkey in the Ouachita mountains of Arkansas. Master thesis University of Arkansas. pp 1-94.

Schultz, C. 1810. Travels on an island voyage through the States of New York, Pennsylvania, Virginia, Kentucky, and Tennessee, II, pp. 182-184. (As quoted by Wright, A. H., 1915. Early records of the wild turkey. Auk, Vol. 32, No. 2, pp. 213-215.)

Smith, Kenneth 1959. Wild turkey in Louisiana. Louisiana Conservationist. November p. 23.

Smith, W. P. and R. D. Teitelbaum 1986. Habitat used by eastern wild turkey hens in southeastern Louisiana. Proceedings of the Annual Conference of the Southeastern Association of Fish and Wildlife Agencies. 40: 405 – 415.

Sonderegger, V. H. 1932. Occurrence of the wild turkey in Louisiana. Louisiana Conservation Review. July pp 8 – 9 & 37.

Steffen, David E., C. Ed Couvillion, and George A. Hurst 1990. Age determination of eastern wild turkey gobblers. Wildlife Society Bulletin 18 (2) pp 119 – 124.

Stafford, David J. 2016. Assessing feral hog (Sus scrofa) population using game cameras and characterizing the associated occurrence of leptospirosis in north central Louisiana on the Jackson-Bienville wildlife management area. M. S. Thesis Louisiana Tech University. May 2016 pp. 1 – 41.

Stafford, Norman J. 2004. Southeast Louisiana poult surveys 1990 – 2004. Unpublished LDWF research.

_____2007. Physical characteristics of wild turkeys in southeast Louisiana. LDWF unpublished research.

_____2015. Louisiana spring food habits 1998 – 2015. LDWF unpublished research.

Stafford, Norman J. III, Richard M. Pace, III, and Michael W. Olinde 1997. Eastern wild turkey gobbler harvest and physical characteristics in southeast Louisiana. Proceedings of the Southeast Association of Fish and Wildlife Agencies Vol. 51: p 381 – 388.

Strelch, Mary M., Andrew R. Little, Michael J. Chamberlain, L. Mike Conner, and Robert J. Warren 2015. Habitat characteristics of eastern wild turkey nest and ground-roost sites in 2 longleaf pine forests. Journal of the Southeast Association of Fish and Wildlife Agencies 2: 164-170.

Stringer, B. D., Jr. 1977. Food habits and behavior of wild turkey poults in east central Mississippi. M. S. Thesis. Mississippi State University, Mississippi State. Pp 31.

Taylor, James H. 1969. A telemetry study of the movements of wild turkey on Jackson-Bienville wildlife management area, Louisiana. Master thesis Louisiana Polytechnic Institute pp 1 – 78.

Thogmartin, Wayne E. and James E. Johnson 1999. Reproduction in a declining population of wild turkeys in Arkansas. Journal of Wildlife Management 63(4): 1281 – 1290.

Timmer, Danny, M. Olinde, M. Roy 1998. The effects of growing season burns on the abundance of various faunal species and nesting and habitat selection of wild turkeys on the Kisatchie National Forest. Louisiana Dept. of Wildlife and Fisheries. Unpublished report pp. 1-6.

USDA Forest Service 2009. Forest inventory and analysis national program. USDA Forest Service publication.

USFWS 2010. Turkey hunting in 2006: an analysis of hunter demographics, trends, and economic impacts. Arlington, Virginia.

Vangilder, L. D. and E. W. Kurzejeski 1995. Population ecology of the eastern wild turkey in northern Missouri. Wildlife Monographs pp 130.

Whitaker, Darroch M., Dean F. Stauffer, and Scott Klopfer 2004. A range-wide meta-analysis of wild turkey breeding phenology. Report to the Northeast Wild Turkey Technical Committee. Pp 1 – 46.

White, Thomas H. Jr., 1986. Effects of selective riverfront timber harvest on habitat use by wild turkeys in the Mississippi delta. Master thesis Louisiana State University, Baton Rouge, Louisiana pp 1 – 119.

Williams, Cliff 1967. The wild turkey in Louisiana. Louisiana Conservationist. Louisiana Dept. of Wildlife and Fisheries magazine March-April issue. p 10.

Williams, Lovett E. Jr., 1991. Managing wild turkeys in Florida. Real Turkeys Publishers for the Florida Chapter of the National Wild Turkey Federation. pp. 1 – 92.

Williams, Lovett E. Jr., 1991. Wild turkey country. Willow Creek Press. Minocqua, WI. Pp 1 – 143.

Wilson, Walker Blake 2005. Seasonal space use, habitat preference and survival of female wild turkeys in a Louisiana bottomland hardwood forest. Master thesis Louisiana State University, Baton Rouge, Louisiana. Pp 1 – 44. Wilson, Walker Blake 2005. Seasonal space use, habitat preference and survival of female wild turkeys in a Louisiana bottomland hardwood forest. Master thesis Louisiana State University, Baton Rouge, Louisiana. Pp 1 – 44.

Wright, A. H. 1914. Early records of the wild turkey. Auk 31: 334-358, 463-473; 32: 61-81, 207-224, 348-366.

Yancey, Richard K. 1969. The vanishing delta hardwoods: Their wildlife resources. Louisiana Wildlife and Fisheries Commission. 1969 Governor's seminar on Mississippi Delta Hardwoods. Little Rock, Ark. p. 14.

Yeldell, Nathan A. 2016. Influence of prescribed fire on reproduction ecology of female eastern wild turkeys in west-central Louisiana. M. S. thesis University of Georgia, Athens, Georgia pp. 1 – 157.

5th Biennial Report 1952 – 53. Various authors. Louisiana Wildlife and Fisheries Commission. Game and Fish Division report. p. 74.

7th Biennial Report 1956 – 57. John D. Newsom. Louisiana Wildlife and Fisheries Commission. Game and Fish Division Report pp. 200 - 201.

11th Biennial Report 1964 – 65. Louis A Pellerin. Louisiana Wildlife and Fisheries Commission. Game and Fish Division Report p. 97.

14th Biennial Report 1970 – 71. Various authors including Charles Smith, Levi McCullin, Cliff Williams, H. C. Beasley, and Marvin Deason,. Louisiana Wildlife and Fisheries Commission. Game and Fish Division Report pp. 112 – 164.

www.ingramcontent.com/pod-product-compliance
Lightning Source LLC
Chambersburg PA
CBHW061223270326
41927CB00024B/3475